From the Door to the Gate

by

Rose Costanza Tangredi

In memory of my parents

Pietro Costanza

and

Maria Salomome Costanza

Special thanks:

To my children who motivated me to begin my Memoir.

To my husband who helped and encouraged me to complete it.

Introduction

This story begins at the "Door", an opening in the wall that protected the Feudal hilltop town in Southern Italy, where I was born. It ends at the electronic "Gate" of a luxury community for active adults.

This book will be of particular interest to all those whose ancestors came to America from Southern Italy, to all who are familiar with the urban public education systems and to those "Baby Boomers" who are curious about future life styles in their golden years.

Printed in the USA 2004

www.Lulu.com

ISBN   1-4116-1940-4

One

When the pains started Maria tied up the kindling twigs she had been gathering, placed the bundle on her head and started up the narrow path that led from *l'orto*, a vegetable plot, to the New Road. The road had been built several years before to accommodate the one daily bus and the occasional car that came to *Noepoli*. Maria knew the road well. As a teenager she had carried baskets of gravel on her head to the men paving it. Soon she reached the bend in the road from where she could see the *Torretta*, Little Tower, the very top of *Noepoli*, a medieval town built on a hill in the southernmost part of the Apennines, the mountain chain that runs north and south through the center of Italy. She looked up towards the *Torretta* where there no longer was a tower but only a stone wall. It was the only reminder of the feudal fortifications that once had been there. The wall circled the flat open area that everyone still referred to as the *Torretta*. Beyond the wall she could see the spire of the ancient church of Our Lady of Constantinople. Praying silently to Saint Anne, patron saint of pregnant women, she continued to walk towards the town. She was relieved to reach the *Fontanino*, Little Fountain, right across from the path that led from the New Road to the upper part of *Noepoli*, *La Terra*. The paved road continued around the base of the hill as if to slice it off from the lower half, the *Casale*, until it came to a dead-end shortly after *La Fontana*, the Large Fountain.

The people who lived in *La Terra* were supposedly better off financially and better educated than the people who lived in the *Casale*. In general that was true but the reality was that very few in all of *Noepoli* were either well-off or well educated.

Maria left the paved road and started to walk up the hard-packed dirt path. On her right was a large barren area with scattered tufts of weeds, stubbornly trying to survive, despite the gravel and loose rocks that rolled down from the wall above. At its edge, overlooking the New Road, was the flour mill. On her left, the path edged a sheer drop into the fields below. As the path rose, it narrowed. It went by the door to the interior spiral staircase of the Vitelli *palazzo* that had its entrance on the *Torretta*. The *palazzo* stood where the feudal castle had once been. Maria walked past the *palazzo* door to a flight of wide stone steps that led to the "Door", the large opening in the crumbling stone wall. Long ago there had been a real door to keep out the intruders. Then, it was just a point of reference. Things were either inside the Door or outside the Door. After going through the opening Maria walked along the narrow, cobble-stone street that wound around the low, attached, stucco houses. She passed several short, dead-end alleys before reaching her house, which was located on the longest and widest street in *Noepoli*.

Maria made it home just in time, on that afternoon of February 4, 1922, for me to be born indoors. Luckily the town's midwife was available. She wrapped me in a long, wide band of cloth, the *fascia*, or swaddling clothes, as mentioned in the Bible: Luke 2:7. The *fascia* was placed at my neck and then wound around to bind my arms and legs, each turn overlapped the previous one until it reached my feet. Then it was securely tucked under and fastened with a pin. Afterwards she performed her other customary duty--pierced my ears.

Because it was winter my mother and I were able to stay home a few days after my birth. But as soon as it got warm enough, my mother had to go back to *l'orto*. Since my mother was my only source of nourishment she had to take me wherever she went. She carried the swaddled me in one arm and balanced a basket on her head with the other. Once there, she placed me on the ground near her. She could easily lift me as she went from one spot to another by simply placing one hand under the *fascia*. Tree branches were my shield against the sun or drizzle.

Even after I was weaned she had to take me along because there was no one in town to take care of me. My grandmother, who lived with us, was needed on the land. As peasants, they had no choice.

At the time I was born, *Noepoli*'s three thousand inhabitants were still divided into well defined social classes. The small gentry and middle classes dominated the largest class, the peasants. As a group, the peasants owned no land, were illiterate, and were resigned to their place in the centuries-old class system, that offered them little hope of a better tomorrow. Men, women and children eked out a living working on other people's lands. Some girls and women were lucky enough to escape the back-breaking work in the fields by working as maids in the houses of the gentry and the middle class. Many peasants barely had enough to eat. Some went to bed without supper, depending on sleep to give them strength for the next day's struggle. Even the peasants who, like my mother's family owned small plots of land, found it difficult to grow enough food.

Besides *l'orto,* my mother's family owned a small vineyard, very far away from town. The vineyard did not require many trips but *l'orto* required almost daily attention. Besides the vegetables, the plot had some fruit trees. There was always some crop that needed attention. Luckily, it was only about a half-hour walk from town. My earliest memories are of my mother, grandmother, a pig and me walking to it. We walked through the Door, went down the hill to the New Road, crossed it to the one-spigot fountain, *Il Fontanino,* (also used as a reference point). There we met other peasants who stopped each morning to water their donkeys in the trough while they filled their small wooden barrels from the spigot.

Most peasants had to leave at daybreak for the one or two hour walk to their destinations. They usually got home after dark, bone tired from their long walk back. Those we met were the lucky few who didn't have too far to walk to their plot of land. Barefoot little girls in their raggedy dresses walked holding on to the torn skirts of their barefoot mothers. The women carried babies in their arms and balanced baskets on their heads. We were a little different. We wore shoes and our dresses were mended.

After walking a little way I would complain that I was tired. To stop my whining, my mother would tell me to look ahead to the landmark she told me to locate on the road ahead of us. When we got there she would pick me up and carry me for a short while. Then she would put me down and give me another spot to look for. We continued in this way until we reached our little plot. As I got older, the landmarks got further and further apart. Eventually they stopped altogether.

We were usually the only ones to take the left fork in the road. The fork was an extension of the main road, built to connect *Noepoli* to other towns higher up in the Apennines. It bent around the low, flat hill with *Noepoli*'s threshing floor, chapel and cemetery. A short distance past the cemetery was the path that led from the road to our property. The road continued past our path for just a short distance, edging a flat, rectangular piece of reddish-brown, parched ground, where the young men played soccer. It ended abruptly at the foot of a craggy hill. Each time the road had been extended past the hill it was either cracked by an earth tremor or disappeared in a landslide. Eventually the project had been abandoned.

We walked down our path, barely visible among the briers, in a single file to a small flat ledge that jutted out of the hill. This sun-baked spot was just big enough to hold several drying racks, made of grass mats, stretched out and held in place by shoulder-high poles. Just behind the racks was the entrance to a small cave. Next to the cave was the brick beehive oven, built right into the hill. The only shade was the shade of the almond tree that grew right at the edge of the narrow, winding path that led further down the hillside to the vegetable plot.

The vegetables were planted on a level piece of land which extended from the foot of our hill to a precipice overlooking a torrent that originated in the higher hills. I heard the water rushing by but I never saw it. I was repeatedly warned by my mother not to go to the very edge. Across the gorge was a hill with caves, the year-round homes of The Cave People, who seldom came to town.

In order to take advantage of every inch of the level and relatively fertile piece of land, the vegetables were planted according to their heights, with shorter ones planted under the taller ones. We grew tomatoes, peppers, eggplants, zucchini, cucumbers, cantaloupes, garlic, onions, and various kinds of beans. At one edge of the vegetable plot there were a plum, a cherry and a peach tree.

We had no set hour for lunch. Whenever it was convenient to leave our work we climbed up to the little flat area and ate our lunch under the almond tree, where there was always a breeze. We brought our lunch from home until the vegetables ripened. Then our daily lunch was the *ciambotta*, a vegetable stew. As soon as we reached *l'orto* we went straight down to pick some of the ripe vegetables and brought them to the flat ledge. My grandmother cut up the vegetables, seasoned them and placed them in a large cast iron pot, while my mother built a fire in a hollow under the tree, set a tripod over it and placed the pot on it. When we were convinced the fire was just right, we left the vegetables to simmer, confident the vegetables would be ready for us whenever we were.

We spent many hours on that small flat ledge, preparing the surplus vegetables for use in the fall and winter. We threaded shoots of *esparto* through the stems of the peppers, garlic and onion as we shaped them into garlands. In the spring, *esparto,* forsythia-like bushes, turned the hillsides golden yellow with their blossoms. After the flowers faded my mother and grandmother cut the shoots, stripped them of their green coverings and then set them out to dry until they were strong and pliable. We hung the garlands of vegetables from the poles that held up the racks. When they were dry we carried them home and hung them from hooks along the rafters in our storeroom.

The hilly ground on the property was not suitable for planting but, it begrudgingly yielded some hard to find *cipolline,* wild onions, greatly sought for omelets. On this part of the property grew several gnarled olive trees, a few fig trees and some oaks. After we were through drying and jarring the vegetables, we took care of the figs, olives and acorns. These chores kept us going daily to *l'orto* until late November.

My mother and grandmother kept me busy by giving me small chores to do. I carried small pails of manure from the bottom of the hill. I checked on the pig to see that it didn't do any damage. I made trips to the almond tree to make sure the *ciambotta* was simmering. In the summer I dug out the *cipolline.* In the fall I gathered the acorns that fell from the trees to feed to the pig in the winter.

At times we stayed in *l'orto* day and night to make sure the vegetables and fruits we had set out to dry weren't spoiled by a sudden rain storm. If we thought the rain seemed imminent, we removed what was on the drying racks and carried them into the cave. When the rain was over, we carried everything out and rearranged them. Often the showers came unexpectedly. The three of us scurried to the racks only to have the rain stop just as we got there. At times, the rain suddenly stopped just as we finished putting everything away. During the summer there were sudden thunder storms severe enough to damage the crops but the rainfall was too unpredictable to be depended on to water the vegetables. Instead, we depended on a communal water supply, a fragile earthen irrigation ditch that often crumbled as we were watering.

The ditch began about a ten minutes walk from our property

at the edge of the soccer field. One of the field's short sides ended at the paved road. The other ended at the edge of a level stretch of the torrent that tumbled from the hill above and down by our property. The women came to this part of the torrent to scrub their clothes on the flat rocks that had been set at its edge. They spread their clothes to dry on the *esparto* bushes that managed to survive or on the many rocks nearby.

The irrigation water had been piped from the torrent to about half-way the long side of the soccer field closest to the vegetable plots. It flowed above a spigot used for drinking. The owners of the vegetable plots were allowed to use the water once a week for a twenty-four hour period. Our allotted time started at noon Tuesday and ended at noon Wednesday. Each Tuesday at noon my mother walked to the source of the water and diverted the flow into the furrow that led to our property. As she walked back she checked the sides of the earthen channel to make sure there were no breaks. Once it reached our property the water was painstakingly guided into each row of vegetables. My mother stood at one end of the row and guided the water with a hoe. My grandmother waited for the water to reach her at the other end of the row and carefully guided it into the next row. And so it went until every row had been watered. Often the water stopped flowing while they were guiding it. They put down their hoes in exasperation. My mother went to retrace the path of the ditch until she found where the water had broken through and carefully repaired the break. The water and my mother would often arrive together. It was bad enough when this happened during the day. When it happened at night, it was even more annoying and time consuming.

The irrigation water was never plentiful. By midsummer, the water dwindled to a mere trickle. Then, it took the whole twenty-four hours just to barely finish the job. On those occasions we spent the night there. My mother and grandmother used the light of the moon or the stars to guide the water into the furrows. Sometimes I fell asleep on the ground nearby, listening to the chirping of the crickets and the soft sound of the water as it gurgled along the narrow, thirsty furrows. Sometimes I slept in the cave. On each side of the entrance was a ledge carved out of the stone wall and covered with straw. The ledge was my bed and the straw my mattress. Each ledge had a niche large

6

enough to hold a clay oil lamp which we used only if absolutely necessary.

Even when we didn't stay overnight we didn't start for home until the moon was high. As we walked by the cemetery, I thought of the story I had heard that someone had actually seen a man turn into a werewolf during the full moon. At other times I thought of the *monachichio*, a tiny gnome, who appeared at crossroads. He would refuse to let you pass unless you gave him your soul. Walking home late one evening I thought of ghosts rising from the graves and said to my mother that I was afraid. Balancing the bundle on her head, and looking straight ahead, she didn't turn her head or miss a step. Very calmly she said,

"Don't worry about the dead. They can't hurt you. It's the living you have to worry about".

Her answer didn't surprise me. I was getting used to her calm, terse answers. Complaining to my mother was usually a waste of time and effort.

As I listened to my mother and grandmother talking during our walks to and from *l'orto* I began to learn about my father and his family.

Two

My father came from *Terranova di Pollino,* about a five hour walk from *Noepoli.* My parents' marriage was arranged by friends of the two families. After the wedding they lived in *Noepoli* with my widowed grandmother in the two room family house.

In *Terranova,* my father had tended sheep for the wealthy land owners. In *Noepoli,* he worked as a day laborer. He desperately wanted to escape the life of the Southern Italian peasants. His only hope was to immigrate to America. If only he could save enough money to buy a steerage ticket! The news reached even remote *Noepoli* that the very restrictive immigration quotas set by the United States were soon to take effect. If my father didn't have the money soon, he could forget his dream forever. Somehow he and my mother managed to save enough for one, one-way ticket. He was one of last Italians to immigrate to the United States before the quotas took effect in 1924.

My father, who had never been on a ship, spent his days on board sucking lemons to calm the nausea that plagued him throughout the long crossing. He was very happy to set foot on Ellis Island in December 1923. With that step, he changed my life forever.

He was met by his mother's sister, Filomena and her husband Giacomo Lufrano. After the emotional encounter and the signing of papers they made their way to Harlem, in New York City. The Lufranos lived with their son John, and their three daughters: Teresa, Lucrezia and Rose, in a tenement building on 118th Street and First Avenue.

My father joined the large number of men who had come to America without their families and who lived as boarders with the families of fellow immigrants. He paid Aunt Filomena a weekly amount to cover rent, laundry and meals. He lived there as a member of the family.

A *paesano* got my father a job in a factory but he worked there for only a few months. He missed the hills, the trees and the fresh air. He could not work eight hours cooped up in a poorly ventilated shop. Other *paesani* found him a job as a hod carrier. He mixed concrete by hand, put it into a hod and carried it on his shoulder to the bricklayers and cement masons. As the buildings got taller, he had to climb more and more ladders. Except for a short lunch break, he worked eight to ten hours a day.

The *paesani*'s aim was to go from job to job without missing a day's work. In a trade of transient workers, reliability was a great asset. A "no-show" upset not only the supervisors' plans, but burdened those who did show up. Both the employers and his friends soon learned that they could depend on my father. He was seldom out of work.

The men who immigrated either to the United States or to South America left with the same purpose. They were going to earn lots of money, return to Italy, give large dowries to their daughters and live a life of ease. These Americans, as they came to be known, soon started to send money to their wives to build new houses and buy land.

My mother started to make plans, not only to replace the old house, but to make the new one as big and as modern as possible. I was too young to remember the actual building, but as I grew older, I heard references to the many difficulties she had in having it built. She had to explain her requirements to the many local artisans involved in building the house and the making of the furniture. Since all the arrangements were made orally, there were many misunderstandings about specifications, prices, deadlines and costs.

She had to give my father progress reports and explain the unmet deadlines and the many cost overruns. Since they were both minimally literate, they had mutual misunderstandings of their own. As if that weren't enough, the Italian postal system compounded their difficulties. Cash in *Noepoli* was so scarce, that the Americans bought Italian stamps in the United States and enclosed them in their letters for their families to use when they answered. Although my mother affixed the stamps, the letters often arrived without a stamp and my father had to pay the postage due. The situation baffled them both but neither knew what to do about it. Finally, the mystery was solved. An ingenious clerk in *Noepoli's* post office steamed off the uncancelled stamps, sold them, and pocketed the money.

Noepoli was a town of cobblestone alleys and narrow streets that snaked into each other with no apparent design. There was only one street that started at the very bottom of the hill at the New Road and wound around the houses to the *Torretta*, at the very top of the town. Our house was located towards the upper end of that street, which, had it had a name, would have been called Main Street. Most houses were huddled together as if to protect themselves against a common enemy, but ours was semi-detached.

It was made of white stucco and had a red tiled roof. Two stone steps from the street led to a solid wooden front door, indicating that we had risen above the horizontally split door of the peasants. The door opened into a small vestibule and three wooden steps led to the kitchen, which like the rest of the rooms, had a rose colored tiled floor. Immediately to the left was a large credenza with a marble top. The credenza wall met the staircase that led to the second floor. The stairwell was divided into two enclosed sections. One section held some guinea pigs and the other, several chickens. Across from the credenza was the wood burning fireplace that provided us with both heat and light and near it were the wooden stools we used instead of chairs. Along the entrance wall and at right angle to the fireplace, was a wooden bench found in almost every kitchen and used as a bed when necessary. In the bench wall, in the sill of the window that overlooked Main Street was a charcoal grill that we hardly ever used. On the other side of the fireplace, under the window that opened onto the alley, stood the wooden frame with our large water barrel. Next to that was the door to my grandmother's bedroom. It was the only room to have cross ventilation, rarely found in the huddled houses in *Noepoli*. Besides the bed and a wardrobe, it had the seldom used table and chairs and my mother's pride and joy, a Singer sewing machine. A trap door in the far corner led to the storeroom.

The two rooms upstairs were separated by the staircase. The master bedroom had two dressers, a wardrobe and my sleeping cot at the foot of the double bed. French doors opened onto a small, iron-railed balcony with a closet containing a toilet seat. *Noepoli* had no running water and no prospect of getting it, but should it ever come, our house was ready. Until then, we flushed the contents of the chamber pots with pails of water. This saved my mother the nightly walk to the edge of town, where the women emptied the discretely covered chamber pots on top of what had been emptied the previous nights.

The other room was a living room with a sofa, two easy chairs and a China closet. Large French doors led to the balcony that went along the width of the house overlooking the street. Pots of flowers and herbs lined up against its black wrought iron fence.

The wine cellar under the kitchen and the storage basement under my grandmother's room had separate doors in the alley way that separated our house from the other houses.

The Americans built better houses or fixed old ones but they were unable to buy what they wanted most - land. There was no land for sale. In ancient times the land had been owned by the monastery built on the spot we knew as the *Torretta*. Later it was owned by the nobles of the various invading countries. Later it was owned by the gentry. When I was born, most of the land was still owned by the descendants of the Vitelli and the Carlomagno families. Bad economic conditions had diminished their wealth but the gentry held on to the land which allowed them to control the affairs of the town.

Throughout the centuries the peasants viewed land ownership as the way out of poverty. Mussolini came into power promising land reforms and forced the gentry to sell some of their land. Finally the day of the sale arrived. Even though not many families were in a position to buy land, the news that a car with two black-suited men had stopped at the *Fontana,* created a great deal of excitement. The curious gathered in the small open area in front of the town hall on Main Street to watch the visitors, escorted by two town officials, walk up the narrow path from the fountain.

Dressed up for the occasion, my mother and I walked down to the town hall, excited at the prospect of buying some land. The black-suited men from "the city" were sitting at a long table, along the far wall of the large room. As we approached we saw that each man had a stack of papers and several ink pads. Each one stamped the document and passed it on to the next for more stamping. Both the guests and our town officials had solemn faces. They looked uncomfortable dealing with us peasants and seemed intent on doing the job as fast as possible.

I felt embarrassed by our lack of education and sorry for my mother as I watched and listened to her struggle to express herself in Italian. When she couldn't find the right word, the town officials were ready to translate the dialect. Despite her language difficulties, my

11

mother realized every peasant's cherished dream. Not only did she have the deed to an arable piece of land, but that land was located just at the bottom of *Noepoli*'s hill.

Shortly after the land sale the town crier announced that there would be a film strip shown in the town hall. As soon as our small group of peasants were seated, one of the two men in charge told us we were about to see pictures showing the latest farming methods. The other man focused the machine on the sheet stretched across the front of the room. We saw pictures of machines we had never seen before, doing the work that we did by hand. We watched men using commercial fertilizer instead of manure. The last few pictures were of crops grown by using these modern methods. We all "oohed" and "aahed". The bunch of white grapes was so big and so plump that it took our breath away.

When the film strip was over the peasants gave each other questioning looks. They murmured to themselves and spoke quietly to each other. Even if they had the money to buy the machinery, they couldn't use it on their small, hilly plots. In fact, they didn't even have the money to buy the good seed or the good fertilizer. The film had changed nothing. They would continue to farm the same way they had always done.

We called the new piece of land the Olive Grove for its many olive trees but it also had many fig trees, a walnut and a chestnut tree. On the land between the trees we grew wheat. One corner had scrub oaks and shrubs.

The euphoria about owning such a seemingly wonderful piece of land did not last long. We realized that owning land was not the answer to eliminating poverty. We couldn't harvest enough crops to pay the taxes on it.

My mother was forced to write to my father for money. He sent the money grudgingly. He couldn't understand why she could not pay the expenses from the crops she sold. I often watched my mother slowly move her lips as she silently read the latest letter. I didn't like to see the unhappy look on her face as she folded the letter and tucked it into her pocket. Later I would hear her discuss the contents with my grandmother. I began to dread the arrival of letters from America.

One day a letter arrived that worried us more than any other. My father was having trouble finding work because of something called the Depression. He warned my mother that he would have to cut down on the money he was sending her.

A while later we received a letter that made the three of us feel much better. My father and all his friends had been hired to work on what was to be the world's tallest building, the Empire State Building in New York City.

Three

My grandmother was small and round. Like the other peasant women, she tucked her colored shirtwaist into the waistband of the full black, ankle-length skirt. A long black apron, tied in the back, protected its front. Her two long braids of wavy, gray hair wound around her head, framed a face etched with wrinkles. Those wrinkles, that moved closer whenever she flashed me her toothless, accepting smile, became part of my earliest memories.

She was cheerful and always ready to dance the lively *Tarantella* and was never idle. She either worked on our land or as a day laborer. In the evenings she sat on a stool near the fire and spun wool into yarn. She fastened a piece of wool fluff on one hook of the spindle, a round slender rod, about a foot long, with a metal hook on each of its ends. She rolled the spindle against her thigh several times, held it suspended waist high and watched the fluff of wool change into a thin white thread as the spindle spun around. She wound the spun thread on the top hook and repeated the procedure with another fluff of wool. When the top hook was bulging with thread, she transferred the thread around a wooden rod, the distaff. In the twentieth century, my grandmother was still following a procedure described about three thousand years before by Homer:..."wove their looms or twirled their distaff".[1] After many evenings she had enough thread to knit a pair of socks or stockings.

My grandfather had been a muleteer for the Vitelli family. He was away for days at the time, transporting goods among the various Vitelli farms and between the farms and the town. Even though he died before my mother married, my mother and grandmother still talked about him very lovingly. They lamented his untimely death brought about by the then untreatable disease of diabetes.

My mother and her three brothers were the only survivors of my grandmother's thirteen children. The oldest, Domenico, fought in the Italo-Turkish War a few years before the start of World War I. He

---

[1] Odyssey, Book 8

immigrated to the United States soon after his discharge and settled in Steubenville, Ohio, near Aliquippa, Pa., where my grandmother's sister, Raffaella, had settled years before. He started to work as a trackman on the Pennsylvania Railroad and sent passage money for my mother and grandmother to join him. But they didn't have the courage to leave the town they knew, for the unknown. They had the fear common to peasants. What could they do in the city if they had no money? Bad as things were, they could always grow something to eat where they were. Domenico continued to send money to my grandmother, making her one of the first Americans in *Noepoli,* as those who received money from a relative in America were called.

My mother's second brother, Antonio, lived in the nearby town of *Senise* with his wife and children but they never came to visit us and we never visited them.

Raffaele, younger than my mother, along with his wife Rosina, their three children, Rosina's nonagenarian father, Francesco and a donkey lived on the piece of land they owned far away from town. During the winter they lived in town on a street used as a short cut to the *Torretta.* They, including the donkey, shared one large, cave-like room with a very low ceiling. The only source of air and natural light was the doorway. The door, typical of peasant houses, opened horizontally. This allowed the peasant to open the top half of the door to get air, light and talk to neighbors, without worrying about the pig and chickens going out. My cousins Rocco, Rosaria and Antonietta, were older than I, but they had never gone to school. They were a little in awe of me because I did. I enjoyed being with them but I didn't like taking the short cut to their house because on the way I had to go by another cave-like one room house. The door was often wide open. A disheveled woman in rags and her little toddler girl, as unkempt as she, sat in the ashes near the fireplace. The room was bare except for some straw in a corner. I felt so sad for them that I avoided going that way.

Francesco, in his nineties and still lucid, rode the donkey back and forth to the farm and often stayed there even when the rest of the family came to town. Even though he needed a cane to get around he continued to make himself useful by doing small chores. He was especially proud of keeping the irrigation ditch in good order. When he was in town he hobbled the short distance from his house to the *piazza*. As soon as he got there, one of the storekeepers put a chair out for him. The group of idling young men stopped their conversation and walked over to him. He was a wonder. Nobody had lived that long in *Noepoli*. The young men surrounded him to ask him about his youth. They had heard the stories before, but to make him feel important, they always asked him to tell them over again. Francesco was happy to oblige. He sat squarely in his chair, stood his cane upright between his knees, placed both hands on the top of the cane and with the rapt look of someone telling a fairy tale, he retold his stories.

As a muleteer for the Carlomagno family he rode through the hills where brigands hid from the police. He was proud of the times he had outwitted them. Sometimes, though, he had to pay "protection" in the form of the goods he was carrying before they would let him go. They swore him to secrecy on penalty of death.

Although Uncle Raffaele was very busy doing his family's work, he could be counted on to help my mother whenever she really needed him. One of those occasions was the killing of the pig. By January the piglet that followed us to the vegetable garden was big and fat. We had taken good care of it. In bad weather and at night we tied it in the storeroom, where it ate acorns and food scraps. We wanted it to be not only big and fat but also healthy until we were ready to make it our meat supply for the coming year. It was almost impossible to replace the pig if it died a month or two before it was to be slaughtered. The only thing worse than the death of fattened pig was the death of a family member.

January was a good time to slaughter the pig. The people, kept home by the bad weather, had the time to do the work and the temperature was cold enough for the meat to keep while it was being prepared. Processing the meat was time-consuming, tiring and boring. It took several days to finish the job. To make this yearly chore more efficient and less boring, relatives gathered to slaughter one family's pig at the time. This arrangement turned the annual chore into a social event.

The actual killing required both strength and expertise. My uncle and my mother trussed the pig in a large wooden vat. While my mother and grandmother held the pig, my uncle expertly plunged the knife in the pig's neck so that it would die as quickly as possible and also allow the maximum amount of blood to flow out. My grandmother held down the pig and my mother held a large pot under it's head to catch the spurting blood. After the blood stopped flowing, both my mother and grandmother took turns dousing the skin of the pig with boiling hot water as Uncle Raffaele scraped off the hair. He worked carefully and methodically, trying not to bruise the precious skin which we used for food. The only of part of the pig that was discarded, was the hair. The organ meats were taken out first. My mother sauteed the liver, heart and lungs with plenty of onions and dried red peppers. As soon as the slaughtering chores allowed it, we sat down around the fire to eat the mixture with crusty bread and red wine.

The intestines were painstakingly washed, salted and rinsed several times before being placed in pans of cold water, ready to be stuffed. When the barrel was empty my mother carried it on her head to the fountain to refill it. Meanwhile, my grandmother diced and seasoned the meat to stuff into the intestines. When the intestines and the meat were ready, my grandmother took an intestine from the pan of cold water and handed it my mother, who, poised over the large bread board set on the table in my grandmother's room, carefully inserted a funnel into one end and pushed the meat through the funnel into the intestine. She had to stuff the meat tightly enough not to leave air pockets and yet gently enough not to break the very delicate and irreplaceable intestine. The stuffed wide intestines became *sopressata,* Italian salami, and the stuffed narrow intestines became various types of sausages. Some of the links were hung from the rafters to dry. Others were put aside until the next day when they were fried and placed in earthen jars, covered with the rendered hog's hot fat. The fried bits of skin strained out of the rendered fat were saved and mixed into the dough of the next batch of bread. The two hind haunches were cut off, salted and hung up to dry to become either *pancetta*, bacon or *prosciutto*, Italian style ham. The bladder was washed and used to store the left-over rendered fat.

But for me, the highlight was the *sanguinaccio*, the blood pudding. My mother hung the kettle with the blood on a hook in the fireplace. She and my grandmother took turns stirring it continuously to mix in the sugar, raisins and pieces of chocolate. We ate some of the pudding by dipping bread in it. The rest was cooked down until it was almost solid and then it was stuffed into an intestine to became a blood sausage.

Besides the *sanguinaccio,* I looked forward to the *cupu-cupu.* It was a kind of drum we made by stretching a dried membrane, from inside the pig, over the open end of a wooden cylinder, the size of a coffee can, and tied a string around it. We placed a reed in the middle of the membrane. I have no translation for *cupu-cupu* but the sounds of the words mimic the monotonous and doleful sounds which we produced when we stroked the reed rhythmically. We played with the *cupu-cupu* all through lent. At Easter we discarded the membrane but saved the cylinder to be used again the next year.

The annual slaughtering of the pig was one of the occasions that kept us in touch with my father's family.

Four

My father's parents and his three brothers lived on the outskirts of *Terranova,* in a hamlet of about thirty widely scattered huts, set in a hollow between two hills. The hamlet was appropriately called, *Le Fosse,* translatable either as Hollows or Graves.

When it was time to kill the pig Grandma Rosa sent my father's younger brother Vincenzo to get us. He would appear in the evening, wrapped in a floor-length black cape, the wide brim of his black hat turned down to meet the collar of his cape, to protect him not only from the cold but from the rain and snow that he often had to walk through. My mother gave him a glass of wine as soon as he sat near the fire. He told us about what was happening in *Le Fosse* while my mother prepared him some food. Barring a heavy snow storm, my mother and I would accompany Uncle Vincenzo back to *Le Fosse* early the next morning. Soon after he finished eating Uncle Vincenzo curled up under some blankets on the wooden bench next to the fireplace, where the fire was banked to keep him warm and we went to bed.

My first recollection of one of these trips was of my mother and Uncle Vincenzo taking turns carrying me. They would put me down for a little while and then my uncle would suddenly swoop me up in his arms to stop me from stepping into a deep pile of snow or into a stream swollen by the melted snow.

When Grandma Rosa needed us in the spring or summer, she didn't send Uncle Vincenzo. She managed to get the message to us and we went as soon as possible as if obeying a royal command. In warm weather we left the house before sunrise. We started out for *Le Fosse* as if we were going to *l'orto.* We walked past our property for a short distance to the base of the hill. We usually got there just as the first rays of the sun peeked over the horizon. The hill, covered with only a few scattered, stunted scrub oaks, was too dangerous to climb in the dark. One side of the narrow, winding path of loose gravel, hugged the hill and the other overlooked a sharp precipice. The path was especially dangerous for women carrying baskets on their heads and for donkeys carrying saddlebags. A bump into one of those crags could be fatal. We were always relieved to reach the top of the hill where the path leveled out into a stretch of woods. In the fall, we broke the silence by crunching the brown, yellow and red leaves on the path. In the spring, the smell from a patch of violets signaled the beginning of the path that led down to the town of *San Costantino Albanese.*

Unlike the rocky, crumbling path up from *Noepoli,* the path down to *San Costantino* cut through evergreens, but it was just as winding and steep. Halfway down the hill the path leveled and widened for a few yards where a spigot come out of the side of the hill. We always stopped to take a drink of the icy-cold water and to rest on some fallen tree trunks for a few minutes. The trees were so tall and the foliage so thick that the rays of the sun never quite reached the ground. No matter how hot, this spot was always cool and breezy. My mother had to coax me to get up by telling me that this spot was about half-way to *Le Fosse.* The sooner we resumed our walk, the sooner we would get there. With renewed purpose we continued down to the bottom of the hill. Mindful of the stories we had heard, we walked quickly on the cobble-stone street that cut through *San Costantino* and didn't slow down until we reached the riverbed on the edge of the town. We crossed into the woods that ended at the riverbed in *Le Fosse.*

As soon as we came to the edge of the riverbed I heard my friends from the previous visits. Four or five barefoot boys and girls, dressed in patched clothes, ran to meet us. I looked forward to seeing them. They always made me feel welcome and special. Besides being the only child from the outside to come to *Le Fosse,* I was also an American. After greeting them and arranging to meet them later, I caught up with my mother and walked with her along the brier-edged lane that ended just as the path reached the hut in which my father was born.

The one room stone hut and its basement were built right into the pine-covered hill. We walked by the basement door and around the side of the hut where we climbed the three stone steps that led to the large room. Its hard-packed dirt floor was swept clean. The wall facing the path had a double bed, a wooden chest and the room's only window. The large fireplace was built in the hill-side wall and on that wall hung three large sheepskin rugs. Near the fireplace were several wooden stools.

Grandma Rosa was also small and round but had a ruddy complexion, flashing dark eyes and thick, black hair braided around her head. She had a fiery temper and a sharp tongue. Grandma was the boss in the family. I was a little afraid of her and when we visited I tried to stay out of her way as much as possible. My favorite refuge was the spring near the hut, halfway up the hill. I sat there, hidden by the shrubs, listening to the rhythmic plopping of the water and to the cicadas sending messages to each other. I watched the birds and the butterflies flitting between the bushes and trees. I didn't leave until I heard someone call me.

My grandfather Giuseppe was a short, thin, quiet man. I think Grandpa was a little afraid of Grandma Rosa too. He was away all day tending the sheep of a nearby farmer. Many nights he stayed with the sheep instead of coming home.

In the evening we sat on the stools around the fireplace and ate our *minestra*, vegetable soup, that varied with the seasons, with wooden utensils, from the wooden bowls that my uncles had carved. We went to bed soon after supper. My mother, my grandmother and I shared the thick corn husk mattress of the double bed. Uncle Vincenzo, Uncle Antonio and my grandfather took down the sheepskin rugs from the wall, stretched them out near the fireplace and went to sleep on them.

If we visited at the right time of the year we saw my father's married brother, Nicola, his wife and their two sons who were a few years older than I. He tended sheep for a landowner in the area. He was away from home from early autumn, when he herded the sheep to the lowlands for winter pasture, until the spring, when he herded them back for summer pasture and shearing. Uncle Nicola was taller than Uncle Antonio and Uncle Vincenzo. He always wore sheepskin pants, with the fur on the outside, and was seldom without his *zampogna*, bagpipe, which he, like the other shepherds, played to relieve the monotony of tending their flocks. Even though Uncle Nicola's family lived nearby, they rarely visited. They stayed away from Grandma as much as possible. Nicola's wife visited only when we were there, trusting my mother to protect her from Grandma Rosa's sharp tongue. The whole family looked to my mother to be the peace-maker between Grandma and other members of the family.

Uncle Gaetano, my father's oldest brother, died in World War 1 on November 3, 1918, the day before Italy signed the Armistice. Every member of the family mourned Gaetano's death, but Grandma never came to terms with it. She became obsessed with the idea of contacting his spirit through mediums. Whenever she heard of a medium she either went alone or summoned my mother to go with her. My mother did not believe in mediums and thought that my grandmother was wasting both time and money but she knew Grandma was beyond reasoning. She humored her and went along with her.

Since Gaetano had no children, Grandma Rosa decided that his brothers should name their first child after him. Nicola's first boy was named Gaetano. My being a girl did not excuse my father. I became Gaetana or Gaetanina. The family and my friends shortened it to Tanina.

Uncle Antonio and Uncle Vincenzo didn't yet have to worry about naming their first child. They were both unmarried and at first they were always home. As time went by, Uncle Antonio was often away tending sheep or doing work for some nearby farmer. Uncle Vincenzo was always there. He took care of the family's vegetable plot, right across the lane from their hut, and shepherded the few family sheep, including the four that belonged to us. The wool from those four sheep kept my grandmother busy with the spindle and distaff. Their milk kept us supplied with small wheels of cheese. I liked watching my uncles make the cheese and waited eagerly to dip some crusty bread into the curds and whey they saved for me.

I was especially fascinated by my uncles' outdoor shaving ritual. They placed a basin of water on one of the hut's holly shaded steps and then stripped to their athletic undershirts. They dipped the bristle brush in the water, swirled it in a cake of soap and then vigorously twirled the soapy brush all over their faces. While the foam soaked their whiskers, they slapped the straight razor over the strop, first on one side then on the other until it was sharp. They took turns peering into the cloudy, cracked mirror hanging from the jamb of the door and carefully scraped off the foam. They finished by splashing water all over their faces and arms, not caring where the water fell.

Uncle Vincenzo was very popular. He was good looking and

he could play the accordion, the only source of dance music in the area. He had no girl friend and was not looking for one. But Uncle Antonio was interested in one girl after another. Grandma Rosa worried about Uncle Antonio.

He romanced several girls and then left them. He had angered several fathers and older brothers who would have liked nothing better than to give him a good thrashing. Grandma worried that sooner or later his luck would run out. She was determined to keep him safe by finding him a wife in *Terranova*. When she found a suitable girl she asked a friend to contact the girl's father, who accepted Uncle Antonio as the suitor. To formalize the arrangement Grandma decided that Uncle Antonio should give the girl a piece of jewelry. She then sent for my mother to go with them to pick out "the gold", a term used to describe any piece of jewelry a young man formally presented to the girl.

Early the morning after we got *Le Fosse*, my grandmother, my mother and I started up the hill to *Terranova*. I followed behind them on the path that was too narrow for the three of us. I trudged along with nothing better to do but listen to their conversation. We were to meet Uncle Antonio in the jewelry store in town. Grandma extolled the virtues of the girl she had chosen for him. I gathered that the girl had been chosen more for her virtue than her beauty. The more she talked about the girl's virtues, the surer I became that Uncle Antonio would not show up. We waited and we waited but he never came. Our walk down the hill was not a happy one. Besides being disappointed, Grandma was worried what the girl's father and brothers might do to Uncle Antonio.

Terranova, higher up in Apennines than *Noepoli*, was built on a hill of the large mountain of *Pollino,* at the southern end of the Apennines. Since it had more rain and snow than *Noepoli*, its landscape was greener with a variety of evergreens and oaks. It was too cold for either olive or fig trees to grow there.

Grandma Rosa's brother Giovanni and his family lived there. They always invited us to stay with them for the annual feast of their patron saint, Our Lady of Mount Carmel. To break up the long trip we left home one day ahead of time and spent the night at *Le Fosse*. But when I was very small, even the walk to *Le Fosse* was too long for me and my mother ended up carrying me most of the way. She looked for an alternative.

Terranova's mail was brought by bus to *Noepoli*. The mailman in *Noepoli* put it into saddlebags and delivered it to *Terranova* by mule. The day before she was planning to be in *Terranova* my mother arranged for him to take me there. I sat behind him and clung to him for dear life, until we reached Giovanni's house. He swung me off the mule and carried me to the top step. He knocked, opened the door just enough to stand me up in the doorway, and left. I felt like a package being dropped off.

As soon as they heard the door, either Giovanni's wife, Brigida, or one of his two teenage daughters, Filomena or Teresa, came to greet me. Their dialect was a little different from ours but I had no trouble understanding them.

The kitchen had wooden floors and was large enough to accommodate a long rectangular table and benches to seat twelve. The cupboards along the walls were filled with dishes, wheels of cheese, dried sausage and rounds of bread. The wall facing the street had a large fireplace and the wall facing a side street had a window. The house was semi-detached and had three levels. A wooden staircase led from the kitchen to the attic where the daughters slept. The master bedroom was off the kitchen. It had a double bed with the thickest cornhusk mattress I had ever seen, which my mother and I shared with Brigida. The storeroom was under the bedroom but could only be reached by a door at the back of the house.

Giovanni was the general manager for one of the biggest landowners in the area. He was a short, stocky, dark-haired, ruddy complexioned man with a handle-bar mustache and lots of confidence. He wore a well-fitting three piece suit and a white shirt with a detachable, stiff, high-collar. His gold watch dangled from a gold chain strung across his ample chest. He was away a great deal of the time, supervising the various properties, the flocks of sheep and herds of cows. When he was home he was usually entertaining businessmen. Brigida was always ready to entertain whomever Giovanni brought home. She was short, slim and lively. Her clothes always looked new and fashionable. Shiny, high-buttoned shoes showed under her long black skirt. Dangling gold earrings danced merrily as she moved and a gold broach sparkled in the center of the high collar of her black bodice. Her shiny, black tresses wound around her head like a halo. The bunch of keys of assorted sizes hung from a chain-linked belt around her waist and jangled with her every move.

The daughters were fair-haired and fair-skinned. Their hands were soft and their nails clean. Even though they belonged to the peasant class they were being raised to attract affluent husbands who would keep them away from the fields. Despite the big difference in our ages, they always made a fuss over me and tried to keep me amused until my mother came.

They took me along to carry an extra jug of water from the fountain. Their fountain was in a tunnel-like concrete structure at the edge of town near a noisy, rushing stream that never went dry. The concrete roof that protected the fountain from rain and snow extended over the large flat stones set along the edge of the river where *Terranova's* women washed their clothes. The kneeling women rubbed the clothes with bars of yellow soap, scrubbed them on the stones, rinsed them in the flowing water, wrung them out and spread them on the nearby bushes to dry. They helped each other fold and arrange the dried clothes in the baskets which they carried back home on their heads. Their laundry facilities were wonderful compared to *Noepoli's* few stones, set haphazardly, on the side of the river near our *orto*.

Brigida took me with her to the storeroom. Finally, I found out why she had all those keys. She lifted up the bunch in one hand and picked out the largest one. While she held the rest of the keys in her clenched hand, she inserted the key into the door's keyhole, turned the large handle and pushed the door into a large and neat room. Two small windows let in enough light for us to see. The shelves were stocked with more cheeses, jars of tomatoes, crocks of rendered fat from the pig and cooked sausages. Garlands of onions, garlic and red peppers hung from the rafters. The big chests along the walls, holding legumes, wheat and flour, had locks. Brigida went from chest to chest and rifled through the keys for the one that fit.

Giovanni's family was also American. Soon after Giovanni and Brigida were married they immigrated to the United States and settled near Giovanni's sister Filomena and her husband Giacomo Lufrano. (The same Lufranos who welcomed my father years later). Giovanni and Brigida lived in Harlem, New York City, for a few years. Their two girls, Filomena and Teresa, were born there but they could not adjust to life in America. While people all over the world would have given anything to come to the United States, Giovanni and Brigida left it to return home. I don't know if they left with lots of money or not. But their two daughters left with a precious possession - American citizenship.

Five

A few months after his no-show at *Terranova*'s jewelry store, Uncle Antonio announced he wanted to marry Mary, a girl from *San Costantino Albanese*. The whole family really started to worry. They feared that this time he might not survive.

San Costantino Albanese was a town of a few hundred attached houses made either of stucco or stones, built in the narrow valley, half-way between *Noepoli* and *Le Fosse*. The town was one of many in Italy that have the word *Albanese* in it. In the sixteenth century many Christian Albanians fled to Italy to escape the invading Muslim Turks. They formed their own towns, kept their own language, customs and religion. Although they continued to worship according to the Byzantine Rites, they were accepted into the Roman Catholic Church. Through the centuries they continued to live isolated from the Italians.

The great majority of the people of *San Costantino* could not speak Italian. Some could not even understand it. Even after the passage of centuries the Italians from surrounding towns knew so little of their culture and history that they referred to them interchangeably as Greeks or Albanians. Sometimes they referred to them as *I Briesci*. That's the closest they came to calling them by their true name, Arbaresh. The general opinion among the Italian neighboring villages was to leave *I Briesci* alone. The men had the reputation of having fiery tempers who preferred to use a knife to settle a dispute rather than to reason. Italians walked through *San Costantino* only when there was no other way to go. They did so quickly, as we did, whenever we went to see Grandma Rosa.

San Costantino was isolated and homogeneous as were the other hill towns of *Lucania*. Throughout the ages *Lucania* had been invaded by so many nations that the residents of its mountain villages distrusted strangers. They learned to rely only on themselves, on their extended families and, only minimally, on the rest of the people of their own towns. The poor roads that were often made worse by earth tremors or washed away by landslides, contributed to their isolation. People who lived in towns far away from each other had trouble understanding one another other. The dialect of each town had traces of Spanish, Portuguese or French, depending on what country had ruled them long ago. The customs and traditions linked them to ancient civilizations and to the Bible.

But despite the family's concerns, Uncle Antonio managed to persuade Grandma Rosa to make the necessary formal arrangements for the wedding. Even after Uncle Antonio had been accepted as the official suitor by Mary's Arbaresh parents, the family was still anxious about the forthcoming wedding.

When my mother and I walked to *San Costantino* for the engagement we realized that we had passed Mary's house every time we had gone to the *Fosse*. The attached, stone house was almost at the very edge of town, just before reaching the riverbed.

After all the stories I had heard and the years of walking fast through the town for fear of antagonizing the townspeople, I was surprised to see all the friendly and smiling members of Mary's family. They greeted us warmly and made us feel at home. I realized they were just like us except they spoke a different language. Mary's grandmother was not much different from my grandmother. She gave me a smile and said a few words in her dialect which I didn't understand. I said something in our dialect which she didn't understand. We just smiled to each other. Mary's mother spoke enough Italian to hold a limited conversation. Mary's father spoke better Italian but he only used infinitives. The older people in *San Costantino* who bothered to learn Italian, found conjugating the verbs just too much trouble. They used the infinitive form of the verb for all cases. Mary, who had gone to school, spoke Italian best of all but spoke it in a sing-song fashion that immediately identified her as Arbaresh.

A few months after the engagement we went to *San Costantino* for the wedding. This time we took our time walking down the street. The bride's father was the first to greet us. He was outside skinning one of the three kids that were hanging from hooks near the door. Inside we found several women getting ready for the next day's wedding reception. Some women were cooking and some were transforming every room into a dining room. My mother quickly joined them in moving tables and spreading white tablecloths. Feeling useless, I decided to go out to see if I could find a playmate. At the

28

doorway, Mary's father stopped skinning the animal, held the knife up in the air close to his chest and started to talk to me. I appreciated his kindness. I sensed that he had stopped his work to talk to me so I wouldn't feel so lonely. After a few words I repaid his kindness by leaving him to finish his work. I started to walk on the road near the riverbed but the road was deserted. After a while I gave up and returned to the bride's house.

My mother wasn't there. She had gone with some other women to a nearby house to prepare the room for the newlyweds. Following their directions I went there. When I opened the door I found the women busily moving things around. Two were kneeling by the bed, about to place a hatchet under it to ward off the evil spirits. My mother told me to keep myself busy outside because she had things to do.

I walked in the dry riverbed overcome by a feeling of a great loss. I realized that I was about to lose Uncle Antonio. He would never again be in *Le Fosse* to fuss over me. The pebbles my feet kicked sent the field mice scurrying in all directions. My sadness intensified when I thought of my last visit to *Le Fosse*. I was happily anticipating hearing the voices of my friends as we neared the edge of the riverbed. Instead there had been absolute silence. I kept turning my head slowly in every direction in the hope of seeing them. I had a foreboding all the way to Grandma's hut. Grandma confirmed my feeling when she told me that the boys were working in the fields and the girls had been sent to various towns to work as maids. I would never see my friends again. The poverty that had ended my friends' childhood so soon had taken part of mine also.

After walking in the riverbed for a while I went back to the bride's house. Everybody was still busy preparing for the wedding the next day.

Mary wore a simple white dress. Her light brown hair, braided around her head was covered by a white veil. The other women wore colorful shirtwaists, long black skirts, gold necklaces and dangling earrings. I wore the dress my mother had made for me just for the occasion. The men wore black suits and white shirts, open at the neck. We all followed the bride and her father to the ancient church of *Santa Maria della Stella.*

The bride and groom joined the priest under the canopy in

the back of the church. Towards the end of the ceremony the couple walked around inside the canopy several times, holding a wedding torte. After putting down the torte, they were each given a glass of wine. They sipped the wine and then tossed the glasses to the ground. After the ceremony we followed the newlyweds back to the bride's house for the wedding feast.

We sat with about ten other guests at a table, covered by a white tablecloth and set with plates and utensils. The happy chatter at the table stopped momentarily as we all watched the black robed priest, who had performed the marriage ceremony, walk quickly and without greeting anyone, to the empty seat at the head of the table. The chatter quickly resumed around me but my full attention was on the priest. He had a long grayish beard, that reached down to the middle of his chest. Under its tip I could see a large cross hanging from a thick gold chain. He put down a golden dish he had brought with him, took a white rolled-up napkin from his wide black sleeve, carefully unrolled it and set out the golden utensils that had been wrapped in it. He sat down and concentrated on his place setting until the platters of *ziti,* the name of the pasta that in our dialect means newlyweds, the bowls of stewed kids, the baskets of bread and bottles of wine were passed around. He helped himself without looking to his right or left. As the guests drank more wine, the conversations around the table became more lively, but the priest just concentrated on his food. When he finished eating he picked up his plate and utensils, wrapped them in his napkin and left as he had come in-- without saying one word.

After dinner one room was cleared for dancing. Cookies and wine were served throughout the evening. The party didn't break up until the newlyweds left for their one room home where they were to spend their one day honeymoon.

In the month of May after the wedding, Uncle Antonio and Aunt Mary invited us to visit them for the feast of their patron saint. At this time of the year the Italians of the neighboring towns put aside their misgivings about *I Briesci.* Several days before the feast day, itinerant merchants traveled to *San Costantino* to sell their wares and the farmers came to buy and sell livestock. Merchants set up tables and booths in an open area just outside the town. The townspeople waited for these merchants from year to year to buy material for

30

clothes and bed linens, lace, buttons, pins, needles, thimbles, combs, hair brushes, jewelry, pots and pans. Over the years the women developed preferences for one vendor over another and patronized their favorites. But no matter how friendly the transaction was, the sale was never made without a bargaining session. No buyer was expected to pay the first price quoted. The sale was not made until both thought they had gotten the better of the other.

The farmers came leading mules, donkeys, cows, sheep, pigs. They staked out a spot in the open area apart from the merchants' stalls. Trading and selling livestock was even more lively. Sometimes the sales generated violent arguments when the animal one farmer bought the year before did not turn out to be as good as the seller had promised.

Although most people went to the feast to buy and sell and to have some fun, some people did go because of their devotion to the saint. They came to pray for a special favor or to thank her for a favor already received. The statue of the saint was in a chapel on top of the hill near the church and could only be reached by climbing a very long flight of steps. During the feast days, black-dressed women prayed the rosary as they climbed the steps on their knees. Glistening beads of perspiration trickled down their devout faces. Occasionally, they paused long enough to take one hand off the rosary beads to wipe the beads of perspiration from their faces. Passers-by stopped to look up at the women and wondered aloud,

"How bad can the situation be for them to pray to the saint like that?"

The sight was so heart-wrenching, that even luke-warm believers stopped to say a prayer on their behalf.

The young of *San Costantino* waited for the feast days to dress up in their traditional costumes. The women wore white blouses trimmed with ruffles upon ruffles of lace and full, ankle-length, woolen skirts. The dark colors of their skirts were almost completely covered by the overlay of either vertical or circular wide, bright-colored satin bands. The rainbow-colored skirts billowed over ruffled petticoats. The women's hair was held in place by a fan-like headpiece made of layers of colored ribbons fastened on each side by a large straight pin with a huge silvery knob. The men wore embroidered black vests over ruffled, long-sleeved white shirts, dark breeches and knee-high white hose. The young people took every opportunity to dance their traditional dances in the open area, at the edge of town.

We spent the night with Uncle Antonio and Aunt Mary. We shared the one bed in their one-room home. I slept against the wall, my mother next to me, Aunt Mary next to her and Uncle Antonio at the outer edge.

After a year or two we had to go for Aunt Mary's grandmother's wake and funeral. The three day wake was held in the same room we had sat in for the marriage meal. One evening, a group of women dressed all in black, skirts touching the floor, both hands holding shawls around their solemn faces, strode in and sat in the empty chairs that had been placed near the coffin. There was a hush of anticipation in the room. They were the professional mourners hired by the family. The women sat erect, eyes on the dead grandmother. As if directed by an invisible conductor, they started to chant in their dialect, shedding tears as they did so. After a while, as if on cue from the same invisible conductor, they stopped singing and crying. They got up in unison and marched out as they had come in.

After a few visits to *San Costantino* the townspeople knew who we were. Whenever we walked through the town on our way to *Le Fosse*, the same people who had looked at us with suspicion before the wedding, smiled and greeted us as friends.

Six

The kindergarten class was a new addition to *Noepoli's* school system, part of the Compulsory Education Act enacted by the Fascist regime. Some peasants didn't send their children to school because they were too poor to buy the books. But even those who could afford it had ambivalent feelings. They respected those who could read and write but they didn't think education was for them. These parents feared that an education might spoil the children for the hard work they were born to do. They told and retold tales of parents who had sacrificed everything to send a son to school only to have that son leave them for a job in the city. The doubts and the expense kept the majority of the peasants from complying with the law. It was easy to do. There was no provision for enforcing the law.

My mother, who didn't let anything stop her from going to the fields, took part of a very sunny day to walk with me on the first day of kindergarten. I knew then just how important my going to school was to her. We took the short cut to the *Fontana*, crossed the road into the *Casale* and quickly came to the house the town had rented from a member of the gentry. We walked up the few stone steps into the reception room with its large wood-burning fireplace full of ashes. The room was the kitchen of the two room house. The room's small window let in very little light. The very young teacher was sitting at the desk near the door. She was not from Southern Italy. She spoke with the beautiful pronunciation that even the educated Southern Italians of the time could not master. Probably this was her first assignment.

Young teachers with the ink on their diplomas still wet and with no say about their assignments, were appointed to staff these classes and the one-room schoolhouses in remote hamlets where no schooling had existed before. The teacher looked up from the papers on her desk and gave us a big smile. She spoke to us slowly and clearly, unsure of whether we would understand her. My mother sensed the young woman's culture shock and tried to reassure her about her stay in *Noepoli*. After the teacher had taken down all the information she led us to the door of the classroom. My mother waited until I sat down. Then she smiled, waved and left.

The teacher's desk was near the only source of light, the French doors to a narrow balcony. We sat two to a wooden table that had an attached bench. The children in the front received some light from the French doors but the rest of us were in perpetual twilight. I sat in the back bench in the darker of the two corners. On rainy days the room was darker and gloomier than ever. There was no bathroom, no heat and no clothing closet. If we needed outer clothing to come to school, we needed it indoors as well. The fireplace in the reception room rarely had a fire in it. The teacher and a few of us carried braziers from home. We held them by their wooden handles so we wouldn't get burned by the charcoal in their metal-lined wooden bowls. We put the braziers under our benches and rested a foot on each handle. The glow from the charcoal barely kept our teeth from chattering. I always had a mustard plaster on my chest. It was my mother's way to keep me from catching colds, bronchitis or pneumonia.

But one day I did catch something and stayed home from school. My mother went for a woman who came in carrying two covered jars containing leeches. I stretched out on the wooden bench near the fireplace, naked to the waist. The woman inverted two cups on my chest and held them tightly over the leeches so they could suck out my bad blood. After a few minutes she lifted the cups with a little explosive pop and moved them to another spot on my chest until the whole area was treated. It wasn't painful but I was cold and uncomfortable.

Another time I had a very painful sore throat. I don't remember seeing the doctor but I remember the foul-tasting medicine he prescribed. My throat had to be swabbed several times a day. It hurt. I clenched my mouth against the medicine. I was uncharacteristically uncooperative. In desperation, my mother asked the young woman who lived with her little girl in the house opposite our storeroom, to apply the medication. She persuaded me to open my mouth and applied the medication so gently that I let her take care of me.

She was a pretty, gentle young woman who was always immaculately dressed in colorful skirts and blouses. Even though she was a peasant she didn't go to the fields. She was one of several

34

women in town who were the publicly acknowledged mistresses of married men. She was supported by the father of her illegitimate daughter. It seemed to me that she lived a better life than the man's wife who had the full responsibility of taking care of the house and the legitimate children. She certainly dressed better and did less hard work than my mother.

Kindergarten was a whole day affair but I have no idea of what we did. We didn't have toys, crayons or drawing paper. I don't remember playing any games. The only thing I remember is the lunch hour. Servants came for the gentry's children and brought them back after lunch. The rest of us brought lunch tied in a cloth or a wooden box. Some of my classmates and I were lucky to supplement our piece of bread with either olives, nuts, dry figs or hard cheese. The teacher told us to put our heads down on the desk and take a nap after we finished eating. She went into the front room to take her *sesta,* nap, that the gentry and some of the middle class took every afternoon. The children who were used to it were home taking their naps. As soon as the teacher left, someone made a noise that brought the teacher back into the room to scold us and repeat her order for us to take a nap.

When I came home in the late afternoon, I could always count on finding my friends Angela and Maria, too poor to go to school, playing in the street. The family had no land. Their father, a day laborer, was usually out of town looking for work. Their older brothers and sisters had left for other towns. Angela and Maria's dresses had so many patches that the original material barely showed. They went barefoot summer and winter. But I envied them as I went by their house and saw their mother, also in a patched ankle-length skirt and barefoot, sitting on their doorstep watching them play. She was always there. She was too sickly to work as a day laborer. (The women whispered that her poor health was brought about by too many pregnancies.) I could depend on her to greet me with a smile and some kind words as I walked towards my house. I knew that neither my mother or grandmother would be home waiting for me. My parents could afford to send me through *Noepoli's* entire school system.- kindergarten through the fifth grade. But I had to take care of myself until my mother and grandmother came home from the fields.

Towards the end of the school year the teacher collected the money for the first grade text books. Each one of us would receive the books by mail.

I had never really paid much attention to the blue-uniformed man who each afternoon walked up the street with his sack on his shoulder and a handful of letters in his hand. Eager to get the books, I started to look for him and wondered how he knew where to bring the letters and packages. The streets had no names, the houses had no numbers and the people knew each other only by their nick names. Many of the family nick names had originated generations before and described the family's origins, occupation or personal traits. We knew them as the "Shoemaker", the "Miller", or the one from *Senise* and so on. Whenever I saw the mailman, I stopped what I was doing to see if he went to our house. I eagerly awaited the arrival of my first books even though the concept of books was a little vague. I couldn't imagine what they would be. The only book I knew was the huge one the priest read at the altar. My mother was one of the few peasants who had gone to school through the second grade and she was eager to get the books too.

When the cardboard box arrived I could hardly wait for my mother to come home to open it. I held my breath as she slit the box with a knife. She lifted the flaps and the smell of sawdust and of freshly printed pages filled the room. The first book she lifted out of the box was a colorfully illustrated copy of *Pinocchio*. I held the book and turned it over to see if there were more pictures on the other side. I couldn't turn the pages. My mother carefully slit the pages with a knife and I gingerly turned the pages. I looked forward to the first grade so I could learn how to read those pages.

Our school week was four and a half days. We had Thursday off but we had to go one-half day on Saturday. The school day was long -- from eight thirty to four o'clock, with a lunch break from twelve to two. The teacher gave us homework to do during the lunch hour while she took her *sesta*.

The first grade had a few peasant children. Otherwise the set-up was similar to the one in kindergarten except that the class was held in a house on a street near us. We walked through the front room with its fire-less fireplace, proudly holding our copy of *Pinocchio,* our notebooks and pencils. The first thing we learned in first grade was to place straight lines, *asti,* evenly spaced between the lines across the page and then all the way down to end of the page. We used every bit of space by leaving no margins. We gradually learned how to write the letters of the alphabet. When we learned the sounds of the letters, we read by sounding out the words in our reader. We practiced writing by taking down the sentences the teacher read to us. After the dictation she called each one to her desk to check the work, while the rest of us quietly waited our turn. We learned simple addition and subtraction. We didn't play any games.

The most memorable event of the first grade was my small pox vaccination. We lined up along the side of the classroom. One by one we stood in front of a man and woman. The woman told me to roll up my right sleeve. She swabbed the upper arm and while she held my arm, the man quickly made three small vertical slashes with a tiny, sharp knife. It hurt but it didn't occur to me to cry out or complain. None of us did. I went back to my seat just like the others and we continued with what we were doing as if nothing had happened.

At the end of the second grade we could decode words, do simple arithmetic and write simple letters. Adults often asked children to read things for them counting on their not understanding what they read. Early one evening, as I was walking home, an elderly middle class lady, dressed all in black, furtively came out of her house and asked me if I could read. When I nodded "Yes" she quickly took my hand and led me in front of the fire. She took a crumbled piece of paper from the deep pocket of her long skirt and asked me to read it to her. The paper had so many wrinkles I could hardly read it when I held it towards the flame. It was an I.O.U.. When I finished, she nodded her head as if she had suspected it's contents all along. She replaced the paper in her pocket with a satisfied look and quickly ushered me out.

Some peasants sent their children to school at least through the second grade in order to eliminate the trips to the letter writers. Whenever they needed to write a letter they had to arrange a mutually convenient time with one of the upper class ladies to write it for them. There were several in town and each had her own following. The ones who could transform the crude dialect into the most flowery Italian had the most followers. These ladies were always approached with the utmost respect. The men, literally, went with hat in hand. If the lady detected any sign of disrespect, she would say that she was too busy to write at that time and that they would have to come back another time. The peasants' time in town was very limited. A postponement was a hardship.

These ladies were paid either with money or produce. Sometimes the peasants had neither. In that case, they asked the *Signora* to write the letter *per favore,* as a favor. She, who also was short of money, would ask the peasants to perform some task for her, also *per favore.* A lot of services were performed *per favore.* This way, people got work done without losing their self respect.

Seven

My vivid recollections of school life start in the third grade which was much smaller than the second. Many of the peasant children had left. The class was taught by *Signora* Cerruti, one of the two permanent teachers in *Noepoli*. Neither she nor her husband were natives of *Noepoli* but they actually liked living in *Noepoli* and they socialized with the upper classes. They had no children. *Signora* Cerruti dressed better than any other woman in town. She wore a fur-trimmed coat over dresses that went down only to mid-calf, used perfume and was the only one with bobbed hair, the flapper style of 1920's.

A woman's hair style was dictated by her social class. The peasants wound their braided hair around their heads, just above the ears. The middle class women arranged their hair in a bun that rested on the back of their necks. The upper class women shaped it into buns on the top of their heads. Bobbing one's hair was scandalous! But the town excused *Signora* Cerruti. After all, she was not a native of *Noepoli* and, presumably, didn't know any better.

In the third grade I became aware of the three portraits that hung under the Crucifix, on the front wall of the room: Pope Pius Xl, Mussolini and King Victor Emmanuel lll. We had to head every page in our notebooks with the calendar date, the year of the Fascist Era, counting from 1922, and the name of the Pope.

The class was held in house near the *Torretta* in a house with its back sitting on the top of the slope that rose behind the *Fontana* on the New Road. For the first time since I started school, my seat was right next to the French doors. Unfortunately, they overlooked the road. The bulge in the hill under the narrow balcony hid the fountain but I had an unobstructed view of the road and the waist high stone wall that separated *La Terra* from the *Casale*. The large opening in the wall was conveniently located across from the *Fontana*, where the bus stopped once a day to deliver the mail. The driver, usually the only one on the bus, took the mail bags out and carried them across the road, down a short flight of stone steps into the post office.

I found watching the coming and going of people on the

road more interesting than the *Signora*'s lessons. I watched the people going to the post office, which also served as a bank and a telegraph office. I day-dreamed of my errands into the *Casale*.

I was often sent to the post office to mail a letter. (There were no mail boxes in town). I handed the letter and the money for the stamp to the clerk and watched him put the stamp on the letter and then toss it into a large box near him.

Near the post office was the store referred to as the tobacco shop but it also sold coffee, sugar and salt. It was the only store in town licensed to sell salt which was so expensive that I went often to buy small amounts at a time. When I stepped inside I had to wait for my eyes to become adjusted to the semi-darkness, before approaching its owner, *Donna* Elvira. She was dressed all in black except for the white kerchief, tied tightly around her forehead. The white kerchief added to the pained look on her face. *Donna* Elvira believed that the shuttered window and the kerchief around her head would relieve the pain of her perennial headaches. The customers respectfully and some, deferentially, routinely asked,

"How's your headache today, *Donna* Elvira?"

They knew what the answer was going to be.

"Still the same!"

Then, again very respectfully, they said that they hoped she'd feel better tomorrow. She'd answer that she doubted that very much.

I sometimes found her holding her hands in a basin of cold water, another remedy for the headaches. She dried her hands, searched through the box of graduated metal weights for the one equal to the amount of salt I had asked for. She placed the weight on one side of the scales, and carefully scooped out a little salt into the other half of the scale. She continued to place small amounts of salt on the scale until the salt was in perfect balance with the metal weight. She then placed the salt in a paper scoop and sent me on my way.

No one could explain *Donna* Elvira's headaches. It was assumed it was the work of The Evil Eye, the explanation given for any misfortune or ailment that could not be otherwise explained. One way to protect yourself against the Evil Eye was to wear a red coral charm in the shape of a twisted horn on a chain around your neck. It was worn by men, women and children. My mother bought me one but neither she nor my grandmother wore one. Another way to protect yourself was to watch out for people who had very thick eyebrows that met over their noses. You also had to watch out for the persons who complimented you on something and did not say, "May God bless you". If you complimented someone, you made sure you said, "God bless" whatever, for fear of being held responsible for casting the Evil Eye on that person.

One evening my mother tied a kerchief tightly around her head and kept her hands in cold water but her headache did not go away. She told me we were going to visit the woman in the *Casale* known for dispelling the Evil Eye.

We entered the small dark room. The old woman sitting by the flickering flames of the fireplace, beckoned to us. Our shadows followed us on the wall. My mother sat directly in front of her and I sat on a stool on the side. The woman looked old but her hair, braided around her head was as black as her shawl that was held in place by a large safety pin. The hem of her full, black skirt reached the floor, hiding her feet. As soon as my mother was seated, the woman reached in her deep pocket and took out a rosary of large black beads. She started to finger the beads and mumble the prayers. After a few mumbles she stopped for a wide but silent yawn. She continued to yawn in between the prayers. With each yawn she crossed herself and made little tiny crosses on my mother's forehead. The more yawns, the more effective her incantations were thought to be. We sat very still and didn't say a word. We listened to the crackling fire and the noise of the beads rubbing against each other as the woman fingered them. She mumbled a combination of prayers to Our Lady and to the occult powers of the Evil Eye. When the woman came to the end of the rosary she crossed herself with the crucifix, kissed it, cupped the beads in her hand and replaced them in her pocket. Without any words she extended her open palm. My mother gladly put some money in it. Her headache was gone.

From time to time *Signora* Cerruti's voice woke me from my wool-gathering. But soon I was daydreaming again. Even though the bulge in the hill obstructed my view, I could see the *Fontana* in my mind's eye. The large, paved, open area around the fountain was the liveliest part of town. There was always a steady stream of women. They came carrying the large wooden barrels balanced on top of a thick wreath of cloth on their heads. The old women held on to the

41

empty barrels with a hand on each side but the young ones walked jauntily, either holding the barrel lightly with one hand or walked proudly with their arms at their side, the barrel perfectly balanced. While they waited to fill their barrels the women chatted and exchanged bits of gossip. Many of them were housemaids and were in no hurry to get back to their mistresses.

Some of the young women lingered hoping to catch a glimpse of their boyfriends. The rules about young men and women talking to each other were so strict, that they tried to figure out ways of meeting as if by chance. Since getting water was a daily chore, the *Fontana* was a perfect place. The young people made arrangements through oral messages delivered by mutual friends, to be at the fountain at a particular time. The young men would casually walk by as the young women filled their barrels.

When the barrels were full, the women carefully rewound the heavy cloths, placed them on top of their heads and helped each other position the barrels on them. Even the jaunty young women carefully positioned a hand at each end of the barrels and walked back home slowly, looking straight ahead, trusting their feet to find secure ground, careful not to lose their balance.

Between my daydreaming I tried to pay attention but I learned little besides the multiplication table which we referred to as the Pythagoric table.

Once a week our priest, *Don* Antonio, dressed in a cassock and black biretta came in smiling. The 1929 Lateran Treaty between Italy and the Vatican had established Roman Catholicism as the official religion of Italy. The priests wore clerical clothes at all times and were allowed to come into the classrooms to teach religion. During each visit *Don* Antonio taught us a part of the Catechism and a prayer. The following week he tested us orally on what he had taught us the previous week. He listened attentively, with his hands deep in the pockets of his cassock. He dug out a religious medal from one of his pockets, and gave it to the ones who recited the prayer without missing one word or hesitation. He dug in his other pocket for a religious picture and gave it the ones who made one mistake. Occasionally I received a picture but never a medal.

Eight

By the fourth grade I was the only peasant child left in school. The fourth and fifth grade classes were so small that they were taught in the same room, by the other permanent teacher, *Don* Francesco, the bachelor son of an upper class family. The other teachers came from the cities and usually left after one year. *Don* Francesco and *Signora* Cerruti were *Noepoli*'s school system. Only once did a supervisor from the City come to visit our classroom. He looked over the few noteboooks *Don* Francesco gave him to inspect and then left without speaking to any of us.

To get to the fourth and fifth grade class I walked past the confectioner's shop, crossed the *piazza* and continued up the winding street into the open area of the *Torretta.* I walked by the church and hurried past the gray, stone walls of the two story prison. I avoided walking too close to its walls. They breathed out a strong smell of stale urine. I was happy to reach the *scaletta,* the narrow, steep, flight of stone steps that went all the way down to the New Road. The *scaletta* separated the prison from the schoolhouse.

The other side of the schoolhouse was attached to the high stone wall of the Vitelli garden. Through its two huge, padlocked iron grilled doors we could see part of the brick path that went past the trees and flowers. It was the place where the Vitellis of old had followed the gentry's time-honored tradition of taking the *passeggiata*, a late afternoon or early evening walk. Past the garden, the wall continued and curved around the outer edge of the *Torretta* and it could be seen from far away. The wall, once part of the medieval fortifications, kept people from falling over the edge of the steep hill. After curving around the edges of the *Torretta,* it ended at the Vitelli *palazzo*, directly opposite their garden. But no one crossed the open area to stroll in it. The *palazzo* was empty. The family had moved away, leaving the garden and the house in charge of a relative.

(In my time the only one who took a *passeggiata* was the priest. He usually could be seen in the late afternoon, walking slowly on the New Road, reading his *Breviario*.)

Before school we ran around on the hard packed dirt

43

between the garden and the *palazzo*. We looked through its bare windows and wished we could go inside and walk down the staircase to the path that led the Door. We tried to scare each other with stories of ghosts haunting its dark passageways. While we ran around we looked out for *Don* Francesco, who lived in a house diagonally across the schoolhouse. *Don* Francesco lived with his widowed mother and two unmarried sisters. His family was typical of the gentry families in *Noepoli*.

The law of primogeniture, that bestowed all property to the eldest son, left the younger sons and daughters completely dependent on the generosity of the oldest brother. Over the years, bad harvests had eroded the gentry's wealth. The younger brothers started to leave for the cities. The ones who remained held all the important jobs in town. Many remained single because the girls in their social class did not have a dowry large enough to make the marriage profitable.

The women of the gentry were completely dependent on the generosity of the males in the family. They had a limited education and no resources. They had no place to go. Whether they got married or not depended entirely on the size of the dowry the eldest brother was willing to give them. Many brothers, faced with the choice of arranging an advantageous marriage for their daughters or giving a generous dowry to the sisters, chose their daughters. Many of the gentry's young women grew old in a male relative's household, as unpaid nannies and servants.

But no matter how poor they were, the gentry maintained their air of superiority and insisted on being addressed by the honorific title of *Don,* for the men and *Donna,* for the women. When the gentry met members of the lower classes, especially the peasants, they expected to be greeted deferentially and be addressed in the very formal third person of *lei.* If the gentry acknowledged the greeting, the peasants felt that a great honor had been bestowed on them. Sometimes the gentry would just go by and ignore the peasants' greeting. They treated us Americans peasants a little better because we had the cash but they resented us for it.

As soon as someone yelled that the teacher was coming, we stopped and ran to the school door. *Don* Francesco walked slowly, deliberately took out his pocket watch and glanced at it. He gave us enough time to get there ahead of him. As soon as he reached us we

44

stood at attention, raised our right arms in the Fascist salute, the Roman salute that Mussolini had adopted as his own, and said, *"Viva il Duce!"*. *Don* Francesco acknowledged our salute and then inserted the key into the door to let us in.

We walked through the front room with its fire-less fireplace and into the classroom. The fourth graders sat on far side and the fifth graders sat on the side near the French doors. (My seat was in the back for both grades). We started each day by standing up, officially saluting the teacher and then singing the Fascist hymn, *Giovinezza,* "Youth".

In the fourth grade we started to write with ink. We made our own ink at home by mixing a black powder with water in just the right proportions or the ink would either become a glob or run off the paper. We carried the ink back and forth to school each day. It often spilled over our hands, our books and our clothes. The pen was a wooden stick, smaller than a pencil, with a tiny slot at one end where we inserted a slotted metal tip. If we didn't dip the tip just so, the writing smeared. I never did master the skill. My writing in school was often messy. The homework I wrote by the firelight was even worse. We all carried our ink bottles with pride. It was a way to show people how far we had progressed in school.

Don Francesco sat at his desk, which had a few books, several notebooks, a ruler and a pointer, and told us what page in what book to turn to. The history text contained several minimally discussed subjects. The history of England was told in two or three pages. I remember it only because of a picture of Elizabeth I wearing a beautifully brocaded black gown with rows of white ruffles around her neck. The design of the dress minimized Elizabeth's waist to almost nothing and I wondered how she could possibly have had such a tiny waist. The only picture of the United States was one showing the traffic on Forty-second Street in New York City. I scrutinized that picture because my father lived in New York. Besides the fact that there were a lot of cars in America I learned that Americans had red skins and straight black hair. I was very confused when *Don* Francesco introduced a new girl and told us she had come from America. She had a very white face and black curly hair. After a while I learned she was born in America of parents from *Noepoli*, who had returned to stay.

45

Our reader dealt with various topics. One story told of *Pierino*'s adventures on his uncle's farm. I looked at the pictures in wonder. I had never seen people so well dressed and farm houses so large. The point of the story was that all these wonderful conditions existed because of the *Duce*'s leadership.

When it was time to read, *Don* Francesco called on one of us to start and then, at random, he called on another to pick up where the other had left off. Before going to lunch he took up one of the several hand-written notebooks on his desk and dictated a few paragraphs for us to memorize at home. When we came back after lunch he called on one of us to start reciting the selection word for word. He would stop us and abruptly call on someone to pick up exactly where the other had stopped. I managed to parrot back the Italian words without fully understanding what I was saying. Before dismissing us for the day, *Don* Francesco dictated some more for us to memorize for the next day. That's how we learned European history from the legendary founding of Rome to Mussolini's *coup*.

The ones who did not pay attention and couldn't pick up the reading or the recitation were called to his desk to receive their punishment. He hit the girls' hands with the ruler and hit the boys' legs with the pointer. The students whose attention span didn't improve were given *Don* Francesco's direst punishment. He ordered the offenders to the corner in the front of the room, to kneel on a handful of dried chick peas.

The only educational tools in the room were a large wall map of the world and a moveable blackboard. To teach geography, *Don* Francesco took the long pointer from the top of his desk, walked over to the map and pointed out various locations on the map. The only thing I learned from those lessons was that the blue represented water. But I couldn't imagine what that water actually looked like. I couldn't imagine any body of water wider than a river. At other times *Don* Francesco went to the blackboard to explain arithmetic problems which I hardly ever fully understood. I don't remember being taught multiplication, long division or fractions but I do remember feeling embarrassed when I was called to the board to solve one of these problems and I couldn't do it.

We had no art, music or physical education. Although Mussolini, a physical fitness enthusiast, who once skied the Alps bare-chested, had mandated a physical fitness program in the schools, there was none in *Noepoli*. The only sport equipment in town was a soccer ball that the young men used on the parched piece of level ground near our *orto*.

In the fourth grade we were automatically enrolled into the Fascist Party and given the credit-card size identification. *Piccola Italiana,* was printed on the girls' cards and *Balilla*, the name of a boy who had defied the occupying Austrians in the eighteenth century, appeared on the boys' cards. Once a week we wore our uniforms. The girls wore a white blouse with a black scarf over a navy skirt. The boys wore black shirts with a white scarf and short black pants. On that day, *Don* Francesco wore his black shirt and black hat. He led us out to the open area in the *Torretta* and marched us around a few times. The exercise didn't do anything towards our indoctrination into Fascism but it was a welcome break from the classroom work.

Aside from the school children, only the town officials belonged to the Party and wore the fascist uniform. The great majority of the people took Fascism in their stride. Since the dawn of history one nation after another had invaded the area. Each succeeding generation had learned the bitter lesson that no matter who was in charge their lot was always the same.

At any rate, Fascism brought about only minimal changes. The people of *Noepoli* quickly learned which rules they had to obey and which they could safely ignore. Mussolini's attempt to change the eating habits of the Southern Italians was a complete failure. He wanted us to eat rice instead of bread because Italy produced abundant rice but not enough wheat. The *Carabinieri* did not even try to persuade the peasants to change. Bread was the only constant in their diet. Any other food was referred to as *companaggio,* literally something eaten with bread.

Two of Mussolini's changes only served to confuse us. In anticipation of reestablishing the Roman Empire, he changed the name of our *Regione* from *Basilicata* to its ancient name of *Lucania*. The other change was welcomed only by the young people, especially the young men. Mussolini wanted to do away with the third person polite address, *lei,* reserved for the gentry and the powerful, and the singular use of *voi,* used to address the old, regardless of social class. The egalitarian *tu* was to be used with everyone. The gentry and the old were annoyed and whispered to each other about it.

It was unlawful for several men to meet and the curfew was strictly enforced. The few men who wanted to talk politics looked for safe ways to do so. A household of only women like ours was perfect. One evening two men came to talk to my mother about pruning some trees. We all sat on the stools near the fireplace. The men and my mother agreed on the price but the men didn't leave. Instead, each man took a twig from the kindling wood near-by and drew pictures in the ashes. As soon as one nodded that he understood the message, the other quickly smeared them. They drew many airplanes. They did a lot of nodding and motioning but never uttered a word. I felt uneasy watching the serious look on the men's faces. I was relieved to see them go.

Nine

The long lunch hour was the loneliest time of the day, especially when I didn't understand the homework. I had nothing to play with except a sock doll. Aside from the text books I had nothing to read except a mail-order catalogue, *La Rinascenza,* that came once a year from Milano. I had no idea where Milano was but I knew it was far away. From the pictures I could see that women there dressed very differently from us. They had bobbed hair like *Signora* Cerruti, wore one piece dresses that reached mid-calf and wore shoes with high heels.

I usually went out hoping to finding Angela and Maria. Otherwise the streets were deserted. The gentry and the middle class were taking their *sesta,* the school children were home with their families and the peasant children were in the fields.

But when I got home in the afternoon, the street was always full of activity. Besides playing with Angela and Maria I also played with three girls, whose father, Carlo, had immigrated to the United States about the same time as my father. The three girls and their mother Isabella lived in three rooms above the butcher shop, directly across from our house. Because of our age differences we were in different grades but we saw plenty of each other after school. We had a special bond because our fathers were friends and lived near each other in New York City. However, when we disagreed about the rules of the game or about who was to do what, they were ready to remind me that their father was a master bricklayer and a member of the middle class and that my father was a hod carrier and a peasant. They referred to their father as Papa' and I by the peasant name of *Tata.*

I tried to minimize our disagreements because, not only did they outnumber me but they would leave me and run home to their mother, who, unlike mine, was usually at home. Isabella rarely went to the fields. She went only if there were any problems with the workers. She had a maid who went to the fountain to get water and to the river to do the laundry. But Isabella didn't get involved in our squabbles. She sent the girls out again to settle our differences by ourselves.

49

We played with our sock dolls, tried to out-do each other in making intricate patterns of the cat's cradle or played Jacks. Our Jacks were round, shiny pebbles. *Noepoli* had so many crumbling stones that finding round pebbles was no problem, but we prided ourselves on owning a set in which all the stones were smooth and fairly uniform in size. We kept them in our pockets at all times. In bad weather we played on the smooth tiles of our kitchen floor. In good weather we played on one of our stone steps. In gathering the widely spread-out pebbles in one scoop, we often scraped our hands on the rough stone. But a little blood didn't stop our game. When there was a large enough group of both girls and boys we played hide-go seek. Otherwise the boys played leap-frog.

As I got older there were fewer and fewer boys on the street. The middle class boys were apprenticed to one of the master craftsmen in town: tailor, shoemaker, carpenter, mason, butcher, blacksmith, cooper, and the barber. They lived in the masters' house and were completely under their authority. Usually only the sons of craftsmen became apprentices. But occasionally a peasant father did manage to do without the son's help in the fields and to pay the tuition.

Whenever an official went by we stopped what we were doing, stood at attention and gave the Fascist salute. We also stopped when we heard the tinkling of the goat's bell. We were curious to see where its owner would stop. Wherever a woman came out with a container he squirted out some milk into it and then kept going. We mostly ignored the pleasant young man who walked by almost every afternoon, talking nonsense to himself and to the people he met. He reminded me of the morning I had rushed out of the house to see what the yelling in the street was all about. Several disheveled women and two men were walking along the street, screaming incoherently. People came out of their houses and others were leaning over their balconies. We all looked on in puzzled silence. Once they passed by, the on-lookers started talking to each other. The family had become deranged during the night while conducting occult rites, chanting incantations and burning cryptic messages in their fireplace. After a few days the whole family, except their son, were back to normal. He became part of the street scene and we just accepted him the way he was.

We were always aware of the women sitting on their front steps. To escape the confines of their one or two room living quarters the peasant women with no land to go to, sat on their front steps. They chatted as they patched and re-patched clothes. Some knitted socks. They threaded the white wool through a huge safety pin on their blouses and clicked the shiny steel needles without tangling the yarn. Mothers openly nursed their babies. The mother's milk was the only food available until the baby could eat soft food. The ones who didn't have enough milk became frantic and looked for the mothers who could spare some. They passed the babies around and whoever had extra milk gladly nursed the hungry babies. When a baby would not stop crying, the mother gave it a *papagna,* a pacifier made of poppy seeds wrapped in a piece of white cloth and shaped like a lolli pop. The mother held on to the cloth until the baby fell asleep. The young mothers gladly gave advice to the young pregnant women who went by. The most common one was not to look at people with physical defects or birth marks. Whatever imperfection the expectant mother looked upon, would surely show up on her newborn. [2]

Even though the women were busy chatting, mending, knitting and feeding their babies and didn't seem to pay attention to us, they influenced our behavior. We felt we were being supervised.

Asides from the women, we were aware of another person. It was a *straniero,* a stranger, who sat on a chair on the stoop of the house attached to ours, where the miller lived with his second wife and his teen-age daughter, Francesca. Whenever I went to visit Francesca I found her step-mother near the fireplace frying slices of potatoes. I smelled them and wished I could eat some. They were a delicacy. She was preparing them especially for one of these boarders who occupied the last and the best of the three interconnecting rooms. The *straniero* usually left after a few months and another came to take his place.

These *stranieri* on the miller's stoop were political *internees* from Italy's industrialized north. Whatever they had done had not been serious enough for a real jail. Sentencing these educated people to spend time under house arrest in *Noepoli* was considered punishment enough. *Noepoli* was Mussolini's Siberia. They sat on the

---

[2]Genesis 30:37-43

stoop, read the day-old paper they received by mail, watched the people go by and exchanged casual conversation with the passers-by. The *internees* couldn't leave the house but the gentry and even the *Carabenieri* often came to visit them. At times, with the tacit approval of the *Carabenieri*, they were invited to spend an evening in the house of one of the gentry.

One of these *internees* was a woman. She was a good-looking, buxom blonde. She sat and read the paper but not too many people stopped to talk to her. The men were afraid of causing a scandal by being friendly to her. The upper class women didn't go walking. The only ones who befriended her were the house maids on their way to do errands.

Most of the *stranieri* stayed only a few months. But there was one who stayed for several years. Unlike the others, he was not educated and too poor to live in the miller's house. He lived with a family in the *Casale*. He was a thin, giant of a man with flaming red hair from far away Venice. He was the tallest and strongest man anyone in *Noepoli* had ever seen. He used his height and strength to earn some money. I saw him carrying bundles too heavy for anybody else in carry. But his shoulders weren't bent so much by the weight but rather by an inner sadness. He was homesick. The peasants understood the depth of his loneliness, treated him with kindness and tried to communicate with him even though his Venetian dialect and *Noepoli*'s dialect were almost mutually unintelligible. In a way, he was like them. He was as helpless to change his fate as they were to change theirs.

One afternoon I smelled the aroma of steaming *puliato* as I opened the door to the kitchen. I became apprehensive. The infusion of this herb was used to treat all types of respiratory problems. My mother was having a bout of malaria. My grandmother sent me to the pharmacy for quinine.

The pharmacy was a small and very bright room in the house of the druggist, *Don* Paolo, the doctor's brother. The entrance wall was all glass except for the door. The wall overlooking the New Road, was half glass. My eyes needed time to adjust to the glare of the glass showcases and the glass shelves behind it. The druggist looked down at me from behind the showcase. When I asked for the quinine he opened the back door of the showcase and took out a bottle. He transferred some of the pills into a small bottle and I had to stand on my toes to take it from him. I walked back home as fast as I could. Quinine was the only thing that would help my mother with her latest bout of malaria, a disease that was thought to be caused by *mal aria*, bad air. I found my mother eating the "soup" prepared from the hot water whose vapors she had inhaled. My grandmother had taken the sprigs of the herb out of the water, dropped morsels of bread in it, and added some oil and salt.

Malaria was common in *Noepoli*. My mother accepted the illness as all the others did. She bundled up to stop the ague, took quinine and waited for it to pass. The townspeople accepted all ailments as something to live through. Toothaches were inevitable. To relieve the ache, the sufferer tied a kerchief around the chin and tied it on top of the head. The kerchief stayed on until either the tooth fell out or someone tied a string around it and yanked it.

Aside from her bouts of malaria and the occasional tooth ache, my mother was in good health. (My grandmother had lost all her teeth before I was born.) Both my mother and grandmother were proud to have survived the Spanish Influenza epidemic of 1918. They ascribed their survival to their diet of hot peppers and red wine.

Sick people seldom went to or sent for the doctor. Few had the money to pay him or the confidence in his skill. Besides, he discouraged people from calling him by the remarks he made when anyone did.

If he was called to take care of an old person he's say,

"Why bother? He or she is going to die soon, anyway."

If he was called to take care of a baby, he'd say,

"Why all the fuss? There'll be another one next year."

When desperation drove people to send for him, they then had to hope they would find him at home. When I was sent by a neighbor to get him, the maid told me the doctor was hunting on his country estate.

"I'll tell him as soon as he comes home."

"When will that be?"

"Maybe tomorrow."

My family was one of the few who paid a yearly fee to *Don Giovanni* for unlimited visits. But I never remember going to his office or his coming to the house.

One afternoon the street scene was different. I sensed something was very wrong. The women weren't sitting and chatting as usual. Instead they were standing in the middle of the street staring at the staircase wedged between two houses. They were solemn and talked quietly to each other. Instead of playing we gathered around the women and heard that the doctor came to see Pino, one of the boys who played hide-go seek with us. We looked at each other fearfully. We all knew what a visit from *Don* Giovanni meant.

As the news spread that the doctor was visiting Pino, more people gathered at the bottom of the stairs.

"What's the matter"?

"Pino's abdomen suddenly started to swell and the swelling spread throughout his whole body".

Some of the neighbors came out of curiosity and some came out in the hopes of getting a free diagnosis. The ones who couldn't afford a doctor's visit hoped to catch him on a sick call. They figured that since they hadn't sent for him he wouldn't charge them for his advice. They waited anxiously for him to come down. Before *Don* Giovanni reached the bottom step, several women started to ask him about a cure for their ailments or the ailments of members of their families. The doctor, used to being cornered like this, quickly diagnosed and prescribed medications and inched himself out of the group.

After he left we heard,

"The doctor can do nothing to save Pino"

Some of us went up to see him. He was lying on his back, on the wooden bench near the fireplace in the kitchen that was no bigger than a vestibule. His body was swollen to twice its normal size. He was too sick to speak or to move. His mother was holding his hand and crying quietly.

For a few days afterwards my friends and I watched women go up the steps to the sick boy's house, sighing and shaking their the heads. When they came down they were holding handkerchiefs to their faces, wiping away tears. A few days later Pino died. The women resigned themselves to Pino's deat as God's will.

Besides playing in the street or running errands for neighbors I often had to tend to supper. When we had no more fresh vegetables to eat, our supper usually consisted of some kind of beans, slow-cooked in the *pignata,* a wide-bellied clay pot with a handle and a removable clay lid. The lid covered a hole just large enough for a long wooden spoon to stir the beans. Before going to bed my mother placed pre-soaked beans, water, salt and oil into the *pignata.* The next morning she started the fire, banked it and set the belly of the *pignata* against the embers. My job was to stir the beans and rotate the pot towards the fire several times during the day. I did it when I got home for lunch and again before leaving for the afternoon session. I went straight home after school to check on the beans. However, no matter how hard I tried, when I got home, sometimes the fire was out. When I couldn't restart it, I ran to Fortunata.

Fortunata was a tiny, spry, cheerful, childless widow whose husband had died before my memory but she still wore black. The dirt floor of her one room house, across the alley from us, was always clean-swept. The room had a double bed, a wooden chest at its foot and a few stools near the fireplace. The shelves on the fireplace wall were lined with small bottles and clay jars. Her wrinkled face broke into a reassuring smile as soon as she saw the panic on my face. She stopped what she was doing and came home with me. She offered encouraging words as she restarted the fire and coaxed the tiny flame by flapping her black apron back and forth. She reset the *pignata,* rearranged the embers around it and assured me that everything would be all right.

We varied the supper by using different beans. We had white, red kidney beans, chick peas, lentils and most often, *fava.* We had *fava* beans three of four times a week. I often heard the young adults say that they would love to leave *Noepoli* just to get away from the *fava.*

One night a week we had pizza. Before going to the fields, my mother mixed and kneaded the dough for the week's supply of bread, ran her oiled hands over it to prevent the dough, as it rose, from sticking to the towels she used to cover it. In the evening, she walked through my grandmother's room, lifted the trapdoor and walked down to the storeroom to make the bread.

First, she lit the wood in the oven and then went to the trough. She put aside a handful to be used as the starter dough the following week To test the oven's temperature and also to prepare our supper she shaped several *pizze,* topped with green peppers and either fresh or jarred tomatoes, according to the season. She carefully positioned each *pizza* on a flat wooden paddle and slid it in the hot oven. My grandmother tended to the *pizze* while my mother shaped several *pitas*, pocket breads, and shaped the rest of the dough into loaves. When the loaves were safely in the oven, we went upstairs carrying the *pizze.*

Before we sat down on our stools near the fireplace to eat the *pizza*, I walked around to the wine cellar to get a bottle of wine. Wine was part of our supper and routinely I was given a small amount. After the meal I brought the bottle back to the wine cellar.

We used the pitas as pockets for the cooked food we took to the fields. When the *pizze* and the *pite* were finished we ate the regular bread. By the end of the week the bread was hard. We fried stale slices in oil. If they were too hard to fry, we sprinkled them with water. We did this carefully so that the bread would be moist enough but not soggy. We sprinkled it with salt, paprika and drizzled it with oil.

For a fast supper, we had *polenta,* a corn meal pudding. We usually ate it just as it came out of the pot or topped with tomato sauce and grated cheese.

When my mother had the time she made different shaped pasta from the coarse wheat bran she sifted out of the flour before making the bread. Occasionally we had a treat from the confectionery store.

The owner of the store on the *Piazza,* not only baked cookies and prepared liqueurs from tiny bottles of extracts for baptisms, engagements and weddings and sold the chocolates, wrapped in red, green and blue glistening foil and the multicolored Jordan almonds that I longingly looked at every time I passed its wide window on my way to school, he also sold groceries. Occasionally, my mother sent me there with the instructions to buy *strozzati*, broken-up spaghetti. The spaghetti were shipped loose in large boxes. By the time they arrived many of them were in pieces. The confectioner separated the broken pieces from the whole ones and sold the *strozzati* at a lower price. When I returned from the store, the water was boiling. While the spaghetti were cooking my grandmother sauteed the garlic to be tossed over them.

Ten

Although I was still in school my mother was thinking ahead to my marriage. Marriages were arranged by the couple's parents along social and economic lines. Peasant men married only peasant women, middle class men married middle class women and the gentry married only within their own class. Even if one of their girls wanted to marry someone from a lower class, the men in her family would not allow her to do so.

Parents of marriageable children were always on the look-out for appropriate mates. The girls' parents looked to marry their daughters to men a little higher in the social scale and the men's parents looked for a girl whose dowry would add to their son's wealth.

When a young man and his parents decided on the appropriate girl they sent a friend to convey their intentions, *ambasciata,* to the girl's parents. When everyone agreed to the marriage, the two sets of parents worked out the financial details. Some couples actually fell in love while all the financial arrangements took place. The ones who did not, married anyway, if the marriage seemed an advantageous one.

There had been occasions when a peasant had been able to give his daughter a big enough dowry to attract a middle class man. My mother hoped the same for me. But if my father could not give me a large dowry, I would have to marry a peasant. To prepare for both situations she found things for me to do in town, as often as possible and took me to the fields only when she had to.

Besides the dowry the girl needed a trousseau. The richer the girl the more elaborate the trousseau. Ideally, she had to have twelve of every personal undergarment and every household linen plus a bedspread or two. The mothers started to save for the trousseau almost as soon as the girls were born. As soon as they saved enough for one item, they went to the fabric store in the *Piazza,* to buy the material.

The item had to be cut and hand stitched. Then each item had to be trimmed with hand-made lace or embroidered or both. Saving the money for the material took time and so did the sewing and embroidering. The girls started to sew their trousseaus as soon as they could thread a needle. They all hoped to be married while still in their teens. My mother became expert at finding the young ladies who needed help with their trousseaus and volunteered my services.

Most often I went to a house half-way between our house and the *Torretta*. The house belonged to an impoverished upper-class widow and her two daughters, *Donna* Giulia and *Donna* Lucia. The mother always greeted me with a big smile and motioned me towards the spacious, rectangular room, brightened by the light from the large French doors in the far wall. The room was intended to be used as both a dining and living room. I could imagine the large group of well dressed and proud men and women graciously eating at the large dining room table and the servants coming and going from the adjoining kitchen. After eating they could sit on comfortable chairs and chat or walk through the French doors and take the air on the wide terrace that overlooked the countryside. But that was before my time.

Usually the two sisters were already at work and gladly gave me the work that was there waiting for me. Most of the times it was just the two sisters and I but some afternoons we were joined by some of their friends who came with their embroidery. In good weather we opened the French doors and sometimes we sat on the terrace. In the spring we lifted our eyes from our stitching to watch the rhythmic movement of the peasant women's bright petticoats as they moved across the fields, cultivating the green wheat plants. At times we heard the faint echoes of their songs. At those times the sisters, living their sheltered lives, looked out onto the fields and said,

"How lucky those peasant girls are."

They envied the peasant women their freedom of movement, their seemingly carefree life and their access to eligible peasant men. Peasant men and women worked side by side and since they were all poor, they had the least trouble marrying the person they really liked.

The two sisters worked on their trousseaus as if their weddings were imminent, when in fact their chances of getting married were next to nil. Besides not having a dowry, they each had a handicap that compounded their problem. *Donna* Giulia was in her twenties and had a limp. The limp alone disqualified her for marriage.

Only an enormous dowry would entice any man to marry her. *Donna* Lucia was pretty, still in her teens and able bodied. But she was handicapped by the Biblical custom[3], still strictly followed, of not marring until her older sister was married.

The family was able to keep up its life style because the sisters' older brother had immigrated to the United States several years before. They talked of the brother's generosity in sending them money but they knew that he would never be able to send them dowries. The brother was just wonderful. The only thing he did wrong was not coming back to *Noepoli*, as it was the custom, to choose a wife. Instead he had married a girl in America. They often talked sorrowfully about their other brother who, years before, had died unexpectedly. One hot summer night he went out on the terrace for some air and got a chill. He ran a fever during the night and in the morning he was dead.

One afternoon two of the sisters' friends came in very excited. Something unheard of was about to take place. A young lady of their class, with no males in the family to stop her, had accepted the proposal of young, handsome and wealthy peasant, rather than to continue to live in genteel poverty with her unmarried sister and widowed mother. The peasant was rich enough to keep all three women in the manner befitting their class. He was so happy to marry into the gentry that he did whatever the three women wanted.

No sooner had the young women reconciled themselves to the fact that nothing as lucky was going to happen to them than another piece of news raised their hopes. A young man who had left *Noepoli* for America years before to escape conscription, was coming back to choose a wife. He had no special girl in mind. *Noepoli's* unmarried young ladies and their mothers started to speculate about his choice and impatiently awaited his arrival A few weeks later, a young man did get off the bus and the news spread like wild fire. The American had finally arrived.

The visitor soon became very visible. Well dressed in a three piece suit, he walked up and down our street, socialized both with the middle class and the gentry. In a few weeks he made his choice. The townspeople were surprised that he had picked a girl without a dowry.

---

[3]Genesis 29:26

The young man had his own shoe repair shop in New York City. He prided himself on being able to afford to choose a girl for herself and not for her dowry. The couple was married within a few weeks and the American stayed long enough to leave a pregnant wife.

Soon after, the arrival of young men in several trucks raised the hopes of the marriageable girls once again and created excitement in the town. They put up poles and strung up wires. *Noepoli* was to be wired for electricity! Those who could afford it had their houses wired. My mother made sure our house was one of them. Finally the night came for the main switch to be turned on. We all went outside to wait. The streets of *Noepoli* echoed with astonished gasps as we beheld the bright light that banished the darkness and brought a glimpse of the twentieth century. The next day the young men left.

The young ladies I embroidered with were disappointed once more. They continued to embroider as a group and continued to hope against hope that somehow a suitor would come. They hoped for a husband who would keep them economically secure and not abuse them. Not to be married was a fate worse than death.

When I didn't go to the sisters' house I went to help Annina. She was the only child of a peasant who had come back from America with enough money to live comfortably and to give his daughter a large dowry. She was in her teens and even though she was not very pretty, she was about to be engaged to a middle class young man.

Annina was usually alone in the two room house. She led me through the kitchen into the family's bedroom. It had a double bed and a narrow bed for Annina. We embroidered in front of the only window. Her descriptions of Vittorio, the young man chosen by her parents, became more glowing with each visit.

One afternoon Annina was not alone. Her parents and Vittorio's parents were sitting at a table near the bedroom door, with a man arranging sheets of papers in front of him. I motioned that I would go away but Annina motioned for me to stay. The two of us sat quietly on straight back chairs at the opposite end of the room. We watched and listened.

I had walked in on the official betrothing ceremony. The notary read off items from a sheet of paper. After each item he asked each set of parents if they agreed or disagreed with what he had just read. Aside from the careful listing of real estate and cash, the notary

60

went down the name and description of every item of Annina's trousseau. Each item was discussed carefully. Annina's mother stopped the notary once to correct the number of the item mentioned. They were giving Annina only ten sheets instead of the twelve listed. The notary public asked Vittorio's parents if they agreed to the number. When this happened we both tensed up and held our breath. Any unresolved differences during this procedure could put an end to the marriage plans. We were both very relieved when Vittorio's parents accepted the ten sheets instead of the twelve listed. We relaxed when we saw the notary hand the parents a pen to sign the documents They all shook hands and Annina's father served *strega,* the popular sweet, yellow liqueur, in thimble-sized glasses. The date for the engagement party was set.

For the party Annina wore a midcalf-length blue dress and arranged her brown hair in a bun on the back of her neck, to denote her new middle class status. The groom and the men wore their black suits, white shirts, opened at the neck and no tie. The guests chatted and sipped liqueur from their tiny glasses and nibbled on the cookies that the confectioner had baked. I looked forward to helping myself to some of the pastel-colored Jordan almonds and the chocolates in the colorful glistening paper that Annina's mother was bringing around on a tray.

A young man started to play the accordion and the guests in the kitchen squeezed together to clear the floor for dancing. The accordionist played the traditional *Tarantella* and the older people got up to dance. When Annina and Vittorio got up to dance the *mazurka,* every eye was on them. They touched the fingers of their outstretched hands and kept their bodies a foot apart all during the dance.

The betrothal was almost as serious as the marriage and Annina took her new role seriously. She was subject to the whims and wishes of her fiancé and his parents. Any perceived impropriety on her part could put an end to the engagement. She and her fiancé could never be left alone. Before Vittorio visited, he had to make sure her parents would be home. Annina had been told to be on guard against the wiles of men in general and her suitor in particular. Even the man you're engaged to might test your resolve to remain a virgin until marriage. She had heard stories where the girls had succumbed to the fiances` wiles and then the suitors broke the engagement because they felt the girls couldn't be trusted to be faithful after marriage. She also knew that when an engagement was broken, the townspeople assumed that to be the reason. The rejected girl usually did not get another offer of marriage. She wanted to be sure to pass her mother-in law's inspection of the sheets the day after the wedding.

With each visit I learned some new detail about their forthcoming marriage. She was ecstatic when Vittorio told her they would have a whole week for a honeymoon and live in a two room house all by themselves. Very few newlyweds had a week for a honeymoon and fewer still could start out in quarters all by themselves. A few days before I had seen the usual way many newlyweds lived. When I delivered a message to a workman, his young bride let me in the one room that she and her husband shared with the husband's father. Their bed was separated from the father's by a blanket hanging from the ceiling.

Eleven

Even though I went to school, helped young ladies embroider their trousseaus and occasionally went to the fields, I still had plenty of time to spend on the street in the front of our house. Since it led to the town hall, the shops, the Church, the prison and the *Torretta,* our front steps and our balcony gave me a front row seat to everything that happened in town.

One of the rare sights was the appearance of a handcuffed man walking between two guards taking him to the prison on the *Torretta.* We children looked on out of curiosity. The adults looked on with sorrowful faces. After the prisoner and the guards had gone by we could hear them mumbling,

"Poor soul".

"I wonder what dire need led him to break the law".

Although the prison served the whole district I didn't see many prisoners being led there. There were never more than one or two in jail at any one time. Sometimes none. On my way to and from school I often saw the jailer take a prisoner for a walk around the prison building.

In the Spring I could looked forward to two visitors. One was the trinket man, who walked up the street calling,

"Any hair to sell. Come and see what you can get for your hair".

He was a small man who seemed to be divided exactly in half by the shallow wooden box he held waist high. The box, suspended by a cord around his neck, was divided into several compartments containing safety pins, straight pins, needles, buttons and rounds of narrow lace.

The women came out of their houses carrying the hair they had saved - the hair that clung to their combs and what they cut off from their long braids. They approached the box with eager anticipation, fondled the various items as they looked up at the man and good-naturedly bargained with him until a bargain was struck.

The other visitor that was welcomed by everyone was the tinker. He came strolling into town carrying pots and pans slung around his neck and shouting,

"Any pots to solder"?

The women came out with their leaky pans as soon as they heard him. As he soldered the leaky pots and pans he talked about what was happening in nearby towns.

The middle class men vied with each other to have him as a house guest because he was a wonderful story teller. The host invited his friends to come over in the evening to listen to the tinker's stories, drink a glass of wine and eat some biscuits.

One year, my godmother's brother, who lived on our street, was the host. We joined the other neighbors around the fireplace, facing the tinker. We listened carefully, watching the firelight play on his face as he told his stories. We, who as a group had never read a story book, were enthralled by the tinker's tales. I didn't understand them all but by the laughs and the comments I could tell that the evening was a huge success. I hoped we would be invited again.

On Thursdays, during the Spring and Summer, the *piazza* was full of activity. The farmers from nearby *Senise* came to sell their produce. Since there was no school on Thursdays I was free to watch the people come and go. The men of the gentry, house maids, middle-class and some peasant women went expectantly, wondering what fresh fruits or vegetables they would be able to buy. The ladies of the gentry were not allowed to go to the *Piazza*. The ones with no men in the family and who couldn't afford a maid, had to depend on the goodness of a peasant woman to go for them *per favore*. These ladies would rather suffer hunger rather than humble themselves by going the *piazza*. The trip to the *piazza* was something more than buying produce. It meant you had something in very short supply in *Noepoli*, cash. Those who went tried their best to make sure that as many people as possible saw them.

At other times, the *piazza* was the refuge of old men who sat on the stone benches under the four spindly trees. Since they were all short of cash, their most enjoyable pastime was tricking each other into treating the others to a glass of wine in the *cantina*, the wine shop in an alley off the *piazza*. They even played a game of cards where the winner had to pay for the wine. When one of them was finally put in a position to either treat them or "lose face", they jauntily walked to the *cantina* and continued to play cards.

Besides the old men, a small group of unemployed young men of the middle class usually loitered in the *piazza*. Since there was no work befitting their class, these young men just did nothing. They either played soccer near *l'orto*, idled in the *piazza* or took long walks in the countryside to look for wild mushrooms and wild asparagus. It was a big accomplishment if they came home with either. Most of the times they came home empty-handed but the search had occupied their day.

The only other people in the *piazza* were the women who went to the dry goods store to buy material for their daughters' dowry or material to make new clothes for the next feast day or black material to make mourning clothes. Black material was bought the most often. The mourning period lasted for one year but if before the year was up, another member of the family died, another year was added. Some women wore black for most of their lives.

To buy material was one of the few reasons the "cave people" occasionally came to town. They walked up the street, looking straight ahead, not bothering to greet anyone, heading directly for the store. Their clothes were even more coarse and more ill-fitting than the ones worn by *Noepoli*'s peasants. Their dialect was farther removed from Italian than ours. The "cave people" had no interest in town life. They returned to their caves as soon as possible. Over two thousand years ago Homer had described them: "...but each one dwells in his mountain cave dealing out rough justice to wife and child indifferent to what others do."[4]

I was out on the street so much that neighbors often asked me to do errands for them or act as a chaperone. Francesca, the miller's daughter next door, was a very unhappy teenager. She did not like her step-mother and resented her father for marrying her. Though she was several years older than I, she was happy to have my company. Her only pleasure was to visit her father's sisters on their farm but both the father and her step-mother did not allow her to go very often. They told her she couldn't go alone and there was no one to go with her.

One summer morning Francesca called to me from her stoop. Her step-mother had finally given her permission to visit her aunts if I

---

[4]Odyssey, Book 9

65

would go with her. It was a long walk to the farm but I said "yes". I didn't have the heart to say "no".

We walked on the New Road, shaded by trees on both sides, for about a half an hour before we reached a break in the trees. Francesca pointed out a low brick house with a red tiled roof in the middle of a green field. It looked like a page from a colorful storybook. We crossed the paved road towards the red brick path, bordered with flowers, that led to the door. The two aunts greeted us warmly as we stepped into the large airy kitchen. It had no frame for the water barrel. Instead, it had something I had never even thought about, a sink and running water. One aunt placed a pot of water on top of a wood burning stove, something else I had never seen, and the other spooned some coarse powder into the two cups she had placed on the table. Reacting to the questioning look on my face she explained she was preparing hot chocolate.

Francesca showed me around the house. It had several rooms built in the shape of a U. Each room had a door to the courtyard. The farm, taken care of by the uncles and their sons, spread out as far as the eye could see. After many years in Argentina the aunts and their husbands returned to *Noepoli* and tried to duplicate the housing and living style they had there. They very rarely came to town. They were Free Masons and were not welcome in the Catholic Church.

One day I was asked to take a message to the priest. The housekeeper led me to a small room where *Don* Antonio was sitting with his head resting on his hands with an ear to a small box from which barely audible words came through a hiss as if coming through water. He looked up just long enough to hear my message and then bent his head down again eager to find out the news that was coming through his precious short-wave radio. It was something I had heard about but I had no idea that one was in *Noepoli.*

Even though the middle class women who lived on our street had a maid they often used me to deliver messages to the other middle class women in town with whom they socialized. I was sent back and forth with messages about arranging for a mutually convenient time for a visit. When the date and time were agreed upon the woman asked me to be her chaperone.

The hostess' maid ushered us into the best spot in the house, usually in front of a French door. The *tondo*, a round table, was set with biscuits, demitasses, and a bowl of sugar cubes. After the women made polite conversation the maid appeared with the *machinetta*, a drip aluminum coffeemaker, and ceremoniously poured the expensive black coffee into the expensive demi-tasses. Then she passed the bowl of the expensive sugar cubes to be delicately stirred by tiny spoons. I wasn't given any coffee but I was given a biscuit or two. I sat in a wooden chair, dangled my feet and nibbled on a biscuit. They spoke as if I weren't there. They exchanged stories about their husbands. They speculated about the embroidery design that *Donna* so-and-so was keeping so secret. They repeated what so-and-so's maid had said to their maid.

After a few of these visits, I realized that the women were gossiping about the women who were not present. I felt uncomfortable listening. It just didn't seem right. I couldn't do any thing about hearing it but I resolved never to repeat it to anyone not even my mother.

Personal messages were sent through children or maids but the general interest news was announced by the town crier who in the evening rang his bell at pre-determined places. When he was satisfied that enough people had gathered, he recited his messages at the top of his lungs. I joined the other children who were sent by adults to bring back the news. Sometimes we went just because we had nothing better to do.

One bit of news we all liked to hear was the announcement of the date a bride would show her trousseau. On the announced day several young women, dressed in their best clothes, walked slowly up our street, balancing on their heads the large, shallow wicker baskets with the linens attractively arranged. Women and their daughters went out on the street or on their balconies to view the quality of the material and the intricacies of the embroidery. They tried to take a good look at the embroidery so they could reproduce some of the designs for themselves. There was no use asking the bride. All brides kept their designs secret.

Stella, one of the brides whose trousseau we had watched go by, lived with her young husband in one room near the *piazza*. About a year after the wedding I noticed that the women on the street were especially friendly to her. They stopped her with some cheerful remark and asked her how she felt. Many times Stella interrupted her answer to cover her mouth with a handkerchief to stifle her cough. After she went by the women's big smiles changed to frowns as they shook their heads. The cough was getting worse and the dreaded word "tuberculosis" was whispered. After a few months she was too sick to go out. The women went to visit her.

One of the women asked me to go with her. Stella was lying in bed, her face as white as the sheet that was covering her. She held a handkerchief balled in her hand, ready to cover her mouth when a fit of cough overcame her. The women seated at the foot of the bed talked with each other and tried to involve Stella in their conversation. They tried to make the time pass as pleasantly as possible while the young woman was dying. The patient was visibly exhausted but she kept up her end of the conversation as best as she could. I was very relieved when the lady I had accompanied decided to leave. Stella died a few days later.

Twelve

On summer days, when I had nothing to do in town, I went along to the fields. By July the green wheat of spring had turned to amber. Fearful of sudden thunderstorms, my mother hired a reaper to harvest it as soon as possible. He wore a brimmed hat, a leather apron and cut-off leather gloves that left the thumbs and fingers free. He bent down at one end of the field, grabbed a handful of wheat stalks with one hand and deftly cut them with the sickle with the other. Then he straightened up and, still holding the sickle in one hand, bound the sheaf with one of its stalks. He dropped the bundle on the stubble behind him as he bent down to cut the next bunch. He worked his way steadily and rhythmically across the field. We followed him, picking up the sheaves and stacking them throughout the field. After two or three days the reaper was done, the sheaves were stacked and the field was ready to be gleaned.

The wealthy still followed the Biblical[5] custom of allowing poor women to glean behind the reapers. But since we needed every ear of wheat we could gather, we did it ourselves. We bent over the stubble to search for any stray ears of wheat and put them in the sack we dragged behind. The kerchiefs tied around our heads were our only protection against the blistering sun.[6] The stubble scratched my hands and legs and the perspiration trickled down my face. I could feel the sweat dripping under my clothes. It was while gleaning that I first caught that worried expression on my mother's face that would always appear whenever she saw me hot and sweaty doing some farm chore. She never said anything as she watched me. The look said it all.

" How are you ever going to make it as a peasant?"

As we gleaned, we picked up the land snails that slithered on the stubble and placed them in a pail of water. At home we rinsed them several times, boiled them and ate them seasoned with sauteed garlic and hot red pepper flakes.

---

[5]Ruth 2: 2-7
[6]Jean- Francois Millet's painting, "The Gleaners".

The church bells struck the hours but we didn't pay much attention. We wouldn't leave until dark. We stopped only when they tolled for a death. Then, we straightened up, bowed our heads, blessed ourselves and mumbled a prayer for the dead. With a sighed "God's will be done", we bent down and resumed our work. We usually were still in the field for the Angelus.[7]

As soon as the reaping was finished my mother arranged for the use of the town's threshing floor. She and my grandmother carried the bundled sheaves on their heads, using both hands to keep them from falling off, unable even to wipe the sweat that ran into their eyes or to push away the stray straws that scratched their necks and faces. I went with them and stayed with the sheaves while they went back and forth until all the sheaves were stacked near the threshing floor. When it was out turn we tossed our sheaves on it. A man walked around its edge, guiding the ox dragging a big, flat, round, mill stone over the sheaves. When one batch was flattened, we tossed in another.

When the threshing was done, we hoped for a good steady breeze. My mother and grandmother took up their pitch forks and started to pick up clumps of chaff and tossed them in the air. If the breeze was just right it would blow the chaff to one side and leave the kernels of wheat on the ground. They paused just long enough to wipe the sweat off their faces or to straighten their backs. They stopped only when the breeze did. They leaned on their pitch forks, and waited to catch the next one. Sometimes they waited in vain. With a discouraged sigh, they put down their pitchforks and sat down nearby. They watched the trees in the distance. When they saw the leaves move, they jumped up, picked up their pitchforks, ready to winnow as the breeze reached them.

We hardly ever finished the job in one day. My mother and grandmother took turns napping, with pitchforks on their sides. As soon as the air stirred one would wake up the other. I watched the winnowing for a while but I eventually fell asleep in the nearby stacks. When the winnowing was over I helped fill the sacks with the wheat and stayed there while my mother and grandmother made their many trips to our storeroom.

The storeroom held our food supply for the year. Wooden

---

[7]Jean-Francois Millet's painting, "The Angelus".

chests along the walls held wheat, flour and various types of beans. Nearby were the liters of oil ready to be sold. Links of sausages, a ham, garlands of dried red peppers, onion and garlic hung from the rafters. In one exterior corner, a small alcove housed the second commode. Near this alcove was the stake where we tied the pig. The opposite outside wall had the brick oven and next to it was a large wooden trough my mother used to knead the dough for our bread.

My mother and grandmother arranged their harvesting chores so that they would not interfere with the celebration of the feast of our patron saint, Our Lady of Constantinople, on August sixth. The feast was the focal date of *Noepoli*'s calendar. People started to prepare for the next one almost as soon as the current celebration was over.

Don Antonio sent out letters to all those who were living in the Americas, asking them for generous contributions. He organized several committees. One arranged for a band to come from out of town and find townspeople to house and feed the musicians for the duration of the celebration. Another arranged for the fireworks and another for a film. Several upper class women got together to sew a new dress for the statue of Our Lady.

The women in town bought material for a new blouse for themselves and their daughters. Families got ready to welcome their out-of-town relatives who had left *Noepoli* but were sure to return for the feast. If ever the relatives came to visit, they came for the feast day.

Three days before the feast, vendors of fruits and vegetables, pottery, dry goods, and ices, set up stands in the open area on the hill that led to the Door. Farmers from the neighboring towns came with their livestock to buy and sell. We went to the fair to buy a watermelon, a fruit we couldn't grow and to which we looked forward from one feast day to another.

We walked along the various stands and the Gypsy wagons. We listened to the Gypsy woman examining the lines in the customer's palm. We watched another turn over the Tarot cards and explain to an anxious woman what each card foretold. Another was delivering a message from a dead relative of the woman facing her. My mother listened with a smile and shook her head. Referring to the Gypsy women she'd say,

"If they could really see the future they would be able to arrange a better life for themselves".

Selling and buying went on outside *Noepoli's* Door and the organ grinder walked up and down the streets attracting the children's attention by cranking the organ and loudly inviting everybody to come see how smart his monkey was. A child put a coin in its cap, the monkey touched a lever and the canary inside the cage picked a piece of paper with the fortune written on it. The organ grinder carefully took the little card from the canary and gave it to the child. If we weren't following the organ grinder we were following the band, marching all through town.

The day before the saint's day, my friends and I went out to the countryside to pick flowers to sprinkle on the statue when the procession went by the next day.

At dusk on the eve of the feast, we carried our chairs and joined the others on the *Torretta*, where a large screen had been set up for the yearly silent movie. Amid remarks of anticipation and the scraping of chairs we tried to find the best spot from which to see the film. A sudden hush came over the crowd when the first squiggles appeared on the screen. The quiet was broken by loud whispers as soon as the dialogue appeared. Those who could, read it for the benefit of those sitting near-by who could not. We empathized with the characters on the screen. We reacted loudly with either sighs or laughter. There was a loud groan when the word *"Finis"* appeared. We were sorry to leave the world of make-believe for the real one. We wouldn't see another movie until the following year.

The next day several men lifted up the statue of the Madonna in her new dress from the niche in church and placed it on a wooden platform. Four men, each holding a corner of the platform, carried the statue down the steps of the church and through the main streets of town.

Angela, Maria and I held our baskets of petals over the railing of our balcony that had been covered with our shiny green bedspread. Waiting for the procession to reach us, we talked across to the three sisters standing on their blanket decorated balcony, with their baskets of petals. After a while we saw the altar boy, carrying a container of holy water, walking along with *Don* Antonio who, in his white robes, embroidered with thick, gold thread, blessed the people standing along the street. He looked up and waved to those of us on the balconies. Some of the petals we sprinkled on the statue fell on the faithful who followed the Madonna barefoot or on their knees.

That day we ate a special meal which we shared with the member of the band, *bandista,* we had housed. (He slept on the wooden bench near the fireplace). We ate around the table in my grandmother's room, covered with a white tablecloth and set with our best dishes. The feast of our patron saint was one of the few days in the year when we had beef from the butcher shop and *ziti,* the store-bought pasta we used for all festive occasions.

Every night of the three day celebration there were fireworks on the *Torretta,* but the most spectacular display was saved for the last night. We were enthralled by the colorful displays that become increasingly more elaborate. When the very elaborate display started to explode and then disintegrate, we knew the show was about to end. Much as we had enjoyed the show, that's how disappointed we were to see it end.

The next day the balconies were again bare and the visitors were gone. The shriveled flower petals on the streets were the only reminders of the feast. When we walked through the Door on our way to the Olive Grove, where the figs were ripe and ready to be picked, the hillside was deserted. The vendors and the Gypsies were on their way to whatever town was celebrating its feast day.

Thirteen

My grandmother and I walked around the trees to pick as many as we could reach. My mother climbed on the branches to reach the figs on the top. We placed the figs in two large, shallow, baskets for my mother and grandmother to carry on their heads to the drying racks in *l'orto*.

There, we carefully sorted the figs. We threaded a strand of *esparto* through each stem of the smaller figs, arranged them either in garlands or in small compact rounds and hung them up to dry. We split the larger ones carefully down the middle, careful not to separate them at the stem, and placed them on the drying rack, flesh side up. When the split figs were dry, we placed an almond in each half and covered it with another split fig, to form a sandwich. We sprinkled the fig sandwiches with sugar and baked them in the brick oven until they were dark brown. They were delicious but we didn't eat too many of them. They were one of our cash crops.

As soon as we finished taking care of the figs we had to get ready for the *vendemmia,* grape-gathering. The vineyard was far away, at the edge of a wide river, the *Fiumara*, which by August was only a dry riverbed. Even though the walk was long I liked going there. I amused myself by crawling under the leafy vines laden with large clusters of white and red grapes. I loved their sweet smell and taste. The only noise under the vines was the buzzing of bees that were so busy sucking the juice form the grapes that they didn't bother to sting me. When I ran out of things to do my mother would send me on a fool's errand. She asked me to walk up and down the river bed to see if I could find some water. I always came back empty handed. Not only was there no water, I couldn't even find a wet spot.

At *vendemmia* time Uncle Raffaele helped us gather the grapes and load them in two panniers on his donkey. My mother and grandmother filled two large baskets to carry on their heads. We started up the narrow, steep path back home. My mother and grandmother, looking straight ahead and holding on to their baskets with both hands, plodded behind Uncle Raffaele's donkey and I trailed behind them. Their feet barely left the ground as they slowly

74

put one foot in front of the other. I was tired and thirsty but I knew better than to complain.

Uncle Raffaele led the donkey to the wine cellar on the side of the house. Its long stone wall had shelves with green liter bottles. Under the shelves were three large casks resting on wooden supports. On the floor were several green, wicker encased demi-john flasks. The opposite two walls were almost completely hidden by a round wooden vat about six feet wide and three feet deep.

The next day, the grapes that had started to dry out were set aside to finish drying as raisins. The rest were pressed into wine. Uncle Raffaele heaped the grapes in the vat. My barefoot mother lifted her skirt above the knees, tucked the hem firmly in its waistband, climbed into the vat and stomped on them. As my mother crushed the grapes, Uncle Raffaele moved the crushed grapes to one side of the vat with a long wooden pitchfork and spread fresh grapes closer to my mother's feet. As she stomped, the juice flowed through the spigot at the bottom of the vat, into the fermenting barrels. When the juice stopped flowing my uncle removed all the skins and stems from the bottom of the vat and put in a fresh batch until all the grapes were pressed.

We put aside some of the juice to be cooked down into *dicotto,* a syrup which we used instead of sugar. Some was put aside and turned into vinegar. We filled a few bottles with the unfermented wine, to drink until the fermented wine was ready. When the fermentation period was over the wine was transferred into the casks against the wall.

At the beginning of Fall we turned our attention once again to the Olive Grove to gather the chestnuts and walnuts. The days were sunny and cool and I enjoyed going there. I picked the nuts on the ground as my mother and grandmother shook them from the trees. I sat down on the ground near my pile of chestnuts and with a sharp stone cracked the prickly coverings. I took out the shiny dark chestnuts carefully, trying to avoid the needles. I removed the thick, soft, green coverings from the walnuts without cracking their shells. The chestnuts pricked my fingers and the walnut juice stained my hands for days. But every year I looked forward to eating the fresh walnuts and chestnuts. We sold most of the walnuts but we boiled the chestnuts and put them in our pockets to eat whenever we got hungry.

In one corner of the Olive Grove there was an incongruous wet spot in which a willow tree surprisingly survived. My mother cut the branches, stripped them, dried them and used them to repair the few caned chairs we had in my grandmother's room. Occasionally she sold some of the dried strips.

When we finished eating the chestnuts we looked for other foods to eat. The green olives were getting plumper but they were hard, bitter and completely inedible. We filled a measure with green olives, covered them with a saline solution and after a few days we rinsed them. For several days we changed the water until the olives tasted just right. The sweet, green olives became part of our daily diet until the ones on the trees turned black in November.

I dreaded November. It didn't snow, but it rained a lot. The rain was a steady, icy drizzle that chilled the bones but it did not stop us from going to the Olive Grove to pick our most important cash crop. Sheets, spread under the trees, caught the plump, black olives that fell as my mother and grandmother shook the trees. They picked up the corners of the sheets and transferred the olives into sacks. My mother hired a man with a donkey to carry the sacks to the oil press at the outskirts of the town.

Once we had stored the oil, we went back to pick the black, wrinkled olives still left on the trees and the stray ones on the ground. They became part of our meals until the summer. We came home drenched and chilled, with stiff backs and red, chapped hands. My mother and my grandmother warmed their aprons in front of the fire. My grandmother wrapped the warm apron around my hands first and then around hers, so that our hands would not sting by being exposed directly to the fire. We soothed our cramped fingers with olive oil.

Fourteen

By end of November we had taken care of all our crops. December was cold and rainy and occasionally snowy. The feast of *Santa* Lucia on December 13 and Christmas made the days less dreary. Saint Lucia, patron saint of eyesight, was not a general holiday but in a town where blindness was dreaded more than death, everyone was devoted to her and celebrated her day in their homes. On the evening of December 12, my mother cooked a few cupfuls of pre-soaked wheat. She left the pot uncovered for the saint to touch when she came during the night to bless our house. The next morning the wheat did have a small depression on it. I knew my mother had done it with the bowl of the wooden spoon but I didn't say anything. Knowing that Saint Lucia had not blessed the wheat did not stop me from enjoying eating it. We ate the cooked wheat for one or two days afterwards. We either sauteed it with onions and pepper flakes or we turned it into a sweet treat by pouring some of the *dicotto* over it.

In preparation for the Christmas service, we planted a handful of wheat in a pot and placed it in a closet in total darkness. We watered the wheat regularly and after a few days the kernels sprouted into pale yellow shoots instead of green. By Christmas, the shoots were over a foot high. My mother tied a ribbon around the wheat, brought the pot to church and placed it among the other pots of yellow wheat at the foot of the altar.

The week before Christmas we got ready to make the traditional foods. The three of us spent hours together near the fireplace as we prepared a different food each evening. We worked by firelight and the flickering wick of the clay oil lamp on the mantelpiece.

The most popular and the least expensive treat, the *zeppole*, were made of very soft bread dough. My mother pulled off a small chunk of the dough from the leavened mass, rolled it carefully between her oiled hands until it was shaped into a narrow rope, pinched the two ends together to form a circle, placed it on a long wooden stick and carefully placed the circle into the hot oil in the cast iron frying pan on the tripod. My grandmother, ready with a very long

77

fork, centered the circle of dough in the pan and as soon as it was golden she removed it to make room for the next one. Over the years they had perfected the procedure so that every movement was perfectly timed. We ate *zeppole* for supper and stored the rest. For the following few days we ate them either plain, sprinkled with sugar or dipped in honey.

Another treat were the *rosette*, or little roses. These were more difficult to make and required eggs, which were scarce. My mother carefully rolled the cookie-like dough into a large, very thin circle on a large wooden board. She used a ridged cutter to cut the dough into long strips about two inches wide. Then she pinched the strip at about one inch intervals and wound it around itself into a shape that had a vague resemblance to a fully opened rose. They were deep fried and sprinkled with sugar.

My favorite were the *calzoncini*, deep fried tiny turnovers, filled with chick pea paste sweetened with sugar and melted chocolate.

Christmas Eve was one of the few times we had fish. Fresh fish was rare in the hill towns of Southern Italy as evidenced by the great many people who had unsightly swollen goiters. The fish that eventually reached *Noepoli* was expensive. My mother bought the cheapest, whiting. She served it in tomato sauce over spaghetti. If we didn't have the whiting, we used a sauce made with stewed *baccala*. *Baccala* was heavily salted cod dried into the hardness of wallboard. To make it edible, the pieces had to be soaked in water and rinsed for several days. The trick was to soak and rinse it just enough to be edible and still be firm.

In winter we usually went to sleep soon after supper. Candles and oil for the lamps were expensive. Firewood was hard to find and it had to be carried long distances. We stayed up late only on rare occasions. One of these was Christmas Eve. It was considered bad luck to return to a dark house after Midnight Mass. My mother carefully gauged the size of the Yule log to last until we got back.[8] Then we bundled up for our walk to church. I knew I was lucky to have a coat and my mother and grandmother were proud to wrap

---

[8]Adaptation of the pagan celebration of the birth of the Sun God on the winter solstice.

themselves in their black, woolen felt *manto,* trimmed in shining black taffeta. The *manto* was a large rectangular cloth that covered the head, reached down to below the waist and was wrapped around the chest by placing both hands under its edges at the chin. It was not much different from the one worn by the women in the Bible. On clear nights, the walk to church was no problem but on overcast or rainy nights, before electricity was installed, it was almost impossible. On those nights we waved a torch in front of us to find our way.

Noepoli was very quiet at night except for the cries of hungry babies. The only people out were the *Carabinieri,* looking for men breaking the curfew, and the shadowy figures of women hurrying to the edge of town to empty their chamber pots.

But on Christmas Eve the streets echoed with the footsteps and the voices of people chatting on their way to Midnight Mass. As we went up the steps of the 400 year old church we had to be careful not to trip over the loose stones or stumble into the hole left by one. We put out the torch and went through the huge wooden doors, we crossed ourselves with the holy water and walked carefully over the white-tiled floor to make sure we didn't trip on a loose one. Near the altar were a few rows of pews that belonged to members of the gentry and the middle class. The rest of us sat on folding metal chairs brought out by the sacristan. We knelt on the hard, cold tile floor. Even though the church was full of people the combined body heat did not keep us warm.

There were more lit candles than usual but the church was still not bright. In an effort to make the altar area look festive, the sacristan had anchored a large, bare olive branch into a wooden vat. From the small limbs dangled a few oranges on strings. In the *creche* under the tree the ceramic Baby Jesus was flanked by the statues of Mary and Joseph.

Don Antonio gave his usual emotional sermon, offering hope for the future. No matter the subject of the sermon. he managed to ask for volunteers to fix the chipped tiles and the loose stones.

After Mass we lit our torch from one nearby and joined the fathers, mothers and older children who carried sleeping toddlers. On the way home we saw lights and heard happy voices from the houses where families were getting together for celebrations. The happy sounds trailed us to our empty house. The Yule log was burning but I didn't feel its warmth. Instead, the crackling sounds of the fire deepened the loneliness.

We heated bricks by the fire, wrapped them up in thick cloths and carried them to our beds. My grandmother took her brick to her bed and my mother and I carried ours upstairs. She rubbed her sheets and I rubbed mine. We quickly got into bed and rested our feet against the warm bricks.

On Christmas morning my mother, with a big smile, handed me an orange,[9] rare at any time but especially so at Christmas time.

---

[9]Another symbol of the Sun God.

Fifteen

The cold, rainy and snowy weather continued into January. But no matter the weather, on January sixth, the Epiphany, *La Befana*, a magical woman dressed in black, came during the night and left a handful of candy to the good children and a handful of coal to the naughty ones.

January ushered in the Carnival. The adults missed not being able to wear costumes, masks and to go about town playing pranks on each other. Mussolini, fearing that political plots could be carried out under the anonymity of costumes and masks, had abolished the practice. But since people were forced to stay in town by the bad weather they tried to amuse themselves as best as they could before Lent started on Ash Wednesday.

The sequential order of slaughtering the pigs gave family and extended family members occasions to socialize. Neighbors got together to talk and sip a glass of wine. The young men went about organizing dances to socialize with the girls. They looked for a host for the dance and a volunteer to play the accordion.

The young ladies arrived chaperoned either by their mothers or older brothers or both. The chaperones took their job very seriously. No matter how much they chatted with each other, they never took their eyes off the young people as they danced. They relaxed only when the couples danced the *Tarantella*. They suddenly became very alert when the couples danced the *polka,* the *mazurka* or the waltz. Body contact was strictly forbidden. A couple who danced too close was immediately punished. The girl was slapped right then and there. She was then dragged home, with the mother still yelling at her. If the girl had a male relative present, he started a fist fight with the offending young man. The dance came to an abrupt end. But no matter how many dances were interrupted by fights, the dances continued to be held.

One day a young couple, who had no relatives in *Noepoli,* suddenly arrived from Argentina. No one knew who they were or why they came. They set up house and were delighted to be in town. The fun-loving couple owned a portable phonograph and dance records.

They gladly agreed to bring them to the next dance. The couple created quite a sensation dancing the latest craze, the *tango*. The older women scowled and whispered to each other :

"What is the world coming to"?

"What a disgrace!"

They made predictions of an approaching moral doomsday.

The young people tried to hide their pleasure in watching the couple dance.

Despite their elders' tongue wagging, the young people asked the couple to all the dances. One day the couple left town just as unexpectedly as they had come and even the disapproving older people missed them.

I didn't mind January's cold and wet weather because my mother and grandmother only went to the fields to gather fire wood. When my mother was in town she took me wherever she went. Even though as a peasant she could go anywhere unchaperoned, she took me along as a precaution. Since my father was away she wanted to avoid behavior that might be remotely interpreted as improper.

One day she went to a neighbor's house without me. When she didn't come back as fast as I thought she should have, I went looking for her. A man answered my knock and opened the top part of the door. His face and his whole body sagged with worry. When I asked about my mother he opened the lower half of the door and motioned to the wooden flight of steps in the far corner of the room. Walking past him into the bare room I saw a little girl on a stool by the fire. She turned a solemn face towards me and her eyes followed me as I climbed the staircase.

When I reached the open doorway at the top of stairs, my mother and the other women told me to get out and stay out. I did leave as fast as I could but not before seeing the swollen belly of the woman on the bed, writhing and groaning in the pain of child birth. I heard the women speak words of advice and encouragement to the woman and a few uncomplimentary ones about the husband's lack of judgment in letting me go up.

The light snow that fell in January usually didn't last long. It was a treat to wake up to see the roofs covered with a few inches of snow. We scooped the crystallized, freshly fallen snow from our window ledges, placed it into bowls and ate it topped with *dicotto*.

On Fat Tuesday, the day before Ash Wednesday, the housewives tried to prepare a meal with meat and lots of fat. Animal fat and meat were strictly forbidden on Wednesdays and Fridays of Lent. We had no trouble observing the Lenten laws.

During the year we occasionally ate a chicken that was too old to lay eggs or a stew made from one of our guinea pigs. We very rarely went to the butcher across the street who was only open when he had meat to sell. Sometimes he had kids, lambs and rabbits hanging from hooks in the window. Occasionally, he had veal or beef. The men of the gentry and the women of the middle class went to buy the meat. It was a job too important to be left to a servant.

Lent was a time for pilgrimages. One year our priest led a small group to see the Passion Play in a town almost a whole day's journey away. My mother and I joined the group with the added purpose of consulting that town's doctor for a pain in my leg that our doctor had not been able to diagnose. Very early in the morning we joined the group in front of the church.

We followed the New Road towards *Senise.* We walked on the bridge over the *Sinni*, the largest body of water I had ever seen, into the outskirts of town. We walked on a dirt road through some woods. By noon, the sun was warm enough for us to look for a shady spot where we could sit down to eat our lunch. *Don* Antonio told us some cheerful anecdotes and whittled a recorder. We sang along as he played.

We reached our destination late in the afternoon and went straight to see the doctor. I have no recollection of the doctor's visit, the diagnosis or the remedy. But I do remember walking from the doctor's office back to the house where we were to have supper and spend the night. It was dusk. The streets were deserted except for a few lone women. They wore floor length black skirts and black shawls that wrapped their upper bodies and their faces, leaving just the eyes uncovered. They walked quickly and furtively, as if running away from some imminent danger. They walked close to the houses, kept their eyes to the ground and hurriedly went in as soon as they found their doors.

We joined the rest of the group in the dining room where two unsmiling women, dressed in black, served us without ever saying a word or looking anybody in the eye. The women in this town were still living with the customs left by the Arabs who had invaded the area hundreds of years before.

After supper we walked a short distance to see the play. We entered a large room with wooden benches facing an elevated stage. The curtains opened on a group of young men in costumes, some dressed as women, and heavily made up. I recognized the familiar words of the Gospels describing the arrest, trial and the crucifixion of Jesus. We were spell-bound. During the crucifixion scene women started to sniffle and to dab their eyes with their handkerchiefs.

The next morning the group met *Don* Antonio for the walk back. My mother took pity on me. She gave me money for lunch and the bus fare. She entrusted me to the adults waiting for the bus. I could understand them even though they were speaking a different dialect. When we got to *Senise* we went into the restaurant nearby to wait for the connecting buses.

It was my first visit to a restaurant. I was impressed by the large room with its two walls of windows. The many tables were covered with white table cloths and set with shiny silverware. The adults hovered over me and helped me order. I don't remember the meal except for the bread. I was used to my mother's coarse bread. The restaurant's had a golden crust and the inside was white as snow.

My bus friends made sure I got on the bus for *Noepoli*. I was the only one to get on. From the bus, the river looked even wider than it had the day before when we had walked across it. All of a sudden I remembered the stories of bridges and roads washed away in rain storms. Even though it was a sunny day I couldn't wait for the bus to get to the other side.

Sixteen

Easter time brought back the good weather and stirred hopes of good crops. To express their optimism most families whitewashed the inside of their houses. We had our house whitewashed and we washed everything that could be washed. My mother soaked the white clothes in boiling hot water mixed with ashes and then carried them to the torrent near our *orto*. She delighted in draping the clean clothes over the bushes, to dry in the sun once again.

At the beginning of Easter Week we baked Easter bread. My mother went to the storeroom to fill a sack of wheat from one of the wooden chests. She scooped out the wheat carefully. She did not want to break any of the eggs we had stored there. She carried the sack through the Door down to the flour mill and returned with a sack of flour. For our weekly batch of bread my mother sifted the flour just once to remove the coarse baker's bran. For the Easter bread she sifted it several times to get as fine a flour as she could. She used mostly eggs to make the dough. She rolled the golden dough into thick ropes. She placed an uncooked egg in the folds as she overlapped one strip over another, and shaped them into stylized dolls or wreaths. Traditionally the dolls were for the females and the wreaths were for the males of the family. She made a doll for each one of us and then a few wreaths for good measure.

My mother asked the priest to include our house in his Easter rounds. The tinkling bell announced the altar boy and the smiling *Don* Antonio, wearing his surplice and carrying a golden wand in his hand. He followed my mother into every room, sprinkling holy water and reciting Latin blessings. He blessed us and went to the next house.

Easter week was a busy time for *Don* Antonio. On Holy Thursday night he held a very solemn and lengthy service in which he re-enacted the ceremony of Jesus washing the disciples' feet. He blessed the water in the Baptismal Font and we filled small bottles to take home. At noon on Good Friday he prayed the Stations of the Cross and afterwards he preached a very emotional homily on a Jesus' three hour agony. On Saturday morning, the sacristan built a big fire in the open area in front of the Church. The priest blessed the

85

fire and the townspeople lit a candle to take home. At noon a joyous series of peals of the church bells announced the end of Lent. To celebrate the Resurrection my mother made a *frittata*, an omelet, made with two foods we hadn't eaten for forty days, eggs and sausage.

By Easter Sunday the houses had been whitewashed, the linens had been washed, the houses had been blessed and even the streets had been swept. Easter and the feast day of our patron saint were the two occasions when the people made a concerted effort to clean up the town, which had no sanitation department and no trash disposal facilities. But the town didn't generate much garbage. The food we bought at the confectioner's store was wrapped in paper or newspapers, which we recycled and eventually threw into the fire. Bottles and containers of any kind were so scarce that we saved them for future use. We fed the table scraps to our pigs, chickens or guinea pigs and we used their droppings as manure. Before my time the domestic animals were allowed to wander the streets at will and the streets were strewn with animal droppings. Under Fascism, the animals were forbidden to roam the streets. If the uniformed guard found one, he lost no time in fining the owner. Since the fine had to be paid in cash, the people complied with the law.

Even the men who didn't bother to attend Mass regularly made an effort to go on Easter Sunday. Women and children dressed in their best clothes. My mother always made me a new dress. She prided herself on doing some embroidery that was unique to my dress. I liked having a new dress but I felt self-conscious when I saw the shabby dresses of my peasant friends. My dresses were often better than most of the upper class girls. But I knew I wasn't their social equal. I felt resented by all three classes.

I became even more self-conscious when my mother cautioned me against the "Evil Eye". Even though I was wearing the twisted red coral horn on a chain around my neck, she instructed me to place one hand behind my back, put my thumb between the index and middle fingers, close the hand into a fist, and keep the fist behind my back all the way to church.

After Mass my mother sent me to pay my respects to *Cumma* Grazia and *Cumpa* Michele, my Confirmation. god-parents. Confirmation takes place at around age twelve, but I was confirmed

86

when I was about two. At that time, my father wrote that he was planning to send for us. The priest was worried that there might not be a Bishop in America to confirm me. After I was confirmed, my father changed his mind.

I liked my godparents but I disliked performing the customary Easter ritual. My mother gave me no choice. I walked down the street slowly, admiring the beautiful spreads covering the railings of the balconies but I eventually got to my godparents' front door and knocked. I wished my god-mother "Happy Easter", bent down, picked up her right hand and kissed it somewhere between the knuckles and the wrist. Her face lit up with pride at my show of respect. She ushered me into the neat one room home and proudly announced my presence to her husband. I bent down, kissed my godfather's hand and wished him a "Happy Easter". As I did so I saw that the faint scar on his temple was still there and I thought of what had happened a few months before.

We were sitting around the fire one cold evening when we heard the knock. My godmother with her *manto* wrapped around a very worried face came in. We made room for her near the fire, wondering what could have brought her out on such a cold night. Her husband Michele was not yet home. Too nervous to stay home by herself, she came to talk to my mother. She was afraid the *Carabinieri* had arrested him for breaking the curfew. My mother tried to reassure her by telling her that her husband had just stayed too long at his mistress' house. The *Carabinieri* would not arrest him and that he would be home soon. My godmother still looked worried but she hoped my mother was right. After a short while she went home for fear that Michele might return and be angry with her for being out.

It turned out that both were right. My godfather had stayed too long at his mistress' house and the *Carabinieri* had seen him walking home. The *Carabinieri* were natives of *Noepoli* and they knew that the men who broke the curfew were not plotting against the government. They were out late either because of some woman or they had been out drinking. Instead of putting Michele in jail (as they were supposed to do), they gave him a beating and sent him on his way. Michele wore a bandage around his head for several days.

As a reward for my visit and paying my respects, my godmother gave me the *strina*, some cookies or some money. I thanked them and left as politely and quickly as I could. Walking back home I was grateful that my baptismal god parents had moved away.

The Monday after Easter was a continuation of the Easter celebration. But my mother and grandmother didn't remain in town. They were eager to get back to the nearby Olive Grove to do the chores they had neglected during Easter week.

As soon as the ground thawed, my mother hired a man with a pair of oxen to plow the ground between the olive trees. We followed the oxen and picked up the stones that cropped up every time the ground was plowed. We carried the rocks to the boundary wall at the edge of the property and stacked them on top of the stones we had carried there before. We were still doing the chore that Homer once described.

"...all being gone that to clear a distant field,
    and drag the stones for a boundary wall".

Once the ground was plowed and the stones stacked, my mother and grandmother criss-crossed the field scattering handfuls of wheat they took out of the large pockets of their cobbler's aprons.

After that, there was nothing to do except pray for rain. There was no water anywhere near the field. But each spring the rain did come. In a few weeks the young wheat plants rippled in the breeze, transforming the brown earth into a sea of green. When the plants were a foot high they had to be weeded and cultivated. The job had to be done carefully and in time to prevent the weeds from choking off the wheat plants. My mother and grandmother carefully stepped between the rows, bent down, pulled out the weeds and then with their hoes, painstakingly broke up the ground around each plant.

To get the job done as quickly as possible, the large landowners hired groups of women to work as a team. Even though my grandmother was old, she was often asked to join the much younger women. When the women got to the field they tied colorful kerchiefs around their heads, removed their black skirts and worked in their multi-colored petticoats. They lined up at the edge of the field and moved rhythmically with each other, lifting and lowering their hoes as they stepped carefully from row to row. To make the job less burdensome, someone would start to sing and the rest joined in. For two or three weeks the whole countryside was dotted with colorful petticoats and the air was filled with songs.

This is what *Donna* Giulia and *Donna* Lucia saw from their terrace. Little did they know how the women's backs ached as they bent over their hoes.

Besides the small wages the owners provided the workers with food. At midday the servants arrived carrying large baskets of food and drink. They appeared again at about four o'clock carrying the food for the traditional afternoon meal, the *mirenda*. This meal was served so that the workers could work until dark. The most generous of the landowners invited the workers to their houses for a late supper. The workers had eaten more food in one day than they were used to. They were happy to follow the Biblical[10] custom of taking a part of their supper home to their families, who might not have had any thing to eat all day. My grandmother always brought me her piece of a soft cheese that I liked.

Until the wheat ripened we spent our time in the vegetable garden which always required a lot of work and a lot of rain. I never really got on my knees to pray for rain but I did say a lot of mental prayers and never more fervently than on Monday nights. I prayed it would rain on Tuesday morning so that my mother and grandmother would not have to go to *l'orto* to irrigate the vegetables. I didn't mind going with them but I didn't like spending the night.

When I went I took over my mother's job of walking along the ditch to mend the breaks. I soon learned every bend and turn of the narrow, shallow, and fragile ditch that was shaded by overhanging tree branches. Once I walked almost all the way to where the ditch began without finding any breaks. I started to worry. What could have caused the stoppage? The tight knot in my stomach became tighter when I saw two uniformed guards. The happy shouts of several young men playing ball and the carefree chatter of women washing clothes in the nearby stream, made me feel worse. When I reached the guards, I tried to keep the fear out of my voice as I asked them the reason for the stoppage.

"The ditch flows above the spigot for the drinking water and it poses a health hazard. According to new sanitary laws passed by *Il Duce*, we have no choice but to shut off the water".

---

[10]Ruth 2:18

" How are we to water our vegetables"?

They just shrugged their shoulders, tilted their heads up with their chins slightly to the side. It was the understood mime for "Who knows?". They clasped their hands behind their backs and stared ahead of them.

I was both worried and scared. I dreaded giving my mother the news. When I did, she and my grandmother were furious. Their faces got red and their eyes flashed. They loudly wished all sorts of horrible calamities upon *Il Duce*. Had anyone reported them they certainly would have been candidates for *Il Duce's* favorite punishment for minor infractions -- a large dose of castor oil.

Fearing the loss of the year's vegetable crop, my mother went to see the guards. They were gone when she got there. She diverted the water to flow our way.

The guards knew the water had been flowing that way ever since they could remember. Periodically, they would divert the water but they didn't linger to see what happened next. After that incident, we started to analyze the water's flow. If the water came in a trickle, we knew it was a break in the ditch. I went to fix it. If the water stopped abruptly, we knew the guards had stopped it. My mother gave the guards enough time to leave and then she went to re-channel the water.

When I started to go to school I couldn't go to *l'orto*. I spent Tuesday nights with Fortunata. She owned some land far away from town but she didn't go there every day and she was usually home. When she did go, she started out in the evenings of moonlit nights. The whole *Terra* knew about her habit. They admired her spirit and her lack of fear of the supernatural. Not only was she not afraid to go by the cemetery at night but she had no fear of the werewolf or the *Monachicchio*.

She went on moonlit nights because she believed the medicinal herbs she picked had special powers if she picked them in the moonlight at midnight. She boiled or dried the herbs into various syrups and salves and stored them in the small bottles and jars that filled the shelves on either side of the fireplace. The neighbors came to her with their ailments. Fortunata looked over the bottles and jars and picked the one she thought might help and generously gave it away.

One evening I burned my knee on a hot coal. My mother went to Fortunata who came right over with a salve and a broad leaf. She spread the salve over the burn, covered it with the leaf and tied it with a strip of cloth. She came to replace the leaf with a new one every day. The scar always reminds me of my dear friend Fortunata.

Each spring a little of her property disappeared in a landslide. But even when the hut was washed away, Fortunata remained undaunted. She retained her cheerfulness, continued her moonlight walks, picked her herbs and continued to supply the neighbors with free homemade remedies.

One Tuesday Fortunata was not home. My friends Angela and Maria, whose father was away, invited me to spend the night with them. Although we played together almost every day I had never been inside their house. I was surprised to see how bare their one large room was. Near the window was a double bed and against one wall was a wooden chest with a large padlock. The chest held the family's entire food supply. The mother kept the food under lock and key and dispensed it as fairly as possible among all the members of the family. The dirt floor was swept clean. The fireplace, swept clean of ashes, gave silent evidence that the family had no wood to burn and no food to cook. The locked chest and the clean-swept fireplace jolted me into a sudden understanding. I knew my friends were very poor but I had never understood just how poor. My mother's words came painfully to mind. Once during harvest time I complained that our house was too cluttered with sacks of produce. With her usual calm and matter of fact voice she said to me,

"If you want an uncluttered house, you'll have to settle for an empty stomach."

When it was time for bed, their mother asked me to share the double bed with her. Not wanting to hurt my friends' feelings I politely refused. I decided to join the girls on the floor and to share their one small blanket. I was at the end and the blanket did not quite fully cover me. After a while I started to get cold and I finally accepted the mother's repeated invitations to share the double bed.

Seventeen

Towards the end of the summer of 1933 a letter from my father arrived addressed, as usual, to Maria Salomone *fu* Rocco. He followed the Italian custom of addressing a married woman's mail by her maiden name and her father's first name. The *fu* indicated the father was dead, a *di* would indicate he was alive. I knew that it was the money my father sent that allowed us to eat and dress better than the other peasants, but I didn't like to see his letters. My mother seldom looked happy after reading them.

I watched my mother slowly and carefully mouth every word of the letter. She looked up stunned. It was so important that she read it aloud to my grandmother and me. My father was planning to visit us! He and his friends had worked on the Empire State Building from the start of the Depression in 1929 until 1931. After the building was finished, they couldn't find work. The Depression had deepened and millions of Americans were unemployed. Men who once had good jobs found themselves on bread lines. Since the economic conditions in America were getting worse, he didn't think he could fulfill his dream of returning a wealthy man. He hoped the visit would help him decide whether or not we should join him in America.

The letter stunned us. I was worried about meeting a father who had left before I was two and of whom I had no recollection. My grandmother was fearful of her position in the household. My mother was a apprehensive. She had been on her own for ten years.

As my father's visit approached, both she and my grandmother tried to anticipate the farm chores that would be neglected during my father's visit. My mother washed every thing that could be washed. My cot was moved from the bottom of the double bed to the bottom of my grandmother's bed.

The nervous anticipation was finally over. My father appeared one day in the fall. He looked like what I thought an American should look like. He had a black coat, black hat and shiny black leather shoes instead of the sturdy brown leather ones worn by peasants who were lucky enough to have shoes.

After greeting my mother and grandmother, he looked at me.

92

I was frozen in place. He smiled at me, wondering what had happened to the toddler he had left behind. He walked towards me and embraced me. I couldn't move. I was relieved when the greetings were over.

A few days later a trunk arrived. My father eagerly opened it to take out the clothes he had brought me. As he took them out I saw the disappointment in his face. The clothes were too small. Then he took out something I had never seen. They were rubber galoshes to be worn over shoes when it rained or snowed. I slowly slipped them on, hoping against hope that they wouldn't fit. I carefully hooked the loops over the buttons of the mid-calf galoshes. I stood up to walk in them. They fit perfectly! I dreaded the moment my friends would see me in them. Especially the ones who had no shoes at all. I knew from the pride that shone on his face that there would be no escape from wearing the galoshes. I prayed for fair weather but the prayers didn't stop the snow and the rain. I obediently put on the galoshes and pretended I didn't mind them.

My father's visit upset our routine. I was used to an empty house at lunch time and after school. I had to watch my every move so as not to do anything wrong even though I had no idea of what that might be. My mother was a little jittery. She'd rather be in the fields. My grandmother tried to stay out of the way as much as possible.

But the middle class men in the neighborhood were happy. They liked to get together in the evenings to talk, play cards and drink some wine. The problem was finding a host. No one really had the money to buy the wine but no one wanted to admit it for fear of losing face, a condition that the poorest peasant as well as the wealthiest member of the gentry went to great lengths to avoid. To save face they made up all kinds of excuses to explain why they couldn't be the hosts for the evening. They had perfected the technique started by Adam. They blamed their wives, who either had work to do, weren't feeling well or they were spendthrift. Every man knew that these were lame excuses but they all pretended to believe them. Each one of them had used the same excuses himself. Eventually some one offered to be the host. Many times no one volunteered and each had to stay in his own house.

When an American came to town, their problem was solved. It was assumed that the American would be the host. My father did

93

not like to play cards and only drank at meal times. Even though he wasn't too happy when the men came to visit he hosted as graciously as possible.

While the men talked and played they debunked the excuses made by those not present. The confectioner was their favorite target. He could not control his women. He was too lenient with his wife, *Donna* Emilia, and their three daughters who were all spendthrifts. They loved to make reference to *Donna* Emilia's latest example of her utter disregard for her husband's wishes.

Donna Emilia wanted to cut her hair in the latest style. The confectioner said "No". It would be scandalous. One day she told her husband she was going to visit a relative in a nearby city. When she returned a few days later she had banks and the hair barely reached her nape. She explained to the shocked husband that she simply had to have her hair cut. Every woman in the city had short hair and she felt out of place. The poor husband pretended to approve to avoid having to punish her. *Donna* Emilia's haircut was the town's topic of conversation for months.

My father felt obligated to have dinner parties, which made my mother nervous. She was used to cooking for the three of us without much thought to menus. We had no regular meal times and we ate around the fireplace, holding our dishes on our lap. For these dinners, not only did my mother use the fireplace but also the two charcoal burners under the kitchen window. She had to set a long table in the living room upstairs. The white tablecloth and napkins had to be washed and ironed. Besides the extra work of cooking, going up and down to serve and the cleaning up afterwards, my mother was in constant fear that the meal would not meet my father's standards.

When the room wasn't used as a dining room it was used for dancing or listening to music. My father had brought a phonograph in a large wooden cabinet. The lid had a picture of a dog with its ear turned towards the bell of a golden horn. It was the RCA- Victor trademark, Nipper, listening to "His Master's Voice". The shelves in the cabinet were full of records. One of them was an Italian poetic recitation of the kidnapping of the Lindberg baby. The women listened in sad fascination. They could not understand how anyone could hurt a baby.

The news of this wonderful instrument reached the gentry. They wanted it in their own homes for a night of dancing and music. One of these gentlemen, who normally would barely acknowledge my father's presence, came to ask if he could borrow the phonograph. When my father agreed, he was asked to go along to operate it.

My father insisted that I go with him. I really did not want to go but I remembered my mother's warnings to be good. We were led to a large room with several men and women I had never seen before. We walked across the room to the corner where the precious cabinet had been placed. I sat on one side of the phonograph and watched my father crank the handle on the other side. When he had wound it up he carefully set the record on the turntable and delicately lowered the needle on it. As soon as the record started to slow down he got up to crank up the handle. His gold watch, strung across his vest, jumped up and down with him. I just sat there and watched the couples dance, talk and sip *risolio*, a sweet, yellow liqueur, from tiny glasses. My father got a glass of the liqueur and I a biscuit. Everyone was having such a good time that no one had time to bother with us. While feeling sorry for myself I caught the lost look on my father's face. His hazel eyes looked around at the gentry, silently asking, "What are we doing here?" I felt the same way but neither one of us knew how to convey that feeling to each other. We just endured the evening in silence.

For the two or three months my father was home I was in fear of saying something wrong. I could see the frustration on his face. He didn't know what to do with this child who didn't respond to him. When my mother told me that my father was returning to America, I felt relieved.

Shortly after, he wrote to tell us he was making arrangements for us to join him. All doubts had been eliminated by the rumors of war in Europe.

My mother started to make arrangements for uncle Raffaele to take care of the property. I often caught sad expressions on the faces of my mother and grandmother as they talked quietly about the radical change that was about to take place. I had misgivings about leaving my grandmother, my friends and the town but I kept all my thoughts and misgivings to myself. Nothing I said would change things.

My imminent departure for America made me an important

person. My fifth grade schoolmates started to pay me a lot of attention. The daughter of one of the Vitelli relatives left in charge of their properties and who lived near the *Palazzo*, invited me to go into the padlocked garden.

It was like stepping into another world. The only greenery in *La Terra* were the four spindly trees in la *piazza* and the plants on people's balconies. In the garden, the trees growing in plots of green grass, were in bloom. The smell of roses carried by a cool breeze was so strong it overcame the fragrance of the other flowers. Cement benches were spaced along the smooth path of red bricks that curved around the trees and flower beds. From the waist-high wall at the edge, the strollers had an unobstructed view of the countryside. To make sure I would not forget her, my classmate plucked a red rose and gave it me.

I went through the last few months of the fifth grade with a variety of feelings. I knew I hadn't learned all that I was supposed to. Long division and fractions were a blur. I wasn't even proficient in the Italian language. I was afraid that once I reached America my ignorance would be quite evident.

Every time *Don* Francesco went to the map of the world, the expanse of water separating Europe and the Western Hemisphere seemed to loom larger and larger. How were we to get across? I didn't dare ask *Don* Francesco. At home my mother was preoccupied with making all kinds of decisions and arrangements and was still doing farm chores. I didn't want to add to her worries. Maybe she was worried about the same thing.

Day by day I tried to learn as much as I could in an effort to make up for lost time but to no avail. Finally the school year was over and the report cards were given out. All the subjects on my report card were marked Satisfactory. I supposed that *Don* Francesco thought that marking the subjects Unsatisfactory, what I really deserved, would have served no purpose.

In preparation for our departure my mother, contrary to my father's advice, began to sew clothes for me which were appropriate for a young lady. We also went to the shoemaker to be measured for new shoes. I sat quietly while he took all sorts of measurements. Then I stepped on the leather stretched out on the floor and the shoemaker traced the shape of my feet with a piece of chalk. I hoped the new

96

shoes would be more comfortable than ones he made for me before.

I still had painful memories of those shoes. My mother and I were returning from the feast of the patron saint of a neighboring town. We joined the wife and young son walking behind the stone-faced peasant who was riding his donkey. The backs of my new shoes had been rubbing against my heels all day but I hadn't said anything to my mother. When she noticed my limping and saw the blood at my heels she asked the man if I could ride on the donkey behind him. The man grudgingly said that I could and since I was riding, his son could ride behind me.

Soon after my father's decision to send for us, my American friends across the street excitedly announced that their father Carlo was coming for one of his periodic visits. They looked forward to his visits. He brought presents, paid up his wife's bills and the family took part in social events that they couldn't attend while he was away.

Carlo told us that my father had entrusted us to his care. As the documents came from America, Carlo made sure everything was filled out correctly.

Finally the steamship tickets and the priceless American passports arrived. Since my father was an American citizen we didn't have to worry about the Italian quota. Carlo arranged for a car to pick us up and take us to *Potenza* where we would board a train to Naples. To make sure that nothing went wrong, he came along with us.

The day before we left, my mother roasted a leg of lamb and boiled lots of eggs. She packed the food in a large white cloth and knotted the opposite ends. Very early the next morning Carlo met us at our door. He carried our valises and my mother carried the bundle of food. Only our footsteps on the cobblestones on the way to the *Fontana* broke the silence of the pre-dawn morning. We spotted a young man standing by a car. After Carlo's introductions we got in the back and Carlo sat next to the driver. At the *Fontanino* I tried to look at the *Torretta,* one last time. But no matter how I craned my neck I couldn't see it. As the car went by the *Fontanino* I kept my head straight ahead, determined not to look back. Instead I started to wonder what lay ahead. Carlo and the driver carried on a conversation. Sometimes my mother was drawn into it. I just listened and tried to imagine what would happen next.

We boarded the crowded train on a very hot and sunny day.

97

All the windows were wide open but the air in the car was stifling. The breeze blew the dust from the parched ground into the car. The passengers started to unwrap their parcels of food. The smell of roast lamb, boiled eggs, salami, cheese, peppers, onions and garlic mingled with the smell of the dust blowing through the window.

In Naples, Carlo led us to a rooming house near the sea. The small boats tied up near the shore increased my fear of crossing the ocean.

Our American passports saved us a great deal of paper work and lots of waiting in offices but we could not escape the US health inspection. We had a long walk to a large gray building. We approached the desk where a young man looked at our passports and told us to wait in the next room for the doctor to examine us. The doctor turned us over to a nurse who checked our hair for lice. Then she ushered us to the showers. The US officials wanted to make sure we would be both healthy and clean when we landed. We were lucky to be examined before leaving our country. I thought of the immigrants who had sold everything to pay for the fare to the US only to be sent back by a doctor of the American Health Department when they set foot on Ellis Island.

The wooden trough I had imagined turned out to be the *Conte di Savoia*, one of the most modern ocean liners at that time. The people boarding proudly discussed the merits of the ship. It was one of the two modern liners owned by Italy. Because of the streamlined design it was able to cross the Atlantic in only eight days. It had stabilizers so that it would be steady even in rough sea. I took courage from the knowledge that we were on such a good ship.

The ship was divided into First, Second and the Third Class. We were in the Third, below the water level. Our small cabin had an upper and lower berth and nothing else. The toilet and shower were across the hall. We left our cabin quickly and we went right up again to the main deck. Soon we heard the announcement that lunch was being served.

The large dining room had huge glass windows and doors that opened onto the deck. We were led to a table for twelve. There was only one child, a boy of about five or six, who was traveling with his well dressed, heavy-set, dark-haired mother. Our fellow diners spoke different dialects but we communicated well enough to make pleasant conversation. Listening to the conversations I realized how very limited our background was. Shortly after lunch, a voice announced the showing of a movie. It was my first "talkie". The actors spoke English, which no one really understood, but we went back every afternoon for the showing of a new movie.

We were kept busy with the regular three meals, the movies and tea after it. One day, as a special treat, the passengers of the Third Class were taken on an escorted tour of the Second Class. The First Class was completely off limits to us.

Our American passports allowed us to land on Manhattan without going through Ellis Island. I wished I didn't have to leave the ship. I knew that the minute I stepped on land my whole life would change. How? I had no idea.

Eighteen

We landed on August 4, 1934. As my mother and I stepped down on the steamy pier my father appeared out of the noisy, waiting crowd. He embraced us and introduced us to the two *paesani* with him. One of them walked over to the street vendor and bought me an ice-cream pop. He didn't buy one for my mother. With that gesture he told me that I was a child and not the young lady I thought I was. He called me Rose. It was the first time anybody had called me by my Americanized version of the unfamiliar name on my passport. In a few minutes Tanina, the young lady, became Rose, the child.

When I was born my parents didn't follow Grandma Rosa's order to call the first child Gaetano. They followed the custom of naming the first girl after the paternal grandmother. Instead of being pleased, Grandma Rosa was furious. To placate her I was given the feminine form of the name, Gaetana, when I was baptized. I never knew that my name was Rosa, until I received my passport.

On our ride up to The Bronx in the *paesano's* car, I was overwhelmed by the noise, the traffic and the tall buildings. I looked for flower pots on balconies. All I saw were iron staircases with landings on each floor.

The car stopped in front of 2120 Crotona Ave, a four story, brick building, at the corner of East 181st Street. The tiled foyer was big and clean. Climbing the steps I smelled foods that I couldn't identify. Each floor had four apartments. We stopped on the third floor and my father opened the door nearest the stairs. The aroma of fried onions and potatoes greeted us as we walked into the small vestibule that led into the kitchen. My father's Aunt Filomena and two of her daughters, Gracie, (Lucrezia) and Rose, welcomed us with lots of warm hugs and kisses. Gracie's husband, Robert, son of Northern Italians, spoke a few words of Italian to welcome us. Rose's husband, Tommy, who was from *Terranova,* spoke cheerful words of welcome in his native dialect.

The kitchen table's shiny ceramic-top was set with a pretty set of dishes, shiny silverware and paper napkins. The two *paesani* joined us for our lunch of potatoes and sauteed chuck steak, smothered with onions. They raised glasses of red wine to wish us good luck in America. My aunt and cousins assured my mother that they would show her where the stores were and to teach her the value of American money.

During the meal I looked around the kitchen in wonder and disbelief. Disposable paper napkins! How could they throw away so much paper! My father took a bottle of cold water and fruit from the icebox, the wooden box next to the table. My cousins washed the dishes in the white, enamel sink with hot and cold running water. They drained the dishes on the grooved enamel cover of the washtub, attached to the sink. They stored the dried dishes on shelves in the built-in closet next to icebox.

The optimism I had felt during lunch disappeared after everybody left. I had doubts and felt uneasy. How were my mother and I to adjust to live with a man who was almost a stranger? How was my father going to adjust to living with us?

I took a good look at our three room railroad apartment. Even though it was sunny outside, we needed the light from the electric bulb in the middle of the ceiling. The bathroom, off the small foyer, had a shiny, white tiled floor, enamel commode, sink and bathtub. The kitchen floor was covered with a bright, shiny waxed linoleum. The window near the sink looked onto the inner courtyard. Ropes on pulleys, spanned the courtyard to the kitchen window of the opposite apartment. Under the window sill was a steam radiator.

Between the kitchen and my parents' bedroom was the living room with a window that also opened on the courtyard. The room had a couch, two easy chairs and a console radio. Against the wall was my bed, a covered, folded up cot, *a branda*. My parents' bedroom had a window with a fire escape, like the iron balconies I had seen on our ride up from the pier. It was the only room touched by the sun that shone across the next apartment house.

That evening I heard the doorbell but no one was at the door. The noise of rattling pulleys and voices came from the wall near the kitchen table. My father opened the small door in the wall, put his head in and yelled down something. The groaning of ropes stopped. He put the bag of garbage on the little platform, level with the tiny window, said something and shut the door. The groaning of the ropes started again. Finally the groaning and voices stopped. The bell was to alert the tenants to be ready to place their garbage on the little platform of the "dumbwaiter". The tenants shouted, "lower," "higher," "wait," or "OK." to guide the super.

The apartment had conveniences I hadn't even dreamt of but I felt confined in it. My uneasiness about the future intensified.

The next day we met the iceman, an immigrant from *Bari*. Using large tongs, he carefully lifted the large block of ice from his well padded shoulder and fitted it snugly into the top part of the icebox. He pocketed the twenty-five cents and repeated my father's warning to be sure to empty the water that dripped into the pan under the icebox, or we'd have a flooded kitchen.

In the next few days, one *paesano* took my father and me to a shoe store to buy me shoes that were soft and didn't pinch my heels. Another *paesano* took us to buy me a dress. Another, gave me a coat, outgrown by one of his daughters. Cousin Rose told me to take off the gold earrings in my pierced ears, which marked me a Greenhorn.

Little by little, Tanina was becoming Rose. Tanina had been economically better off than most in *Noepoli*. Rose had joined the great number of the poor of the Great Depression.

In the next few days we got used to the noise of the large metal cans scraping the cement in the courtyard. The super dragged the heavy garbage cans and the cans filled with ashes from the coal furnace, up the steps to the front of the building for the Sanitation Department to collect.

We heard the out of work men who went from courtyard to courtyard. They sang a song holding a hat in front of them. After their song, they begged for coins. Most of the times they were met by absolute silence. Occasionally some coins clinked on the cement. When that happened, they lavishly blessed those who had dropped them.

We visited the Lufranos, who lived a few blocks away, on tree lined Bathgate Avenue, in an attached, two-family, Victorian-style house, built during the boom of the 1920's. A wide flight of wooden steps led to a small porch covered by the overhang of the second floor. From the vestibule we walked into the hallway. To our immediate right was the door to the front parlor. I later learned that the houses of the period were so designed to allow the guests to go directly into the parlor, which was always kept ready for company,

102

without going through any other part of the house. But at that time, the parlor was Rose and Tommy's bedroom. We walked on the shiny linoleum of the hallway, along the well polished staircase that led to the tenant's apartment. At the head of the stairs, was a small room, *u stanzino*, usually retained by the owner and rented to a boarder. My father had slept in *u stanzino*, until we came.

The dining room had an ornate, glass covered, mahogany table. Several golden trophies were displayed on the glass covered server. They were the prizes that Tommy had won in dancing contests before he got married. In one corner was a pianola, a piano that automatically played music, when perforated rolls of music were inserted into it. An archway separated the dining room from the kitchen and the white, tiled bathroom. They both looked as new as the day they had been built. Outside the kitchen door was a small concrete patio, bordered by beds of herbs and flowers. A wire mesh fence separated it from the patios of the attached houses on either side and from the patio of the house in the back.

The first time we went there for Sunday dinner we walked down the few steps from the sidewalk, right into the large kitchen in the basement. The round table, that easily sat twelve, was all set. Aunt Filomena had invited the whole family to meet us. A bathroom had been built in the unfinished part of the basement, next to the coal furnace. The kitchen and the upstairs bath were rarely used.

The few blocks that separated us from the Lufranos had apartment houses and only a few private houses. The owners of the private houses and the tenants of the apartment houses were immigrants or children of immigrants. Our apartment house was typical. We had immigrant Jewish, German and Italian families. On the second floor lived an Italian[11] couple with two girls about my age. In the front four room apartment, on our floor, lived a young couple from *Abruzzi,* with their two small children. A couple from *Bari* and their two redheaded children, lived in the apartment on the ground floor, facing the street. There was only one American family. That meant they spoke English without an accent and nobody knew where their ancestors had come from. Their blonde, unmarried daughter was

---

[11]For convenience I use Italian instead of Italo-American. Same for other nationalities.

referred to, in awe, as the "Nurse".

Most of the immigrants in the neighborhood had come at the beginning of the 1900's. Some came after World War I, but none had come after 1924. The older adults spoke with accents but their American born children and grandchildren spoke English. My mother blended right in but I stood out like a sore thumb.

On September 1 we met the woman we would see every first of the month thereafter. At first I thought I was seeing my friend Fortunata. Like Fortunata she was small, dressed all in black and had as many wrinkles but not her smile. She was a Jewish immigrant. Her wrinkles sagged from past troubles and her eyes were wary of possible troubles ahead. She clutched a large, black, leather bag with many metal clasps, as if afraid someone might grab it from her. She barely said "Hello" as she came in and waited, standing up, while my mother got the money for the month's rent. She took a receipt out of one of the compartments of her bag, handed it my mother, said "Good-by" and left.

Nineteen

All through August, as I walked to and from Aunt Filomena's house I went by the large, three floor, brick, school building, P.S. 57 across the street from our building. I saw children playing in the large concrete yard that was enclosed by a tall chain link fence and wondered what it would be like to go to school in such a building.

In early September, Cousin Gracie, my mother and I walked across the street to register for school. None of the women in the office spoke Italian and none had ever dealt with a non-English speaking child. One of them tried to figure out my grade level by writing some fractions on the board. Oh, how I wished I had paid attention to *Don* Francesco! Since I couldn't do them, she placed me in the first grade. She gave my mother a piece of paper with the number of my classroom on it.

On the first day of school we went to the room and my mother gave the teacher the piece of paper. The teacher smiled at her and conveyed the message that she could go. Used to always sitting in a dark classroom I could not believe the amount of light in the room. Large windows, with shades to regulate the light, took up the upper half of a whole wall. Under each window was a huge radiator. As if the windows weren't enough, the ceiling was full of electric lights. The children looked at me with smiling faces as they listened to the teacher, who I assumed, gave me a flattering introduction. She assigned me to a combination seat-desk in the back of the room. The top of the desk had grooves for the pencils and a hole on the top right hand side, with a tiny glass container in it. All the seats were bolted to the floor, in six rows. A seat for each child! The front wall was covered by blackboards and above them was a picture of George Washington and a large American flag. The door wall had a clothes closet. The teacher gave out paper, pencils and crayons. Later, we each got a reader. After a while the teacher lined us up to go to the bathroom and then to play in the school yard.

At three o'clock, when I crossed the street to our apartment house, I saw the *Barese*, resting her arms on a pillow, waiting for her children. As I went by she smiled and spoke a few encouraging words in her dialect. From that day on, I could count on her to give me a big "Hello" when I came back from school, just as the mother of my friends Angela and Maria had done in *Noepoli*.

She was one of the wives whose husbands had a good job and didn't allow their wives to go anywhere without them. The husband brought home a bag of groceries when he came home. Every time I went in or out, I saw her sitting at the open window, resting her arms on a pillow. She watched the children play and chatted with the passers-by.

The girls in the building played on the sidewalk and always asked me to join them. Sometimes I did but most of the times I didn't. I was afraid of making a fool of myself. I couldn't play ball or skip rope. I hesitated to play jacks with the unfamiliar metal ones and the little rubber ball. I usually made excuses that I had to go upstairs.

The two Italian sisters on the second floor reminded me of Angela and Maria, but unlike them, they were not resigned to being poor. They were bitter beyond their years. One of their complaints was that their step-father didn't buy them the nice dresses and hats they needed for church. They resented those of us who had them.

I went to the nine o'clock, children's mass, at the nearest church, St. Martin of Tours. It had a long middle aisle and rows and rows of wooden benches on either side. No crumbling stones or broken tiles. I sat in one of the back pews that weren't roped off. For the first time in my life I saw nuns, in their long, black habits. They led their classes from the nearby Catholic School to the cordoned-off pews. The children marched in perfect order and during the mass they obeyed the nuns' terse orders like robots. I was familiar with the Latin mass but I didn't understand one word of the English homily.

After a few Sundays I became bored with the children's Mass and started to go to the adults' mass. I listened to the weekly sermons that were completely new to me, about making generous, silent contributions when the collection basket came around. There had been no collection baskets in *Noepoli*.

My mother, like the other Italian immigrants, went to the Italian Church of Our Lady of Mount Carmel in the Italian section of Arthur Avenue. There, the women felt comfortable wearing kerchiefs instead of hats. They could beat their breasts and pray aloud without fear of criticism from the unemotional American, mostly Irish, parishioners of St. Martin of Tours.

One afternoon, instead of joining the girls on the sidewalk, I went upstairs and as if to justify my not playing, I turned on the radio. I discovered that station WOV had several Italian language programs. The first one I tuned in was from 5 to 5:15 and was the serialized version of Shakespeare's "Othello", acted by the many members of the Minciotti family. I recognized it as one of the stories the tinker had told. The program was interrupted several times for commercials for pasta and olive oil. The commercials took so much of the fifteen minutes that the story went on for months.

After school I sometimes went to see Frances, our neighbor from *Abruzzi*. She and her husband had emigrated separately from different towns in *Abruzzi* and each lived as a boarder with a *paesano's* family. They had met by chance, fell in love and got married without consulting either set of parents. Her husband, Ettore, a tall, athletic muscular man, earned a very good salary as a sand-hog. Sand-hogs worked in compression chambers under water, digging tunnels and subway lines. Many died on their way up from a condition called the Bends. The job was so dangerous that it was done mostly by immigrants.

Frances was always happy to see me. I would help her with her two small children. Sometimes I baby sat for her, *per favore*. One afternoon she told me that a radio had been invented that allowed you to see the people talking. I looked at her in disbelief. Even after she assured me that it was true, I didn't believe her.

On weekends my father took us to different places like the Bronx Zoo and the Bronx Botanical Gardens. One Saturday he took us on the Third Avenue El to visit some *paesani* on E.118th St. in Harlem. Many of the Southern Italians who came to America at the beginning of the twentieth century, settled there. Then, the old immigrants sent for their relatives and helped them find housing and jobs. New immigrants settled near their *paesani*. Finding themselves in a strange land, not knowing English and uncomfortable with people from other countries, they lived near each other. They continued to speak their dialects, to eat their native foods and held on to their customs. They built their own church, Our Lady of Mount Carmel. The *paesani* organized a Mutual Aid Society to help each other during sicknesses and other emergencies. There was no need to learn English well. The stores were owned by fellow immigrants. The men learned just enough English to function on their jobs. The women who worked as operators in the garment industry didn't need much English either. Many of the supervisors were *paesani.* .

The streets in Little Italy were noisy and crowded. Garbage from the overflowing cans against the buildings littered the sidewalks and streets. As we climbed the stairs of the tenement building, we passed garbage bags resting near the doorways of the apartments. But the apartment of our *Terranova* friends was immaculate. The linoleum floors were waxed to a high shine.

The Italian immigrant colony was still very large. The residents felt comfortable in the old surroundings and didn't want to leave. Only a few families had moved to better neighborhoods.

During the 1920's the Lufranos had been among the first to move up from Harlem's crowded streets to the Bronx's tree lined blocks. At first, they hesitated even to walk around the neighborhood. They felt they were not good enough to live among the Americans, which meant anybody not from Southern Italy. During those boom years, Aunt Filomena eagerly awaited Uncle Giacomo to come home from work with *i casicavall.* She held up her apron for him to drop in the money he took out of his bulging pockets. I couldn't imagine what he did with *i casicavall,* (the dialect for *cacicavalli),* long Italian cheeses. I eventually found out that they were referring to the pins that Uncle Giacomo re-set in a Bowling Alley. His pockets held the generous tips he received.

The 1929 Wall Street crash, and later, the automatic reset button eliminated his job. When we came Uncle Giacomo had a steady job as a packer in a factory where his son-in-law Tommy was the foreman. He earned enough to continue to pay the monthly obligation to a mysterious person, Aunt Filomena referred to *u monich,* a monk. It took me a while to realize that Aunt Filomena was referring to the mortage they still had on the house.

My father had lived as a boarder with the Lufranos both in Harlem and in the Bronx. He was determined not to go back to Harlem. Gracie and Rose helped him find the apartment, cleaned it and helped him choose the used furniture for it.

During the fall we received an invitation to have Sunday

dinner at *Don* Carlo's house. I couldn't wait for the day to come. I was actually going to meet the older brother of *Donna* Giulia and *Donna* Lucia, of whom I had heard so much while we embroidered. We took a train and a bus to Flushing, a middle class suburb of New York City. We walked along a few tree-lined blocks of attached, private houses. A well dressed man in his middle thirties, about my father's age, but with delicate features and rimless glasses, answered the door bell. He greeted us very graciously in the Italianized form of the dialect that the gentry used to talk to the peasants.

His wife came out of the kitchen wearing a fancy apron to protect her good dress. She was a far cry from the housewives I had met so far who wore sturdy bib aprons over their cotton house dresses. Her parents were northern Italian immigrants but she spoke very little Italian. She went back to the kitchen and *Don* Carlo ushered us into the combination living-dining room. The huge window overlooked the street. The fire in the neat fireplace was not for heat but for atmosphere. The mantelpiece was immaculate and held several framed pictures. Nothing like the fireplaces full of ashes and the sooty mantelpieces of *Noepoli*.

We sat down at the table, set with matching dishes, glassware and silverware *a la Conte di Savoia*. The smaller glasses were filled with a bright red liquid. *Don* Carlo told us the red liquid was tomato juice. He said it as if he were apologizing for his wife's lack of judgment for serving a drink so alien to our background. My mother and father dutifully drank it. *Don* Carlo noticed my hesitation and very kindly said to that it was all right not to drink it.

The wife taught Home Economics in High School. She prepared her meals according to the proper nutritional standards and didn't allow for cultural differences in the eating habits of the peasant *paesani* that her husband occasionally invited. The *paesani* belittled her job. The thought of going to school to learn to cook from a book, was ridiculous. *Don* Carlo was caught between loyalty to his wife and the *noblesse oblige* ingrained in him as a member of the gentry. He felt obligated, on certain occasions, to invite the lower class *paesani,* even though he knew they criticized him when they left.

Don Carlo was a life insurance agent for The Metropolitan Life Insurance Company. He was one of the educated immigrants who had come to America with no intention of returning to Italy. He became Americanized as soon as possible. He learned English, got a good job and married a wife with no ties to *Noepoli*. *Donna* Giulia and *Donna* Lucia would wait for him in vain.

The *paesani* who like the Lufranos had bought two-family homes in the Bronx, invited us to their houses. None of them lived near a trolley car route. We walked everywhere. Every family we visited proudly showed us around their houses. We walked through the immaculate, fancy parlors and dining rooms but we were always entertained in the basement kitchens. Before we visited, my father told me about the educational accomplishments of their American born children. Unlike the many Southern Italian immigrants who sent their children to work instead of to school, our *paesani* sent their children through High School. Some had sent their sons to college to become doctors and lawyers. Their daughters did not work in sweat shops. They were clerks in banks or with the telephone company. But none had gone to college.

The longest and most pleasant walk was the one we took through Bronx Park, to visit Aunt Filomena's other daughter, Tessie, in the Woodlawn section of the Bronx. On summer afternoons the park was full of immigrants. To escape the heat of their crowded apartments fellow countrymen gathered for picnics under the trees they staked out. As we walked by, we heard the different languages and smelled the different foods. Italian men walked through the trees carrying sacks or large paper bags looking for dandelions or mushrooms.

Tessie was married to Tony, a cement mason from *Terranova*. They lived in a detached, one family house with a garage. They were among the very few people who owned a car. We ate lunch on the picnic table, under a large grape harbor in the backyard. Their two boys, about my age, spoke the few dialect words they knew, to teach me new English words.

Twenty

By the fall I had learned the American money, abandoned the metric system and become familiar with the new meanings of certain calendar days. October 12 had never meant anything to me in *Noepoli*. I didn't really grasp the meaning of Halloween. Armistice Day was on November 11 instead of November 4. Aunt Filomena invited us for Thanksgiving dinner and I ate turkey for the first time. Tessie's boys told me about the Santa Claus and I heard my classmates talk about him. The windows of the shops on East Tremont Avenue were brightly lit and glittered with tinsel. Pictures of Santa Claus were everywhere.

My father's co-workers from *Terranova* and *Noepoli* came to visit. I recognized some of them from a picture I had seen. They were standing with my father by an American flag raised on top of the Empire State Building on their last day of work. The smiles showed pride and gratitude. Pride for having been a part of the construction of such an historic building and gratitude for having survived. Many workers had not.

Carlo, the bricklayer who had escorted us to Naples, lived with Millie and her husband in a three room apartment in Harlem. The *paesani* had a great deal of respect for him because he was a master bricklayer and could easily figure out mathematical problems. Whenever anyone posed a problem to him he pushed his hat back on his head, tilted his head, put his cigarette to one side of his mouth and pulled out a small, black address book out of his shirt pocket. He removed the numerous rubber bands around it to take out the stub of a pencil and one of the many business cards inside its pages. He made tiny calculations on the card while talking through one side of his mouth and squinting through the smoke of his cigarette. After he gave the answer to the question he bundled everything back again. Nobody ever figured out what all those business cards were for.

Gino, a bachelor mason, who lived with his sister and her husband, came visiting in a well tailored three piece suit, tie knotted tight around his starched collar. He was the picture of a dignified and successful business man. His suit jacket pocket was never without an expensive fountain pen and pencil set. Because he was illiterate, the pen and pencil set never failed to draw comments from the *paesani*.

Pan'asciutto, dry bread, a mason from *Terranova*, was short, very wiry and had a high pitched voice. For some dietary reason, known only to himself, he ate just dry bread for lunch. He was also referred to as *Rosa Mea,* My Rose. No matter what the topic under discussion was, somehow he would find a way to point out that his wife Rosa, could do it better.

Other friends who had emigrated without their families visited regularly. One of them was Joe, the shoemaker, who had come to Noepoli and married a girl without a dowry. He lived by himself in a furnished room and was well known for preparing a delicious dish of spaghetti in fifteen minutes. Since he got home from work at ten o'clock at night, that was his usual supper. He followed the ritual of other men whose families were still in Italy. Each Sunday morning he visited one or two families. When all the families had been visited, he started the rounds again. Wherever he went he was offered a glass of whiskey from the bottle the *paesani* prominently displayed every Sunday morning, in anticipation of these visits. The hosts, as a matter of form, routinely invited him to stay for Sunday dinner, usually served about 2:00 PM. The extending and accepting of the invitation followed a certain ritual of polite offers and polite refusals until the invitation was finally accepted or definitely refused.

Another of our regular visitors was Rocco, from *San Giorgio*, who lived as a boarder in a *paisano's* house in Harlem. My mother and I had often visited his family on their feast day. His wife and daughter Angelina, my age, had visited us on our feast day. Rocco had a routine all his own. My father had loaned him some money, *per favore*, (no interest). He came every Saturday morning carrying a bag of quality fruit. Along with the bag of fruit he discreetly paid back a few dollars and then sat down to smoke his pipe. He tried to convince my father to join the Communist Party and to subscribe to the Italian language Communist paper, *Il Lavoratore*. He talked at length of capitalism's injustices towards the workers. My father listened and tried to point out fallacies in his arguments but to no avail.

Every time the men who still had families in Italy came to visit, my father urged them to bring them to America as soon as possible or they would be caught in the war that was sure to break out. He had served four years in W.W.I and knew first hand how bad things could be.

By December I welcomed the hissing sound of the steam in the radiators. I enjoyed doing my homework on the table in the warm kitchen without crouching near a fireplace. I really missed the heat when it was shut off at ten o'clock.

The fire escape balcony on which my father had often spent the stifling nights of summer, held our winter icebox. The metal box with sliding doors held the perishable food and a bottle of non-homogenized milk. Before we used the milk we had to shake the bottle to make sure that the cream at the top was equally distributed through the whole bottle. This was very annoying on the mornings when the cream had frozen at the top during the night. Not shaking the bottle properly caused many family fights. We had no problem. My father and I were the only ones to use milk in our morning coffee. My mother didn't like coffee or milk.

I found out that the school year was divided into two semesters: A and B. The A was taught by one teacher and lasted from September through January. The B term was taught by a different teacher and lasted from February until June.

By February of my first school year I had gone through 1A, 1B, 2A and was in 2B. The teacher asked the class to write a report on Abraham Lincoln. My father told me he would take me to the library. I had no idea what that was, but I was too timid to ask. I still felt uneasy with him. I was always afraid of saying or doing something wrong. I had the feeling he was just as wary of me as I was of him.

The next Saturday morning we walked on Crotona Avenue to East Tremont Avenue, under the Third Avenue El to Washington Avenue to a massive, gray, dingy, corner building with huge windows. We climbed the wide stone flight of steps into an enormous, high-ceilinged room, that despite the huge windows, was not bright. It was filled with so many free standing bookcases, placed back to back, that it took me a while to realize that the walls were also lined with books. My father walked me around the room and in between the stacks. I gaped at the sheer number of books. When he thought I had been sufficiently impressed he stopped between two stacks. He looked at me and as if stating a religious belief, he said,

"Everything you want to know is in these books, which you can borrow for nothing. It's up to you to read them. No one can do it for you. "

We picked out a book on Lincoln and brought it to the librarian to check out. She checked out the book on my father's card and explained that the first floor was for adults only. With a smile she told me that in the future I was to use the Children's Library upstairs, by using the stairway around the corner. The steps near her desk were cordoned off and were used only by the librarians.

On our walk back my father told me again how lucky I was to be in America. If I studied hard I could be whatever I wanted. He had no money to pay for college but if I got good grades in High School I could go to one of the tuition-free City Colleges. Although he never said it, I knew he wanted me to be the first of the *paesani's* daughters to go to college.

I understood very little of what I read about Lincoln but I couldn't wait to return to the library to visit the children's section, which was open only after school. I joined the long line of children there ahead of me, eagerly waiting for the librarian to open the doors. When she appeared at the head of the wide spiral staircase, she cautioned us not to push the child ahead of us in our eagerness to get upstairs. Huge windows on three sides of the room made the second floor much brighter than the first. We had no trouble reaching the books in the child size, free-standing bookcases. I leafed through them looking for clues about the subject of the book. Sometimes a child near me whispered a suggestion. Often I decided by the few black and white pictures in the them. I chose *Michael Strogoff* because of the black and white sketch of a man wrapped in heavy overcoat riding furiously through a sheet of snow. I took the books home and read them. That is, I looked at all the words on the page and I was happy if I understood a few. Evidently I understood enough to motivate me to return to the Library as often as I could. At the suggestion of one of my schoolmates I took out *Tales of a Thousand and One Nights.*

Some afternoons I went from school with the children who took the short-cut through Crotona Park. We walked on the red, brick path between the flower beds and around the gurgling fountain. When I got home from the Library my mother was home. No matter where she went during the day, she made sure she was home in time to greet my father at 4:30. Since the building trades had unionized, the long work day had been shortened to seven hours.

My father, covered from head to toe with fine cement dust, walked straight into the bathroom and started to run the water in the tub. Then he came into the kitchen, had a drink of water, took the towels and clean clothes from my mother and went back into the bathroom. Soon we heard his sighs of relief as the warm water soothed the aches of the day's work.

When my father came out into the kitchen my mother had the boiled water ready in which he stirred the boric acid he used to wash his irritated eyes while he soaked his aching feet in a basin of warm water into which my mother had diluted some Epsom salt. She was ready to apply iodine on the bruises and cuts.

Before sitting down to supper at 5:30, my father brought the bottle of red wine to the table. My mother had a glass and I drank a small amount. My father never drank more than two or three glasses. Some nights he was so tired, he barely finished eating before falling asleep at the dinner table.

Twenty-one

During our the first winter in America my mother got sick with erysipelas, a contagious and potentially fatal disease. Her face was covered with sores and scales and so swollen that her eyes were almost completely closed. After a few days she lost all her hair.

The doctor, a *paesano* who lived in Harlem, was addressed as *Don* Lorenzo just as if they were all still in *Terranova*. He was a slight man with a gentle manner and wore rimless glasses. As he snapped shut his black bag he told us that there was no medicine for the disease. He prescribed a daily teaspoon of whiskey and complete bed rest. He notified the Board of Health and a Quarantine sign was placed on our door. My father and I were allowed to go out but no one, except the doctor, could come in. Every time I went in or out that sign reinforced my feeling of being different and not fitting in.

Don Lorenzo came every day and repeated his order for the daily dose of whiskey and complete bed rest. My mother could not be left alone. To make sure I would not miss school my father asked for a night job. He was such a reliable worker that the boss, not wanting to lose him to another contractor, gave him a job as a night watchman. My father shopped, cooked, cleaned and washed clothes for the weeks my mother was confined to bed. After a few weeks *Don* Lorenzo told us my mother was no longer in danger. Miraculously, she survived without any scars and her hair grew in just as wavy as it had been.

By late Spring my father's friends and coworkers resumed visiting. Usually, the men visited in the evenings, without their wives. It was rare for entire families to visit. Preparing a whole family to pay a visit was just too much trouble. Visiting meant getting dressed up. Not every member of the family might have dress-up clothes to wear, all at the same time. Silk stockings were expensive. Many of the women were overweight and had to lace themselves in whalebone corsets. One obese woman made a lasting impression. The corset was laced so tight that once she sat down she couldn't move. The tips of the stays held her breasts so rigidly that she couldn't lower her head to sip the tiny glass of *strega*. I vowed then that I would never get fat.

If families visited, it was on Sunday afternoons. They came

unannounced. It was bad manners to let the hosts know ahead of time. The prior notice would obligate the hosts to entertain the guests lavishly. By arriving unannounced, the hosts could save face in case they didn't have any refreshments to serve.

My mother got back to trying to follow the American housewife's routine. Monday was wash day. She scrubbed the clothes on a washboard in the tub attached to the sink, boiled the white clothes in a big tin tub on top of the stove and then rinsed them. She hung the wash on the clothes line with clothespins she took from a canvas bag hung by the window and slowly moved the line through the pulleys. We had gotten accustomed to the noise of the pulleys creaking as the housewives moved the laundry across to the opposite windows.

The women prided themselves on getting their white clothes really white. They listened to the soap commercials that promised to get rid of the tattle tale gray. Rinso promised to get clothes Rinso White. The commercials were so convincing that little by little the women stopped using the yellow bars of soap and bought the new powdered products. One day a Southern Italian immigrant came around, selling gallons of *biancolina*, bleach, that would eliminate boiling the white clothes. Then, to eliminate the yellow tinge left by the *biancolina,* my mother dissolved a little bag of bluing in the last rinse.

Washing clothes in America was much easier than taking the clothes to the river but it still took the whole day. So did making chicken soup, from the large, tough soup chickens. The housewives combined the two time-consuming chores by making chicken soup for Monday night's supper. My mother started to simmer the chicken before she started the laundry. She divided her attention between the laundry and skimming the broth.

Tuesday was the official ironing day. All washables were made of cotton and needed to be starched with homemade starch. My mother was happy to use the flat, electric iron instead of the one she used in *Noepoli*. (That iron had a slotted compartment for live coals. She had to be sure none of the ashes spilled over the clothes as she moved the iron over them). Housewives with large families could never finish the job in one day. One of our relatives, Jimmy *Nuost,* Our Jimmy, father of three school aged girls, was usually referred to as "She's ironing". It was the answer he always gave whenever anyone asked about his wife.

Women had to shop for food every day. Some families did not have the 25 cents for a block of ice. Even those who used iceboxes couldn't depend on them to keep perishables fresh for more than a day. Food shopping and its preparation, child care, and housework took almost the whole day. In the afternoon, after the housework was done, friends in the same building got together for coffee, cake and conversation. But they didn't linger too long. They made sure to be in their kitchens, preparing supper, when their husbands came home.

Knowing that the housewives were usually in their apartments, vendors of all kinds of services went door to door to sell their products. We got used to the Fuller Brush Man, carrying his sample case from door to door, trying to convince the housewives to buy his household gadgets.

My mother, used to being in the fields all day, could not spend a whole day in the three room apartment, much less, sit, chat, and drink coffee. She found reasons to go out. She made friends with the shopkeepers and the women she met on the way to the stores. Unlike most of the other Italian immigrant housewives, my mother was free to come and go as she pleased - just so she was home when my father came home. My father was not like many of the *paesani* who, did not want their wives to have jobs and who jealously guarded their wives' comings an goings. I think he realized it would have been a waste of effort. My mother had been on her own for so long, she wasn't going to change her ways. Besides, he had been very impressed by her determination and resourcefulness. Shortly after we arrived she took the Third Avenue El to a specialty store on East 14th Street, to buy the embroidered Altar cloth she had promised to send to our priest.

The husbands controlled the money and gave their wives a household allowance. My father did the opposite. He kept just enough cash for his daily expenses and gave the rest to my mother to manage. He trusted her to spend it wisely and also to save some of it. He used to joke with his friends who kept their wives on allowances. He was sure that if a wife wanted to skim money from the allowance she would find a way. And many did.

In June, we received a letter from our priest, asking for a contribution for the feast of our patron saint. By then I no longer received letters from my friends in *Noepoli*. I stopped answering them when they asked me for silk underwear for their trousseaus. They thought that everybody in America was rich. There was no way I could convince them that I was too poor to send them anything. My mother kept getting letters from Uncle Raffaele which I soon started to dislike as much as I had disliked the ones from my father when we were in *Noepoli*. The letters always had explanations as to why Uncle Raffaele couldn't pay the rent on the property. Either the taxes went up or the crop failed or both. Every time a letter arrived she dreaded having to show it to my father. I hated the tension and the quarrels they created. I started to dislike owning property.

That summer my mother's brother Domenick (Domenico) came from Steubenville, Ohio, to visit us. He was handsome, with a rosy complexion and shiny light brown, wavy hair. He was friendly and Americanized. Although his English was not perfect, it was evident he spoke English most of the time. He mixed our dialect with American expressions. The dialect no longer was natural to him.

Through him we found out that Uncle Michele, my grandmother's younger brother, was living in the Rosedale section of the Bronx, where there still was open land. He had white, wavy hair and looked like and older version of Uncle Domenick. He left *Noepoli* to escape his shrewish wife and settled in Louisiana where he married a non Italian and raised a family. He moved his family to New York at the beginning of the Depression in the hope of finding a better life. He too, spoke English all the time, except with us.

Twenty-two

Often I wished I could ask my father to help me with my homework. I didn't because I sensed that it would only embarrass him to admit he couldn't help me. But he made sure I was doing my work. One morning, my elderly 3B teacher stopped in the middle of the lesson to see what the man at the door wanted. When she opened the door my heart skipped a beat. The man was my father. The teacher looked as concerned as I felt. Parents rarely went to school. When they did, it was either to complain or because they had been called by the principal. My father, wearing a white shirt, tie and his one black, three piece suit, smiled at the teacher and simply asked her how I was doing. The relieved teacher turned towards me, smiled and assured my father that I was doing very well. My father smiled his shy smile at me, waved and left. My classmates didn't understand what was happening but I got the message loud and clear. My education was very important to him and that I'd better do well.

At the end of the third grade we received a notice that in September all the grades through the sixth had to report to a brand new school, P.S.92, a few blocks from our house. P.S. 57 would become a Junior High School, for seventh, eighth and ninth graders. Whereas P.S. 57 had no greenery around it, the new school was on a street with trees and it had shrubs, grass and flower beds. Their sight brought back memories of the open spaces that I missed.

The homogeneous classes had about 35 students. Each class on the grade had a numerical exponent, starting with 1 for the brightest. Some grades had so many classes that the exponents got up to 8. I was usually placed in a class with an exponent of three or four. For arithmetic and spelling, the teachers divided the class into three groups. The smartest sat in the first two rows, near the clothing closet, the middle group in the two middle rows and slower group sat in the last two rows, near the windows. I always sat somewhere in the back seat of the first or second row.

The first thing I remember in P.S. 92 is the Assembly period. Every Friday the girls had to wear a navy skirt and a middy blouse with a red scarf. The boys had to wear long pants, a white shirt and

120

tie. The classes marched quietly to their assigned seats under the watchful eye of their teachers. Talking during Assembly was unthinkable. We stood at attention while the color guard marched to the front. We saluted the flag and sang the Star Spangled Banner. After the flag was very reverently returned to its place on the side of the stage, the teacher in charge stepped to the lectern. She solemnly opened up the Bible to the marked passage from the Old Testament, read it with great dignity and then shut the book, without comment. During the reading you could hear the proverbial pin drop. The Bible reading meant nothing to me. I wasn't familiar with any of the passages. I don't think it meant much to any of us beyond the fact it was a time we had to be very quiet.

The next vivid memory is of Class 5B. I was transferred to it from 5A a few weeks after school year started. As soon as the teacher showed me my seat, she asked if any one could speak Italian. A girl raised her hand. We smiled at each other. The teacher was delighted. From then on, I was that classmate's problem, not hers.

I was impressed by the number of text books I was given. The reader had many stories and at regular intervals, at the bottom of the page, were proverbs like "A rolling stone gathers no moss". The history book was a thin volume with many black and white pictures of Indians, log cabins, and Pilgrims, trudging through the deep snow. At the end of each story was a "fill the blank" test. We had to copy the whole sentence and write in the missing word. The arithmetic book had word problems and all types of addition, multiplication, division and fractions problems. We had to multiply and divide fractions like 367/950.

We had to write with pen and ink but I didn't have to bring the ink from home. A monitor periodically poured ink in the tiny glass container in the hole on top of the desk that I had noticed that first day of school. The pens were the same as the ones I had used in Italy. I still didn't like writing with pen and ink, especially during the penmanship lessons. The Palmer Method was the opposite of what I had been taught. In Italy, we picked up our pen after each letter. In America, I had to maintain a continuous stroke for the whole word.

One morning, the class became very excited when the teacher announced it was time for sewing. They had been sewing a garment cover, barely big enough to cover the shoulders of a dress.

The teacher handed me two pieces of blue cotton, thread and a needle and left me to fend for myself. The girl next to me, who always wore a knit cap and who was usually ignored by or made fun of, by the other classmates, felt sorry for me. She very kindly showed me her work and tried to explain what I had to do. I smiled and nodded that I understood. In one period I did more than the class had done in weeks. The girl glared at me. Why had I wasted her time? I wished I could explain how I had learned to sew.

When the teacher saw how well I sewed, she brought several head scarves for me to hem, in preparation for her summer cruise. Then she brought some of her friends' scarves.

The teacher spent most of her time at her desk, in front of the room. She stood only to write assignments on the blackboard for us to do at our desks. Each morning at 10 o'clock, she sent her pet, a girl in the front seat, to the corner grocery store, to buy one orange. While we did our work she cut the orange and squeezed it over a glass orange juicer and poured it into a tall glass. After each sip, she delicately removed the pips from her mouth.

At lunch time I walked home with a Jewish girl who lived on the second floor of our apartment house. When her mother opened the door the smell of a baked potato filled the air. I felt a bit of envy as I walked up to our apartment. I was almost sure my mother would not be home. She seldom was. After she did her housework she walked to the open air market on Arthur Avenue where the vendors were all Italian immigrants, to buy fruits, vegetables and fresh bread. Then she walked to the grocery store and the butcher. Some times she had to make two trips because there was just so much she could carry in two shopping bags. She didn't even try to coordinate her errands to be home when I came home for lunch. Once I had the courage to ask her why. She looked at me as if the idea had never occurred to her. After all, I had managed very well on my own all through the long lunch hours in *Noepoli*. She felt that leaving me lunch was enough. Knowing how hard it was for her to be cooped up in the three room apartment, I never mentioned it again.

One lunch hour still lingers in my mind. I was about to take out the dish of lentil soup from the icebox when the doorbell rang. A tall, heavyset woman and three children were at the door. As I greeted them, their family history flashed through my mind. She and her

122

husband came from a town near *Noepoli*. They had many children and the money they received from the Home Relief Agency wasn't enough. The husband rode the Staten Island Ferry playing the accordion, hoping the passengers would drop some coins in his hat. At lunch time, the wife took her three youngest children to a *paesano's* house, counting on the Southern code of hospitality. You don't eat unless you invite your guests to join you.

My brain was processing all this. I said that my mother was not home. The woman just smiled and proceeded to come in with the three children in tow. We sat in the kitchen making conversation. I didn't have enough food to feed them. I didn't dare heat up my small dish of soup. I couldn't possibly eat while four pairs of hungry eyes watched me. We chit-chatted a while and when I said it was time for me to go back to school they waited for me to stand up and followed me out.

I joined the other children on the sidewalk outside the school. The boys ran around and the girls skipped rope. I just chatted with whomever was near. They didn't know quite what to make of me but they all liked to talk to me and be my friends. No one made fun of my mistakes.

That particular lunch hour I wished I had some money to buy something from the peddler who appeared regularly with his glass-enclosed push cart. He sold candy for a penny, slices of coconut for two cents, and baked, sweet potatoes for a nickel. In warm weather he sold ice cream pops for a nickel. Just as I had never bought anything at the confectioner's shop in *Noepoli*, I didn't buy anything from the peddler. I never mentioned him to my parents. I didn't want to embarrass them in case they didn't have the money to give me.

I ignored my hunger pangs and chatted with the other children until the bell rang. We scurried to our class' designated spot in the yard. We lined up in two lines, in size places, boys and girls separate. When the teacher blew the whistle we stood straight and shut our mouths. We walked silently to our classrooms, going up the Up staircase. No one wanted to risk punishment for talking in the halls.

On her walks back and forth to the various stores, my mother became friends with two Southern Italian sisters who were subcontractors for a clothing manufacturer. The economic conditions were so bad that many immigrant husbands had no choice but to send their wives and daughters to work as sewing machine operators in sweat shops. But, no matter how poor, women with small children couldn't leave them to work in the factories. The factory owners found a way to bring the work to them. They subcontracted the work to enterprising women in the community who parceled it out to their friends and neighbors to sew in their homes. The homeworkers were paid by the number of pieces they finished. In their eagerness to earn as much as possible, some neglected their homes and their children. Their school children did piece work instead of homework.

. The were happy to give my mother a bundle of tablecloths and napkins to embroider. She stitched early in the morning and late in the evening but she never asked me to help. She insisted that my job was to study. But I helped her whenever I could. She was very proud to receive her small, brown pay envelope with her name on it. She became a preferred customer of the two sisters until the practice was abolished several years later.

I seldom asked Josephine, my Italian classmate, for help in the classroom but we became friends after school. She invited me to her house, a block away from the school, to meet her family. They lived in the lower apartment of a two family house her parents owned. The father sold bananas on a cart that he pushed from street to street. Josephine and her four siblings were all American born, spoke English, but understood their parents' dialect. Her parents came from *Le Puglie* but we could understand each other. We visited each other's houses and did things after school.

On Saturday mornings we went to the run-down *De Luxe* for the 10 o'clock show. We went early, hoping to be among the first 100 on line, to qualify for the day's prize. We paid our ten cents and were ushered into the children's section by a white uniformed matron, who patrolled the aisles to make sure no one sneaked into the adult section in the balcony. We saw two features, cartoons, the newsreel and a chapter of a serial which always stopped with Flash Gordon at the mercy of Ming the Merciless. We couldn't wait for the next episode to see how Flash Gordon got out of danger.

When I came home one Saturday afternoon, Rocco was there with his last bag of fruit and his last payment. His wife, two teenage sons and Angelina were coming to America. The oldest son remained

124

in Italy. Shortly after they arrived we went to visit them in their cold water flat in Harlem where they had to share the hall bathroom with the other tenants on the floor. Angelina and I were going to live different lives. Instead of going to school, she was going to work.

At the beginning of the sixth grade I was still the only foreign born student in the school. Shortly into the term a girl from Milan was placed in another sixth grade class. Her father, finally convinced that there was going to be a war, sent for her and her mother. I immediately felt inferior to her. Not only did she speak beautiful Italian, she also spoke good English. She walked proudly through the halls and talked confidently to all the teachers. I was always unsure of myself and afraid of making mistakes.

One of the big events of the sixth grade was getting our copy of *My Weekly Reader*. We saw pictures and read stories about the first successful flight of a helicopter. We were enthralled with the pictures of the smiling, sixteen year old King Farouk, "Boy King" of Egypt, recognized throughout the world by his distinctive red fez. I wasn't too happy when they wrote about Mussolini. He was belittled when they compared him to Hitler. Hitler was impressing the world but Mussolini was being made fun of. I felt that all of Italy was being belittled.

The Sunny Italy section of our geography book added to my insecurity. The description of the country and the happy, smiling people were not how I remembered them.

The school not only took care of our education but also of our health. The nurse examined my teeth and referred me to a dentist on East Tremont Avenue, who treated the poor school children. I didn't know what to expect. I had never been to a dentist. My father walked the several blocks with me to meet the dentist who turned out to be a wonderful husband and wife team.

I had twelve cavities. Each cavity required at least two visits. The painful drilling and the temporary filling took up the first visit. A week later, the permanent mercury filling was put in. I spent many afternoons in that office. Sometimes Dr. Riis worked on me and sometimes his wife, Dr. Rae. In the spring they began to talk about their two week summer vacation in the Adirondack Mountains. The resort limousine would take them and their only son to and from the resort. For weeks after they got back they talked about the mountains, the lake and the hotel on its bank. I listened in wonder. I didn't know anyone who went on a vacation.

The nurse also referred me to an optician who fitted me with a pair of silver, metal rimmed glasses to correct my astigmatism and near-sighted vision. Fortunately, I was not the only one with glasses. The teachers went out of their way to tell us how nice we looked.

At the end of the sixth grade I was placed in the Rapid Advance class. It was made up of the smartest six graders from the several elementary schools that fed into Junior High 57. We were grouped together in one class, to cover an enriched three year program in only two.

Twenty-three

During that summer my mother and I boarded a train at Pensylvania Station to visit Uncle Domenick and his family, in Steubenville, Ohio. The breeze from the open windows brought relief from the heat but it also brought soot from the smoke stack of the coal-fired engine. The rattling of the wheels was almost deafening as the train meandered through forests, rode over mountains or crossed them through tunnels. We were ready to get off the train as soon as the conductor announced that Steubenville was the next stop.

Patsy, a relative we had never met, had no trouble spotting us when we got off. As we walked up the street that gradually rose up a hill, I noticed that the tallest buildings were only three stories high and those few, were business establishments. There were no apartment houses, only unattached, single family homes. My uncle's house, similar to all the others on the street, was almost at the very top of the hill.

The two-story frame house had one porch in the front, and one in the back. The front parlor had a fireplace and was kept immaculate at all times. Always ready for company. The house had cold running water, no central heating and no bathroom. The outhouse was at the far end of the back yard.

Uncle Domenick's wife, Aunt Grace (daughter of Sicilian immigrants) and the four children, Rocco, Angelo, Sam and Mary were there to greet us with open arms. Rocco had finished High School and the others were still attending. All the boys belonged to the school band and Mary took piano lessons from the woman next door.

During our visit I watched Aunt Grace go through her weekly routines. Monday was wash day but hers took longer than ours. Not only did she have laundry for six people but she had to first heat the water on the stove. Aunt Grace was one of the few proud owners of a washing machine which consisted of a wooden tub with an electrical activated agitator in the center. When the clothes had been agitated enough, Aunt Grace picked one item at the time and carefully passed it through the manually operated wringer at the side of the tub. Tuesday was ironing day, Wednesday was mending and sewing, Thursday was for baking bread and pies and Friday was general housecleaning day. Dusting was a daily job. Fine soot spewed by coal fired trains that went through Steubenville three or four times a day, was everywhere.

Saturday was bath day. The same large wooden tub that was used for the laundry on Monday doubled as bath tub on Saturday. Since the tub was in the kitchen next to the stove, a schedule had to be followed so that each person would have privacy. Sunday was the day to dress up, go to Church in the morning and go visiting or receive visitors in the afternoon.

Aunt Grace had something noone we knew in New York had - a telephone. When it rang, she listened to make sure it was her ring and not the ring assigned to another family on the party line. She sat in the parlor and spoke with complete ease as she visited with one of her friends or one of her many siblings.

Unemployment in Steubenville was as high as it was in the rest of the country. Even the men who had jobs either with the railroad, coal mines or the steel mill, did not earn enough to support their families. They usually did not have the money to pay for all the groceries they bought. From the shelf under the counter the storekeeper carefully took out a large notebook with a pencil dangling from a string and carefully noted the items that were bought on credit. At the end of the month the families paid what they could and carried the balance until the next month. To supplement his wages as a trackman my uncle cultivated a vegetable garden, a few blocks away from home.

Most of the young women in Steubenvile did not have jobs. They did household chores, and like the young women in *Noepoli*, thought about getting married. Meanwhile, they worried about where to get the money for silk stockings which were very expensive and delicate. As soon as there was a run in a stocking it had to be discarded. If the run was not visible they stopped it from spreading by applying colorless nail polish.

During our visit we went to see Aunt Raffaella, my grandmother's sister in Aliquippa, Pa., where she and her husband had settled at the turn of the century. The car we rode in pulled up to the others parked in front of the three story brick house. Aunt

128

Raffaella, a heavyset, jovial woman had the same wavy hair of my mother's family. The house was full of people gathered there to meet us. She introduced us to her daughter, who was two or three years older than I, the three married sons and their wives and several other guests. They all spoke English to each other but spoke the Americanized dialect with us.

After all the introductions and embraces we climbed to the second floor where dishes of food were lined up on the long table set for the large group that sat down to it. As the dishes of food were passed around I noticed that Aunt Raffaella made sure the daughters-in-law saw to all the guests' needs. They didn't look too happy about it. The husbands, caught between their domineering mother and their unhappy wives pretended not to see or hear. One of the sons and his wife lived in the same house with Aunt Raffaella. The other two and their wives lived in houses nearby. They all depended on Aunt Raffaella's generosity to supplement their meager incomes.

When Aunt Raffaella was left a widow many years before, she kept several boarders, who, lonely for their own families, helped her to raise her children and her sister's young son, Michael. Michael was left an orphan when Aunt Raffaella's sister died by asphyxiation due to a faulty gas jet.

Little Michael had grown into the serious, good-looking bachelor, in his early thirties, who sat in a prominent place at the table. He had a full head of brown hair that touched the wide collar of his white shirt. He wore an out style wide black cravat instead of a tie. Everyone was very deferential and addressed him as the "Judge".[12] I found out later that while still in his twenties, he had been part of the defense team for Sacco and Vanzetti. He wrote letters to the Judge to spare the two but to no avail. They were given the death sentence. (Many years later they were exonorated)

Sitting near the judge was the widower and his little girl who lived across the street. When he and my mother first greeted each other they both looked sheepish. I soon found out why. Had my mother and grandmother come to America when Uncle Domenick had sent them the passage money he was the man she would have married. The man was very nice and for a few minutes I wondered how

---

[12] www.library.duq/specialcollections/musmanno

different I would be, if my mother had married him.

We enjoyed the visit but we were happy to be back home, in our three rooms. I appreciated the bathroom with the tub and the hot water even more than before my trip. My father was happy to welcome us back and we all resumed our routines.

In September I'd be returning to the school building across from our apartment house. I wondered what Jr. High would be like.

Twenty-four

On the first day of school I walked across the street into the school yard and joined the other children milling around looking for our classes. I found the monitor holding the sign for my class and joined the group. Soon all 35 of us arrived. Because it was made up of students from various neighborhoods I didn't know anyone except one girl. She was the daughter of the German immigrant who owned the bakery on the corner of our block. We were all a little nervous and tried to make conversation. When I looked around at the lines of regular seventh graders I couldn't help but notice how much younger my classmates looked. I was about a year and half older than the average seventh grader but they were at least a year or maybe two years younger than average because they had skipped a grade or two.

Just before the bell rang our homeroom teacher stood at the head of the line and led us to our home room. Mr.Corday took the attendance and gave us our schedule of classes. We stayed together as we moved to our different subjects. Before we left one classroom for the next, we lined up according to our height, boys and girls in separate lines. (Luckily, I was not the tallest). The teacher escorted us to the next class. We returned to the homeroom for dismissal.

Everyone noticed us as we walked through the halls. We were the youngest, had the straightest lines and were the quietest. We hated to meet one class of ninth graders. They had been left back a few times, were almost as tall as the teachers and were loud. The big girls at the end of the line loved to taunt us by calling us "Babies". When they were out of ear shot, we called them "dumb".

Since we came from different neighborhoods and had lots of homework, we seldom saw see each other after school. In the morning we socialized outside the wire fence until the bell rang. My classmates were the children or grandchildren of Italian, German, Polish and Jewish. immigrants. Most of them were children of professionals, shopkeepers and tradesmen. I was the only foreign born and the poorest.

Some waited for me to compare their Latin homework with mine. Mr. Corday, who was also our Latin teacher, often quoted

Cicero and Caesar but did very little teaching. He assigned a few pages in the grammar text for homework and we were on own to figure everything out. Even though my Italian wasn't perfect, it gave me a slight edge over the rest of the class. Sometimes my classmates talked about the radio programs they listened to and retold the jokes they heard on the *Eddie Cantor, Fibber McGee and Molly* and the *Jack Benny* shows. On the 1938 Halloween morning, my classmates were excitedly talking about men form Mars invading a town in New Jersey. By not listening to *The War of Worlds* the evening before, I had missed the panic the radio show had created. The listeners had been fooled into thinking they were listening to an actual news program.

I didn't know any of the programs. We only listened to the nightly, fifteen minute news program with H.V. Kaltenborne and another fifteen minutes with Walter Winchell. I continued to listen to the five o'clock Italian dramatizations of Shakespeare's plays and other stories. During the week-ends we listened to some Italian comedies and to *Don Peppe u Rusicatore*, an Italian political satirist, who interjected a few southern dialect phrases in his caustic comments about Mussolini's attack on Ethiopia and his part in the Spanish Civil War. By then, even Mussolini's sympathizers were losing respect for him.

I finally persuaded my father, who thought that listening to the American comedy programs was a waste of time, to let me listen to them so I could discuss them with my classmates.

Besides the radio programs they talked about the adventures of Dick Tracy, in the comics.

I couldn't do anything about the comics. The only paper we bought was *Il Progresso Italo Americano,* which my father read carefully, every day.

Helen, one of the girls who waited for me to check her Latin homework, was pert and slim. Her black, Persian Lamb-like hair set her apart from the rest of us, who had long, straight hair. She was the youngest of four sisters, born of Sicilian immigrants. They owned a two family home, similar to the Lufranos. Some mornings Helen looked quite upset. Two of her sisters and their father were having bitter arguments. The oldest sister had a limp and did not have a boyfriend. The younger sisters had boyfriends and wanted to get

132

married. The father, still following the Biblical custom, insisted that the oldest had to be married first. Towards the end of the year the younger sisters had had enough. They were going to get married regardless of what the father said.

During our Civics class the teacher asked if any of our parents had health insurance. We looked around at each other to see if anybody knew what she was talking about. Only one boy, the son of a lawyer, raised his hand. The teacher explained the advantages and benefits of health insurance. All I learned was that we couldn't afford it.

For music we went to the Auditorium along with other classes where the music teacher taught songs to the whole group. In December we started to practice religious Christmas Carols like Silent Night. I didn't know much about religion but I knew that most of my class was made up of Jewish children. I felt very uneasy when I noticed that they were singing *Round Virgin and Child* just as loudly as the Christian children. It just didn't seem right that they had to sing Christian songs.

My father didn't have a steady job but he earned enough for us to live very frugally. As soon as President Roosevelt's administration created the Public Works Administration or WPA, my father applied for a job. The WPA workers became the favorite butts of jokes. They were pictured as spending more time leaning on their shovels than actually digging with them. But my father was not bothered by the jokes. He was happy to work for the $48 a month, instead of receiving Home Relief. He was among the very first to join the Social Security System, after it was created in 1935. It was a revolutionary program intended to help ordinary working people plan for their old age.

My mother was always ready to work at odd jobs. After the embroidery piece work was abolished, she rolled cigars for a Sicilian, who manufactured them in a little store in the neighborhood. She learned to arrange flowers for a Florentine florist who called on her whenever he a had a wedding or a funeral. My father's steady job and the money she earned, gave my mother the confidence to do what she had wanted to do for a long time. She looked for a four room, front, non-railroad apartment. She found one on the top floor of a five-story walk-up, on Arthur Avenue near East 179th St.

133

The frayed awnings, shielding the front rooms from the summer sun, were reminders that at one time the building had been occupied by affluent tenants. The awnings didn't do much to keep the apartment cool. During the first summer we learned just how sweltering the apartment, under the flat, tar roof, could be. It was a struggle to keep things cold in the icebox. When the landlord, a very tall, pleasant Jewish man who spouted Schopenhauer, offered us a refrigerator for two more dollars a month, my parents accepted. The freezer compartment was big enough for two ice cube trays. (Frozen foods were not even a thought in the housewives' mind). No more pans to empty. No more chipping ice. We could have ice any time we wanted.

The front apartment allowed us to see and hear what was happening in the street. We could hear the cries of the push cart vendors hawking their products. One of the favorites was Joe the fisherman.

After a few months, a stranger came around to collect the rent instead of the landlord. More and more owners chose agents to collect the rents. They didn't want to hear their tenants' complaints or listen to their hard luck stories when they didn't have the rent.

My room was the corner room on the unattached side of the building, the tallest on the three blocks that separated us from Crotona Park. There were no buffers to deflect the cold winter winds. When the heat was shut off at ten o'clock, my room quickly became an icebox.. On very cold nights I put my coat on top of all the blankets but I couldn't do anything about my nose. It got so cold that it woke me up.

We started to have fresh killed chickens as soon as my mother found out about the Jewish chicken market, two blocks away on La Fontaine Ave. The market was a huge, cavernous room, filled with cages of cackling chickens of all sizes. A man asked you if you wanted to make soup, stew or fry? He then led you to the appropriate cages. He took the chicken out of its cage and held it up, so you could feel it. He kept taking them out until you found the one you liked. He took the chicken you chose to one of the many deep sinks along the outside wall. There, he expertly twisted its neck, ran it under the scalding hot water, and quickly and deftly plucked off the feathers. He left the pin feathers for you to pluck out and jokingly

134

warned you to make sure to take the entrails out, before cooking the chicken. A favorite joke was about the bride who cooked the chicken with the entrails still in it..

I enjoyed going to school. Except for our Latin teacher, the others made their subjects interesting. We always had lively discussions in our Social Studies class. "Should the USA lift the embargo on Japan?", was one of liveliest. One boy in particular, stood up and argued emotionally for lifting the sanctions. The only effect of the embargo that I understood was that because we were no longer buying Japan's silk, the ladies' stockings were getting too expensive. Women hated those made from heavy, lisle thread. During the warm months some opted to use tan make-up on their legs. I liked the discussions but I didn't like the Scrap Book assignments. We did not subscribe to any magazines. I had nowhere to go to look for pictures.

The discovery of King Tut's tomb, the ancient Boy King, in 1922, was still generating a great deal of interest. I didn't know what to do when we had to arrange a scrapbook on ancient Egypt. Gaetano, the tenant in the Lufrano's house, an agent for the Prudential Life Insurance Co., invited me to his house to look through the back issues of the *National Geographic,* whenever I needed pictures.

Like *Don* Carlo, Gaetano had gone to school in Italy and was able to get a job with an insurance company. Selling life insurance policies to the poor was a relatively new concept. Insurance companies welcomed educated men who could speak their clients' language to inspire confidence in the husbands to buy the policies and in their wives to let them in every week to collect the quarter for each policy. Dressed in dark suits and ties and carrying their black Debit books, these agents were familiar figures in the neighborhood. They often had to make repeat visits because the housewife did not have the quarter to give them the first time they went. After a while the insurance agent became almost like a member of the family.

Gaetano and his wife came from *Terranova.* They had two American born children, Larry, an under-employed lawyer, and Clara, a high school graduate who worked in an office. Clara, pretty, soft-spoken, often sat on the porch to wait for her boyfriend, son of Italian immigrants, named Larry like her brother, and like him, was an under-employed lawyer. Clara always had a smile for me but there was sadness in her smile. She and Larry had been engaged for years,

135

but marriage was not in sight. Larry did not earn enough to support her. They saw each other on the week-ends and Wednesday evenings, the designated week-day date night for couples who were serious about each other.

They, like the other couples, usually went to the movies. They were affordable and offered escape from their dull lives. The films featured handsome men and beautiful women whose problems were resolved at the end of the film, and then lived happily ever after. The women loved to see the fashionable clothes worn by the women stars and fantasized about the male stars. They still mourned the romantic matinee idol, Southern Italian, Rudolph Valentino, who had died a few years before, at the age of 31.

Even though the movies were not expensive, the movie houses were usually empty during the week, when they showed their B (budget) films. To attract the women who normally would not go to the movies, they started "Dish Nights". They displayed a complete set of very attractive dishes in the lobby. The women received a free dish every time they bought a ticket. The offer was irresistible to the women like my mother who, didn't own a matching set and had no hopes of buying one. She went every dish night, regardless of what was playing, until she had collected the complete set for twelve.

My father did not trust salesmen and never bought a life insurance policy, even though the agent was a *paesano*. But the day a total stranger, carrying a case in one hand and a book in the other, rang the bell, he let him in. My father was still earning only $48 a month but he bought the complete set of Dickens and a set of *The Wonderland of Knowledge*. As a bonus, we received an enormous two volume unabridged dictionary.

We stored the encyclopedia and dictionary in the living room and I placed the set of Dickens on the two glass enclosed shelves of the secretary in my room. Even though I froze in winter and sweltered in summer, I was very happy to have a room of my own. I could shut the door and stay up as long as I needed to do my homework, without disturbing my parents.

Moving to the new apartment meant I had to walk a few blocks to school. Walking back and forth I went by a store that had been converted into a factory. My friend Angelina was working there as a sewing machine operator. Her family had moved from their cold

136

water apartment in Harlem to an apartment near us. By then Angelina was the only sibling living at home. Her brother Ferdinand was being treated for tuberculosis in a sanitarium in Lake Placid, New York. Her brother Tony was serving in the CCC, Civilian Conservation Corps, another New Deal program to help the poor youth.

One hot June afternoon, the factory's door was wide open. I stepped in to say "Hello". I almost fainted. The only air was what came in from the front and back doors. The whirring noise of the machines, set next to each other, with just enough space between the rows for the floor lady to reach each operator, was deafening. The women sat with their heads bent low over the machines and their fingers fed the material as fast as their feet could pedal. They didn't even lift their heads when the finished pieces were picked up and the ones to be sewn were left in their places. They were paid by the piece and every minute was precious. The floor lady stopped me from going toward my friend and told me to leave immediately. She didn't want a child near the place for fear of attracting attention. Angelina was under age and should not have been working. They hid her whenever the government inspector came around. Angelina never even lifted her head.

As Junior High was coming to an end I began to dread having to go to the district High School, Theodore Roosevelt, near Fordham Road. The school, about a four mile walk from home, was the one where all the Junior High schools in the district had to send their graduates. It had a very poor academic program and was well known for its discipline problems. There was no way to avoid going there.

One day Mr. Silverman, my mathematics teacher, told me that he was recommending me and three other girls to take the entrance exam to the all girl Hunter College High School. He explained that if we graduated from there we would be assured admission to the all women, tuition free, Hunter College. My heart almost stopped with both anticipation and fear. We were to meet with him the next afternoon so that he could give us some pointers about taking the test.

Twenty-five

The morning of the test, Louise, who lived in the next building, Marie, who lived a few blocks away, both daughters of Southern Italian immigrants, and I walked together to the 179th station of the Third Avenue El. We got in the third car of the 7:30 train. Janet, who lived in the Jewish section around East 174th St., joined us at the next station. We talked nervously about the test until we got off at the 68th St. station. We walked over to Lexington Avenue, to an old, red brick building attached to the tall, modern, Hunter College.

The dimly lit Auditorium was filling up with girls, chatting just as nervously as we were. We listened to the student leaders make encouraging welcoming remarks and then we went to different rooms for the test. All the way home we went over the test, alternating between hope and despair. A few weeks later I was notified I had passed the test. A great number had failed it. Luise was one of them.

We were assigned to three different classes but we rode the train together. After a few days we were relaxed enough to notice the other riders on the 7:30 train. Morning after morning, they were the same riders, sitting in the same seats, doing the same things. The men buried their faces in the *Daily News.* Even the ones who seemed to be reading *The New York Times* usually had the *Daily News* tucked in it. The *Times* had all the "news fit to print" but what *The Daily News* printed was more interesting. Some men wore work clothes. Others wore suits, ties and starched, white shirts. The young women office workers wore dark dresses with detachable, starched, white collars and cuffs.

My homeroom class was an older version of my Junior High class. We were either daughters or granddaughters of immigrants. We represented almost all the countries of Europe. My Junior High class came from several neighborhoods. My High School class came from all the five boroughs of New York City. On Monday mornings, a few Irish girls who sat together in the front, talked about the boys they saw on the week-end. They talked to each other but loudly enough for all of us to hear. We just listened in awe. Except for Dorothy, who told me about the "I said" and "he said" conversations she had with the *The Bronx Home News* delivery boy, no one else had any boys to talk about.

Dorothy lived in a tenement amidst the fire gutted ones of the South Bronx. She was a tall, pretty girl, with almond shaped eyes and shiny brown hair. Every day of that first year she wore the same starched, tan cotton dress, with small yellow flowers. How she managed to launder it and starch it so often, I never found out. As the months went by, Dorothy got taller and the dress got shorter. By the spring, it was high above her knees. When the teacher asked her to go to the board, she walked with great dignity, standing tall, seemingly unembarrassed by the shortness of the dress. She rarely mentioned her family except for her mother, an Hungarian immigrant to whom she was devoted. Dorothy and I became close friends mainly because we were the poorest in the class and both our mothers communicated with smiles and nods rather than words.

When the term started I was the only foreign student in the whole school. A few months later, a very friendly and confident Jewish girl, speaking heavily German accented English, came carrying a bulging briefcase. Her family was one of the relatively few who had foreseen further troubles for the Jews and left Germany.

The increasing tensions in Europe finally convinced Joe, the shoemaker, to send for his wife and small boy. By *Noepoli*'s standards, the wife had been living a very comfortable life with the money her husband sent her. Anticipating a luxurious life style, the young wife stepped off the boat in a stylish dress and a boa around her neck. The rude awakening came when she climbed up the grimy stairs to their cold water, railroad flat apartment, in a tenement in crowded Harlem. The bathtub was bolted to the kitchen floor and the toilet was in a small closet. Carlo, the most urbane of all the *paesani,* was the only one who did not listen to my father's advice. He clung to his dream of returning to Italy a rich man.

Although Hunter College High School was a school for the gifted, (I didn't realize it at the time), its physical conditions were no better than the tenements. The rooms were stark and needed painting. The only furniture were the movable chair-desk combinations for the students and the bare metal desks for the teachers. The teachers moved from room to room as we did. No one had the incentive to decorate the rooms. The gym was a bare, windowless room in the basement. The only apparatus was the small drum the young teacher beat to set the tempo for our exercises. The cafeteria was a counter in a corner of a large room where two ladies, wearing white aprons and hair nets, prepared sandwiches on request. Small containers of milk and ice-cream pops were available.

Those of us who brown bagged had been told not to leave our lunches in our lockers for fear of roaches. We carried our lunches along with our books. We ate breakfast so early, that we were ready for lunch after the first period. We nibbled at our sandwiches as we walked from one class to another. We usually had nothing left by lunchtime. Sometimes we splurged and spent a nickel for an ice cream pop. But when the price went up to six cents, we didn't buy them as often. That extra penny broke up the nickel we needed for the fare home.

We didn't spend too much time complaining about the physical conditions of the school. We were too busy doing our work to make sure we wouldn't be expelled. A few months into the semester several girls were asked to leave. Some found the work so difficult that they left voluntarily. My class had a set of twins who didn't return for the second semester. I was in constant fear that I might not be able to do the work.

The first class trip was to The World's Fair which opened in the Spring of 1939, in Flushing Meadows, Queens. The Fair helped us, temporarily at least, to forget the Depression. Pictures and statuettes of its logo, the Trylon and Perisphere, were everywhere. The ads and news articles promised the visitors a glimpse into the *World of Tomorrow.*

We stood in a long line on the ramp to see General Motors' *Futurama,* an utopian view of the future transportation patterns. In another building we saw a model of an under water city that was to be our home in the near future. Dupont had *The Wonder World of Chemistry* where they made *Better Things For Better Living-Through Chemistry.* Through the large window we could see an upholstered chair hanging in midair as if by magic. A close look revealed that the chair was suspended by a single thread of the new, man-made miracle fiber - nylon. General Electric displayed its electric refrigerators to entice the women to get rid of their iceboxes. R.C.A waited for the opening of the Fair to broadcast its first commercial TV program, for the select few who had TV sets. We walked by the Borden's display and saw Elsie, their famous cow.

Except for the Lagoon of Nations, where I visited the wonderful Italian pavilion, everything was American. The Fair was a miniature American universe. It was designed to make us proud to be Americans by promoting all things American. But the more I saw, the more foreign I felt. I couldn't identify with the young employees who were blond, slim, and who wore trim, tan uniforms, to accentuate their blondness.

The Fair promoted the *Melting Pot* ideal of American society by encouraging immigrants to accept American foods and American customs as soon as possible. We immigrants embraced the same ideal. In public, we were American and at home and with our fellow immigrants, we were ethnic. In school I kept quiet when the girls talked about mustard, mayonnaise and milk. I didn't mention that I never drank milk and that at supper, I had a few sips of wine. We wanted to be Americans as soon as possible and tried to minimize our foreign backgrounds. But it was easier said than done. Despite our outward Americanization, we could not hide our diverse ethnic backgrounds at school functions where so many of our parents spoke with foreign accents.

The technology displayed at the fair was creeping into the classroom. The teachers no longer accepted hand written assignments. Our papers had to be typed. My parents bought me a Royal portable. That summer I enrolled in a free typing course, one of the many courses, offered in a high school in Harlem, through the Works Program Administration. A group of us, trying to do something meaningful, started a club. We met after classes in a small room in the neighborhood. The dirt on its only window was so thick, it stopped the light from coming in. While everybody was talking about what to do, I took it upon myself to go out to clean the window. When I came back in, I was told I had been elected president. They really didn't know me. I had shown no leadership qualities. I guess they felt that if I was willing to wash the window, I must deserve to be president.

I was very uncomfortable throughout my presidency. I had never been in charge of anything. I really didn't know what I was doing. When we disbanded at the end of the summer I had no idea of

141

what we had accomplished but I had the distinct feeling that I had been the president of group of communist sympathizers.

Stark as Hunter High's physical conditions had been, they worsened when I returned that September. The juniors were transferred to the ninth floor of an old warehouse on 32nd St. on the East River. We took the Third Avenue El, transferred to the Second Avenue El and then walked down a very long, steep, block to the river front. To get to the elevator, programmed to stop only on the ninth floor, we had to walk past men loading and unloading crates. There were no lockers. Besides our lunches, we had to carry our coats and books, as we moved from room to room. Our lunches hardly ever lasted beyond the first period.

At three o'clock, Marie, Janet, Shirley, daughter of Estonia Jews and Edith, daughter of Latvian Jews, and I, walked up the hill to the Second Avenue El. Walking up the long block, our hungry stomachs were assaulted by the aromas from the Italian restaurant at the top of the hill. The smell of roasting *capozzelle*, sheep's heads, which I didn't particularly like, was so appetizing that I would gladly have eaten a whole one. My friends didn't know what they were smelling but the smell was so good, they too, groaned with hunger.

We returned the 68th St. building for the senior year. We complained to each other about the physical conditions and the enormous amount of homework, but we were happy and proud. We were getting a good education and in the process earning admission to Hunter College. The curriculum was extensive and difficult. We had to study Math, English Literature and Grammar, Social Studies, Physics, one modern language, plus, either Latin or Greek, Music, Art, Hygiene and a brand new subject, Phonetics.

One of our history teachers, a large woman with bulges from her throat to her knees, was one of old teachers who had started to teach when teachers were not allowed to marry. She had a very long Dutch name which we abbreviated to VP. She wore the long version of the Flapper dresses of the twenties, with the built-in belt just above her knees. Ropes of different colored beads dangled from her ample bosom. We always found her at her desk, either cutting articles from the newspapers spread out in front of her or sharpening pencils with a penknife. She didn't stop when we went in. She just looked at us over the rims of her glasses.

She started the lesson by asking a question that had a one word answer. After a while we found out that she used the same question for all her classes for that day. We waited for the class ahead of us to come out and asked them for the word of the day. One day the word was "Pope". When VP stood up in front of the room to ask the first question we didn't bother to pay attention. We knew the answer. The girl she called on, stood up in the aisle and confidently answered, "Pope". VP lowered her chin to her chest, looked at her over her glasses and with her characteristic derisive cackle mimicked,

"Pope!. Well! I changed the question and the answer is not "Pope".

She opened her marking book, found the girl's name, and announced "zero". We watched her carefully make the small circle with her pencil.

Sooner or later we were all in a similar position. Once, VP asked me the importance of Puerto Rico to the United States. I stood up in the aisle and answered, "For its strategic position".

She gave me the same look and cackled,

"And pray, what does strategic mean"? I was so stunned by the question that I was tongue-tied. I watched her open her book and make that deliberate circle. But I learned a lesson I haven't forgotten. You don't understand a concept until you can explain it in little words.

We soon learned that VP's cackles were those of a mother hen. She became one of our favorite teachers. When we graduated we gave her a small, hand held pencil sharpener.

The other history teacher, Mrs. Russel, was a young, tall and thin as a reed. Her hair was as golden as the corn silk of her native Iowa. She stood out as a ray of sunshine among us, mostly brunettes. We went to her class right after lunch. The lunch tray on her desk always had the crusts of a peanut butter and jelly sandwich and the shell of a baked potato, which the women in the lunchroom prepared for her in a metal gadget that fitted over a burner. She ate that every day, hoping to put on weight. She never gained an ounce. Her specialty was the Time Line. We had to place all events in the appropriate sequence in the Time Line. We had trouble finding space to put the items under 1848. I still remember that in that year, every country in Europe was having some kind of revolution or disturbance.

We always found Miss Fields, one of our English teachers, (same generation as VP), sitting at her desk reading a book. Each time we went to her class we wondered if she'd be wearing the same dress. Day in and day out, throughout the whole year, she wore a woolen, long-sleeved ankle length, green dress. After a while we decided that she must have two identical dresses. She wore one, while the other was being cleaned. She taught from her desk. She only went to the board to diagram a sentence. The books we read in her class, *Silas Marner* and *Mill on the Floss* were as dull as her wardrobe.

Our Social Studies teacher was the antithesis of Miss Fields. She was young, pretty and very vibrant. She spent most of her salary on dresses and shoes. To those of us whose wardrobe was only slightly better than Miss Fields', the Social Studies class was a fashion show. If we found her sitting at her desk, we craned our necks to get a peek at her shoes. She waited until all of us were seated. Then she got up, stood where we could all see, and with a flourish, she'd say,

"I know you won't pay any attention until you see my new shoes".

No matter the subject of discussion, she interjected the idea that women should not give up their jobs as soon as they got married, as most husbands expected them to do.

"How long does it take to clean a three room apartment"?, she would ask us rhetorically.

The question in our mind was rather whether we would ever find a job. The Depression lingered on. Movies, articles and books dealt with the plight of people coping with all sorts of privations brought on by lack of work and natural disasters. One day we saw Marilyn sneaking a glimpse at a book she hid under her desk. We wondered what it could be that she didn't want the teacher to see. She was reading *The Grapes of Wrath,* covered to look like a text book. She read a page or two in between classes. She bought the book but kept it a friend's house overnight. "My mother would kill me if she knew". Steinbeck's best seller captured the suffering of the people driven off the their land by the severe droughts. It was banned in some places because of the graphic description of the Okies, such as the woman breast feeding a hungry adult male.

The young Hygiene teacher was afraid to discuss anything

144

more controversial than whether to dust before or after vacuuming.

There was very little after school life at H.C.H.S. Except for a few who stayed for an occasional club meeting, everyone rushed out at three o'clock. We all had long trips home. Some had to ride the subways and then buses to get home. I didn't have the time to participate.

I qualified for the New Deal Administration's works program for needy students. I received six dollars a month for working in the school library during my study periods and two afternoons a week. On those afternoons I rode the train without my friends. In the winter I got home after dark. I started my homework as soon as I could. Some evenings I didn't finish until almost midnight.

Even though college was free, Dorothy's family was too poor to send her. The rest of us were eager to start college in September. We expected to date the young men from Hunter's brother college, The College of the City of New York, CCNY. We had full confidence that we would be married as soon as we finished college. Despite our social studies teacher's admonitions, we still placed a good marriage ahead of a career.

Twenty-six

In September 1941, Marie and I met Janet on the 7:30 train for our first day at Hunter College. We separated as soon as we entered the modern multi-storied building to go to our different classes. In my first class I spotted only one familiar face. We had seen each other in the halls of Hunter High, but Regone and I had never spoken. In a roomful of strangers we approached each other as friends.

Regone and I happened to have several classes together. I invited her to our house but she didn't dare invite me to hers. Mussolini had invaded Greece and the Greeks hated the Italians.

She and her younger brother lived with their parents in Manhattan, in a neighborhood of Greek immigrants. Her father had a job with the New York City Department of Sewers. Regone, like the other children of Greek immigrants, went to Greek school on Saturday mornings. If I could learn to read Greek, egone's mother would assume I was Greek. We met before, in-between and after classes, for Regone to teach me the Greek alphabet. After a few weeks she brought the Greek newspaper for me to read aloud. Since Greek is very phonetic, I was able to decode the words without understanding any of them. After a few weeks, Regone invited me to her home. She told her mother that I could read the Greek newspaper. he mother was thrilled. Using the Italian intonation, I read a couple of paragraphs. Convinced that I was the daughter of Greeks, she welcomed me and served her delicious rice pudding. A few visits later we told her the truth. She accepted her defeat graciously.

I met Regone's friends at the youth meetings held in her church and I participated in their non-religious activities. During those meetings I noticed that, under their Americanized and Christianized exteriors, their souls were still with the ancient gods on Mount Olympus.

A few weeks after classes started I visited the Guidance Counselor to ask if I could carry extra credits to finish college in three and a half years. She could not give me an answer until she saw my grades at the end of the first semester. She had seen too many freshmen leave during the first six months because they could not keep up with the work.

I registered with the College Employment Office. My father paid the semester's book fee of five dollars and fifty cents, but I needed to earn spending money. Some of the miracles predicted in the World's Fair were becoming a reality. That magic nylon thread was being spun into nylon stockings. They were not as luxurious as the silk ones but they were wonderful compared to the heavy lisle ones. It would be nice to buy a pair of nylons once in a while.

One of my first jobs was taking care of four year old Toby, who lived with his parents in an apartment on Lexington Avenue. A stately West Indian woman, wearing a starched white lace cap and a white, starched, lace-edged apron, over her black uniform, formally let me in. Toby's mother explained my duties and told me her husband had an important job in Washington, DC. On the days I took care of Toby she went shopping or met friends. On nice days Toby and I walked to the playground in Central Park.

One day, Toby's mother gave me cab fare for the short ride to his grandparents, who lived on East 78th St. and Madison Avenue. The private elevator doors opened into the room-sized entry foyer. The apartment took the whole floor. Doorways from the foyer led to the living room, the library, dining room and kitchen. Each of the several bedrooms had a private bath. In one of the bedrooms lived the elderly Nanny who had taken care of all the children. The room was her private domain and she was treated as a cherished member of the family. On the next few visits I met the two cleaning women, two laundresses, the cook and the woman who just came in to serve dinner. They came and went by the service elevator in the kitchen.

Occasionally, I slept at Toby's house on Saturday nights. When I stepped into the car on the Third Ave El, on my way home the afternoon of Sunday, December 7, 1941, everybody was gloomily reading a newspaper. I was stunned to see the huge headlines "US AT WAR". My heart sank. How could this be?

We in the United States were well aware of the war in Europe. The daily newspapers were full of war stories. Radio news programs broadcast war stories every night. Thanks to the Movietone news reels shown in movie houses ahead of the feature film, we were familiar with Hitler's Charlie Chaplin mustache and his Goose

Stepping troops; Mussolini, on the Quirinale balcony, arms akimbo, addressing the crowds and his profile showing his upturned defiant chin; the cigar-smoking Winston Churchill and other world leaders. But we didn't worry about anyone attacking us. We felt safe. We were between two oceans.

I realized that the vision I had of what my college years were going to be like, had suddenly blurred. The best way to cope with the situation was to keep busy and to do my assignments as thoroughly as I knew how.

That first semester we were expected to attend Chapel but noone really checked and at the end of the semester the practice was stopped. At the end of the semester we voted "No" on whether we wanted to keep the course that taught us how to set a proper table for serving tea.

At the end of the semester I returned to the Guidance Counselor. She took out my records. She looked up in surprise. I had the highest average in the entire freshman class. I would be allowed to take an extra three credits per semester, as long as I continued to get good grades. If I also took summer courses, I would be able to graduate in three and a half years.

One Saturday morning, a few weeks later, my father went out to do an errand. To cut down on the times we went up and down the four flights of steps, we planned our errands carefully. I was very surprised to see him come back a few minutes later, with storm clouds on his face and a business-sized envelope in his hand. The letter was from the Office of the Dean and was addressed to me. As he handed me the letter he said,

"Why would the Dean of the College write to you"?

I became just as concerned as he. I couldn't imagine what I had done wrong. My father didn't budge and kept staring at the letter as I nervously opened it. He looked sheepish when I told him that I had made the Dean's list. From then on, he looked for that letter at the end of each semester.

Shortly after that, when I went to baby-sit, Toby's mother opened the door. The stately maid had left for a better job. During the next few weeks, the door was opened by a series of women, without uniforms. Toby's mother's complained about the caliber of help. Servants were leaving for war -created jobs that paid better and had

148

benefits.

Toby's grandmother was even more distraught. She was furious with President Roosevelt's administration for lowering the personal income cap to include them. Up to then, only the very wealthy had paid personal income tax. She didn't know how she was to continue to run the household without the money they would have to pay in taxes. I couldn't really sympathize. The people we knew barely had an income. The next time I saw her, she proudly told me how she had resolved her problem. She had dismissed the woman who served dinner. The family had decided that after the cook placed the food on the table, they would pass the food around to each other, family style. She paused for me to congratulate her on her brilliant solution. I said the appropriate words and controlled my urge to laugh.

Louise (who had failed the entrance test for Hunter HS) and I saw each other socially all through High School. When I started college her mother was delighted to tell me that Louise had a good job in an office, earning a good salary, while we in college were penniless. As if that weren't enough, she smugly informed me that Louise's office was a good place to meet young men.

We at Hunter weren't earning much money and weren't having many dates. Hunter College and CCNY tried to ignore the war by continuing the periodic dances that traditionally had been jointly sponsored. I went to the first one. The war cast a pall on everyone. The dances were abandoned for the duration of the war.

Some women left college to join the WAC, the women's branch of the Army or the WAVES, the women's branch of the Navy. Some volunteered in the USO clubs to entertain the service men.

This upset my Italian professor, an immigrant from Milan. Women should be kept in their places. Granting the vote to women was a waste of effort. Everyone knew that women always voted the way their husbands did. We took our little revenge by snickering whenever he repeated one of his many sayings, " *moglie e buoi dai paesi tuoi"*, when it comes to buying cattle or choosing a wife, its best to get them from your own town. We all knew he had married a non Italian.

Meanwhile, the *paesani*'s daughters were earning huge salaries as sewing machine operators but many had to hand the small brown pay envelopes, unopened, to their fathers. The fathers, at their discretion, gave them a small amount of cash out of it. The supervisors, Southern Italian immigrants themselves, kept both fathers and daughters happy by making out two envelopes. The larger amount went in the official envelope for the fathers and, unknown to them, a smaller amount into the envelope for the daughters.

More and more men were called into the service. Soon, the only men around were the old, the married, and 4-F (the ones with some physical defect). The 4-F men became the butt of jokes. Although they felt awkward about their status, they made the most of it. They were the only young men around in a country of lonely women and unfilled jobs.

To keep up the soldiers' morale, relatives recruited pen pals for them. A friend gave me the name of her cousin from California. I wrote about my activities, usually by V-mail, and he described all the places he went to.

The man shortage was bad enough for all women but for us Southern Italian girls, it was worse. We couldn't accept casual dates. Our fathers expected *n'ambasciata,* the message from the young man's father, sent through a *paesano,* asking permission to date us. It was understood that the dating would lead to marriage. To avoid the Southern Italian fathers, both Italian and non-Italian young men preferred to date non-Italian girls. Those who did date Italian girls, made arrangements to meet somewhere away from home. The girls made up stories and depended on friends to cover for them. When I accepted a date with a soldier I met at a dance, I told my father that he was coming to the house. I convinced him that it was safer than meeting him at some street corner. My father was not happy but he understood. He also knew that he could not keep track of all my movements.

Despite the war we tried to live the college years as best as we could. I received an invitation to join the Italian Sorority, made up of Italian majors. As they talked and explained their activities, I realized I couldn't join. The extra credits I carried and my part time jobs left me little spare time. Besides, I didn't have the money to participate in their activities.

I continued to do my assignments as thoroughly as I knew how. I was never sure when they were good enough. One day our history teacher gave us a test which consisted of comparing the

Industrial Revolution, the American Revolution and the French Revolution. My mind just froze. I could not think of a thing to write. I stared at the yellow, legal pad sheet and twirled my pen. I looked around at my classmates who were busily writing. Finally, I wrote a very short paragraph for each Revolution. There was room to spare on the paper. When I saw some classmates going up to get more paper I started to feel ill. I could no longer bear the agony. I gave in my single piece of paper and left while everybody was still busily writing. I was so sure that I had failed the test that, for the first time ever, I cut the next class. Later in the day I met several of my classmates who told me that it was too bad I had missed the class. The teacher read my paper to the class. It was the best answer she had ever received.

Women started to fill jobs traditionally held by men. They worked in plants making guns, airplanes and tanks. They became mechanics to maintain them. The metaphor for all of them was *Rosie the Riviter*, a woman wearing pants, a man's shirt and a colorful bandanna around her head, created by Norman Rockwell for the cover of the *Saturday Evening Post*. As the war continued, more jobs became available. I got a job as a salesclerk in the W.T. Grant store on East Tremont Avenue, a few blocks from home. I worked Thursday evenings and all day Saturday, until the store closed at 10 o'clock, for four dollars and sixty-five cents a week. It put an end to my traveling all over the city to fill the one or two day jobs I was sent to by the College Employment office.

I was assigned to the shoe department, the most disliked department in the store. Customers, aware that once they used their ration coupons, they couldn't buy another pair until the next year, tried pair after pair, before buying. The number of pairs I showed were never enough. I had to go down to the stockroom to get more. After all that, most left without buying and I had shoes strewn all over the floor. No sooner did I put all the boxes back in place, than another customer would walk in.

Bad as that was, it was preferable to the cold winter nights when no one came into the store. The manager and the assistant manager, the only male employees in the store, stayed away from us as much as possible but watched us from the vantage point of their office, in the open loft at the back of the store. They could see every nook and cranny of the large store. We had to appear to be busy at all time. We went from counter to counter arranging things, disarranging them to rearrange again. The evening was never-ending.

One Saturday afternoon, a young woman came in and walked up to me with a big smile of recognition and called me by name. She was the girl with the wool cap who had tried to help me with the sewing project in the fifth grade. I was glad to see she had nice brown hair and no cap. She said she was happy to see me so she could apologize. Through the years she had been feeling guilty for hating me so much for sewing so well. I told her that I was sorry, too. A big weight seemed to lift from her shoulders.

Walking to and from my job I would see some men carrying large signs protesting a store's unfair treatment of the workers. Passersby either ignored them or called them trouble making communists.

There seemed to be no end to the war. Casualties were so high that the married men with children and those who had been considered too old at the beginning of the war, were drafted. Few men were left. One Saturday morning, one of the sales women was in tears. The assistant manager had been drafted. We found out then, that he was her husband. During the Depression husbands and wives were not allowed to work for the same company. They kept their marriage a secret for fear of losing a job. None of us had ever suspected anything. They always came and went separately.

When Millie's husband was drafted, Carlo continued to live in the apartment with her. He referred to her as *a bossa,* the name given by boarders to the woman who took care of them. He took her with him when he visited the *paesani.* Millie was American born but spoke the dialect very well and enjoyed making the rounds with Carlo.

No matter what we did, we could not forget the war. The pictures and stories of the war were on the front pages of the newspapers. The love songs about separated lovers were intermingled with the war news broadcasts. Housewives couldn't go shopping without their ration coupons for meat, sugar and clothing. Bill boards reminded us that "Loose lips sink ships". A bearded Uncle Sam pointed a finger over the giant letters "Uncle Sam Wants You". Movie stars held rallies to sell US Bonds. Signs in first floor windows of apartments houses asked for Quiet, to remind the passersby that a night defense worker was trying to sleep. The quiet of the night was often shattered by the shrill sirens for lights out. We were cautioned daily, that even the glow of a cigarette could pinpoint a target for an enemy bomber. Sitting in the dark, waiting for the all clear siren, we heard the building's air raid warden shout, "Hey you in 4B put the light out! You in 5C put the light out".

As the war dragged on, food shortages became more severe. There were signs urging everybody to grow Victory Gardens. Finally the Italian immigrants could have the last laugh. For decades they had been laughed at by the Americans for planting vegetable gardens wherever they found an abandoned plot of land. My parents had been planting vegetables for several years on a plot of land in Rosedale, near Uncle Michele's house. Now they were admired for their work.

The war fueled the economy. The WPA and the other Depression programs stopped. My father found work with large contractors and worked every day. My parents bought a fifty year old, two family, detached, house, on the next street, one block closer to the park. My mother's wish of owning a detached house, finally came true. It had a front porch and a backyard where my father planted a fig tree and both of them planted tomatoes, peppers and string beans. They no longer had to take the street car to the plot near Uncle Michele's house. My father filed for a permit to make wine. He bought the paraphernalia that he needed, set them in the basement and in the fall bought the grapes.

Everyone suffered during the war but the Italians suffered even more. Italy as a member of the Axis, became an enemy of the United States as soon as Japan attacked Pearl Harbor. The Italian immigrants who were not American citizens were declared enemy aliens. Most were given identification cards and ordered to report regularly to the authorities but some were interned in camps, far away from their homes.

It was particularly painful during the invasion of Italy. We read and heard about the Allied forces bombarding familiar towns in Southern Italy. Italians flying the planes for the US were bombarding the towns their relatives had come from. My friend Angelina was torn between worrying about her brother Michele, in the Italian Army, and her brother Tony, in the American Army.

Italian prisoners of war were sent to a POW camp in New

Jersey. One of them was a young man from *Noepoli*. It was impossible to think of him as an enemy. We took turns visiting him and brought him Italian foods.

These events dramatized more than ever the importance of being an American citizen. Even the men who had come to America alone years ago, with the intention of returning to Italy with lots of money, knew the value of American Citizenship. As soon as the mandatory five years residency provision was over, they had filed for their certificates. My father had been one of them. Since I was a minor at the time I became an American citizen through him. I was a naturalized citizen but to prove it I needed to show his certificate. As soon as I became 21, my father insisted I get my own certificate of derivative citizenship.

I took the ferry to Ellis Island, which was no longer used to process immigrants. The long exterior stairs of the red brick building were in disrepair. The large hall was intimidating. I was directed to one of the cubbyhole offices along the wall. A woman went over some papers, asked me several questions and then told me I would receive my certificate in a few days.

My father and I encouraged my mother to attend a citizenship class at the nearby school. When she went for the test, the judge asked her a few questions, like who was the first president and what is the most important right granted by American citizenship. Then he asked her about her children. When she proudly said I was going to Hunter College, he stopped questioning her and granted her citizenship papers.

At the beginning of my junior year those of us who wanted to teach had to decide whether we wanted to take the education courses to teach in high schools or in the elementary schools. Actually, it was not a choice at all. Everybody would have preferred to teach in high school. The job was better paid and had more prestige. But only those with at least an index of 2.5 (out of 4) were allowed to take the high school education courses. Although I had chosen Italian as major so I could teach it in high school and had an index of 3.7, I chose the elementary school education courses. My woman Italian professor and my classmates thought I was completely mad. According to one classmate *La Signora,* a small energetic woman, dramatically put her hands through her hair and said, "What a waste of a wonderful brain"!

But I didn't have the confidence that I would be able to use my wonderful brain to earn a living. My goal was to get a secure, steady job, as soon as I got out of college. Since Italy was an enemy of the United States, I didn't think a test for a permanent license to teach Italian in high school would be given any time soon. On the other hand, there hadn't been a test for elementary school teachers since the early thirties. The rising birthrate would soon create a shortage of elementary school teachers.

Besides all the courses in methodology, I had to spend several hours a week as a Student Teacher. The concept of homogeneous classes that I was used to in the Elementary Schools had been abandoned for the new concept - heterogeneous grouping. I was assigned to a third grade class, taught by a teacher who excelled the new method of teaching the class according to ability groups, rather than teaching the class as a whole. My assignment was to observe the teacher's management techniques for keeping the two groups working independently, while she taught the third group.

My plan to finish college in three and half years, almost came to nothing. In the last semester I developed bronchitis, for which there was no cure except bed rest for six weeks. The professors accepted no excuses for late assignments. For each day late, they lowered the grade by one. After a few days, you automatically failed the course or opted to repeat it. I could not do the assignments without the reference books from the college library which, could be borrowed for only one or two days at a time. The late fee for each book was five dollars per day and the diploma would be denied if you owed money to the library. My fifth grade friend, Josephine, was then at Hunter. She took it upon herself to get my assignments and to borrow the books from the library. She then turned in my finished assignments and returned the library books on time.

At the end of November, a few days after I was back in school, my psychology professor handed me a small envelope containing an invitation to tea. When she saw the perplexed look on my face, she grinned and explained that I was invited to join the prestigious academic society, Phi Beta Kappa.

I went to the tea but in order to be officially enrolled, I needed the five dollar initiation fee. My father thought it was a waste

155

of money. He said that being nominated was honor enough. I finally convinced him to give me the money. I didn't bother to ask for the ten dollars I needed for the Phi Beta Kappa key. The induction ceremony became memorable in retrospect, because Bess Meyerson, the future Miss America, played the flute.

I looked forward to graduation but just as in High School I didn't get caught up in the usual excitement. I bought the year book but I couldn't afford the twenty five dollar class ring. I went to the Prom in a borrowed dress with the son of friends, who had not gone to college and was just thrilled to be invited.

My parents gave me a Bulova wrist watch. Finally I could go to work.

Twenty-seven

On the day after I received my Substitute Teacher certificate I walked into the office of P.S. 92. The two Irish secretaries were sitting at their shiny desks, facing each other, with hands folded and chatting. The only items on the desks were the ridged pen and pencil holders. The table near the door held nothing but the sign-in book and a pen. At 8:40 one of the secretaries got up with a red pencil in hand and stood guard over the sign-in book. If a teacher signed in at 8:41, she was ready to highlight the lateness.

P.S. 92 had not changed much since my student days. Many of my teachers were still there. Except for two Jewish teachers, they were all Irish. Most of them were part of the original group of teachers. The first principal, given complete control of staffing the school, decided to hire only beautiful young teachers. The school looked like a residence for aging movie stars. But even though they were pretty, many had not married. After the Wall Street crash of 1929, few eligible young men had a steady job. The only ones with steady jobs were teachers, policemen, firemen and other municipal workers. The married teachers were married to firemen or policemen, who as a group, were also mostly Irish. One of the Jewish teachers was married to an unemployed lawyer.

The halls were just as quiet as I remembered. Classes tip-toed through the halls in a double line. In the morning, the Principal walked the halls, looked through the small window in each classroom door and then returned to her office. Sure that all was well, she stayed there. Some teachers still taught the whole class from the front of the room. They wrote the assignments on the board and then sat at their desks, confident that the children would do the work without uttering a word to their neighbors. The children then went up to the teacher's desk to have their work checked.

The school had many Jewish children. They and the two Jewish teachers stayed home for the Jewish Holydays. So many children were absent, that several classes were combined into one, freeing as many teachers as possible, to report to the neighboring schools where there were several Jewish teachers and very few Jewish children.

One morning there was no vacancy at P.S. 92. I didn't worry. All the schools were feeling the teacher shortage. If one school didn't have an opening, the school near it, did. I walked into a problem school in the Arthur Avenue section and was given a fifth grade class for two weeks, while the teacher recuperated from a broken leg.

Most of the students were the children of Italian immigrants. The conflicts between the values of the old world generation and their new world children created many of the discipline problems. It was one of the schools that sent its graduates to the Roosevelt High School that I had dreaded attending.

After an hour in the class I wondered whether the teacher had broken her leg on purpose. At lunch time, one boy came to me and brashly announced,

"I'm not coming back this afternoon."

I didn't answer him but I sincerely hoped he would carry out his threat.

He came back in the afternoon and at dismissal he threatened again, "I'm not coming tomorrow".

When he said it the next day, I told him that he'd be doing me a big favor. Then he threatened to bring his uncle to school.

" Please do. I'd love to meet your uncle."

He was a notorious truant but he came to school every day of the two weeks I was there. I never got to meet his uncle.

After the two weeks were up, I walked a few blocks to the Third Ave El, used a nickel to ride the trolley to a school on E. 174th St., also known for its discipline problems and its chronic teacher absenteeism. The principal greeted me as if I were the answer to his prayers. I had just saved him the unpleasant task of dividing a class among the other classes on the grade. At the end of the day he asked me to please report every day. He was sure that there would be at least one vacancy a day. But one morning all the teachers were there. For fear I would stay at the school that hired me that day, he kept me on as the Assistant Principal, who was absent. I stayed in the office and sent all messages to the principal. Whenever there was no class for me, he hired me for whatever position was unfilled for the day.

Even though I had State certification to be a permanent

158

teacher anywhere in New York State, I could not be a permanent teacher in New York City without passing a test administered by its Board of Education. There hadn't been one given since the 1930's. The teacher shortage prodded the Board to give one in the Spring of 1945. Not only did the recent college graduates file for it but also all the teachers who had been teaching as substitutes for years.

I got up almost at dawn to be sure I'd be on time to take the written test scheduled for nine o'clock, at a High School in Brooklyn. The test consisted of a three hundred item multiple choice test in the morning, and a three hour methodology essay test in the afternoon. I returned home after dark, exhausted and bleary-eyed.

Shortly after the test, articles in the newspapers described it as the most difficult ever given. So many had failed it that, another test would have to be scheduled. Without being notified whether I had passed or failed the written part, I received letters notifying me of the dates and places for the other parts of the test.

I had to appear before a panel of the Board of Examiners to be tested orally on methodology. Then I had to read aloud a passage I had never seen before, to check my pronunciation. On another day, I had to report to the Board's headquarters in Brooklyn, for a medical examination.

My anxiety about the results of the test was forgotten on E-Day, May 8, 1945. The war in Europe was over!

In early June I received a thick letter from the Board. I opened it with trembling fingers. My marks were excellent on all parts except the speech test. In reading the selection aloud, I had mispronounced omniscient, prescient and flaccid and dentalized, (didn't raise my tongue high enough when pronouncing "ds" and "ts"). Because I had failed the speech test I would have to take all the parts of the test again. I stared at the letter in disbelief. What possible damage could my low "ds" and "ts" do to elementary grade children? When in the elementary curriculum, would I have to pronounce those three words?

While I was trying to come to terms with the vanished dream of a secure job, a dull pain in my right side persisted for a few days. I finally went to Dr. Soscia, whose office was in the middle of the Italian colony of Arthur Avenue. The Doctor's immigrant father, who lived in the building, unlocked the door to the office. While we waited

159

for the doctor, we chatted in our respective dialects and he told me how the doctor almost married a nurse in the hospital. No Doctor son of his was going to marry a lowly nurse. He had arranged matters so that the son married the daughter of an Italian surgeon.

I was still the only patient when the doctor came in. Except for the examination table and two chairs, the office was bare. There were no cabinets or files. After the doctor felt my lower abdomen, he told me he was quite sure I had chronic appendicitis. The condition was especially dangerous because it could easily be ignored. I did not have the usual severe pains and nausea associated with appendicitis. The only way he could be positive was to examine me internally. But no Italian doctor was going to examine an unmarried Italian girl internally He told me to go the hospital that afternoon for the operation the next day. There was no time to waste. If the appendix burst, it could be fatal. One of a *paesano's* sons had recently died from a burst appendix. I handed him a five dollar bill. He held it in one hand while he dug in his pocket for a big wad of bills and peeled off the two dollars change.

I was in the hospital for a week. We had no health insurance. My parents had to dip into their meager savings to pay the three hundred dollar bill. Had I been in *Noepoli* I would have been dead. The reason? A belly-ache!

I felt miserable and discouraged. But what I felt was nothing compared to what the whole world felt on August 6, when the first atomic bomb was dropped over Hiroshima. Most people didn't know that such a bomb even existed. The devastation it caused challenged our imagination. Our consciences felt a little better a few weeks later, when Japan surrendered because of it.

The bomb ended the war but it also raised the specter of global atomic destruction. Survivalists dug bomb shelters and stocked them with food. In school we held periodic air shelter drills. When they heard the siren the children crouched under their desks, facing away from the windows, to protect themselves from shattered glass.

That September I found a six month position to teach a fifth grade at a school a short distance away by trolley. My classroom neighbors were three young, Jewish teachers. At lunch time we walked to the small delicatessen across the street, where the owners, a Jewish immigrant couple, treated us with deference. I discovered tomato sardine sandwiches and ate them often. The four of us talked about our classes but eventually we got to the subject of men. I didn't have much to say. I didn't have a boyfriend. Elaine was approaching thirty, was not married and blamed it on the war. She talked wistfully about marriage as if it were going to continue to elude her. The recently married Shirley could not stop talking about her wonderful Jack. Jean, living in an apartment with her mother, talked of the imminent discharge of her tall, dark, handsome husband. They were hoping to find a place of their own. A few weeks after he returned Jean seemed distracted. After a few more weeks, she started to complain about him. A few months later, she announced they were getting divorced.

As the service men returned to their wives and girlfriends, the couples realized just how much the long separation had strained their relationships. Many marriages ended in divorces and many engagements were broken. The pen pals who had fallen in love, made arrangements to meet. Some of the meetings ended in marriages and others ended in disappointment. Others got cold feet at the last minute and never kept the appointments. When my pen-pal docked in New York he came to see me before returning to California. We spent a nice evening together and then we shook hands at the bottom of the steps to the Third Ave El.

The Nuremberg war crimes trials to punish the people responsible for the atrocities of W.W.II, started. We read about them in the *Progresso Italo Americano*, which periodically published the accounts written by our relative, Judge Michael Musmanno, one of the presiding judges.

But the future punishment of those who had committed the war crimes would not bring back the men who been killed. There were few eligible men to go around. Although the war had made women more independent and they no longer were as submissive as before the war, their ultimate goal was still marriage.

I set aside my worries about marriage to prepare for the repeat test. One of my colleagues, a Speech major, coached me on the proper placement of the tongue for the "ts and ds" and listened to me read. I retook all the parts of the test and hoped for the best.

On Sunday morning, August 26, 1946, I heard the ring of our newly installed phone. I was still getting used to its sound. Before the war we couldn't afford a phone and during the war we couldn't get one. My friend Margaret asked me to go along with her and her sister to her friend's wedding reception, that evening. Maybe, we would meet some nice young men. I didn't know the couple and I didn't want to go. She persisted but I still said, "No". I thought of the last time I had gone to a dance. The young man I danced with me handed me a piece of paper with his name and phone number, in case I wanted to see him again. I was not prepared for such a change from the way things were before the war. The young men called the girls. Not the other way around. I was so upset that I decided not to go to any more dances.

But Margaret did not give up. She called several times predicting a fate worse than death. If I didn't change my attitude I was going to end up an Old Maid. Late that afternoon I gave in.

The three of us walked up to East Tremont Ave and turned on Washington Avenue to the Winter Garden Ballroom. By walking into the spacious foyer, with its sofas and chairs, I determined the rest of my life.

The huge ballroom had been transformed into a dining room. The three piece band was playing. We milled around with the other guests until we found seats at one of the large round tables. The newlyweds marched up to the dais to the tune of *Here Comes the Bride*. The relatives of the couple brought an assortment of sodas to the tables.

Later, the bride's mother and father, each carrying one end of a huge tray, stacked with wrapped sandwiches, came to the table. The relative escorting them picked up a sandwich, looked through the wrapping and announced, *Ham* and handed it over to whomever wanted it. If the person was too far, he threw it across the table, for the guest to catch. He continued to pick up another and announced, *Salami, Provolone,* and all the combinations of fillings. He either handed over the sandwiches or tossed them, until all the guests at the table had been served. An Italian stand-up comic referred to them as *football weddings*.

Couples got up to dance. But no one asked us. Towards the end of the evening the couples at the table started to whisper to each other and glanced towards the bride. The women took out sealed envelopes from their pocket books and the couples walked up to

162

bridal table. As they offered their best wishes they handed the envelope, *a busta*, containing a cash gift. The bride thanked them for their good wishes and handed them a small amount of Jordan almonds, wrapped in white netting, tied with a narrow white ribbon. Then she handed the *buste*, containing ten, five or two dollars, to her mother, seated next to her, who stuffed them into a large, white satin bag with a draw string.

We too, went up to congratulate the couple. As friends of the couple's siblings we were not expected to bring a gift. But only the ones who brought *a busta*, received the Jordan almonds.

On our way out, we were so busy discussing our dismal evening that we didn't notice the three young men coming out with us. We turned when we heard them agree with our assessment of the evening. We sat down in the foyer to continue the conversation. The three came from Brooklyn and were attending the College of the City of New York on the GI Bill of Rights. Al, a college friend of the groom's brother, hadn't wanted to take the long train ride to the Bronx by himself. He convinced the reluctant Joe and George to go with him. We ended up by making dates, not sure whether they would keep them. It was well known that men didn't make casual dates with women who lived in another Borough. It was a long train ride from Brooklyn to the Bronx.

In the next few days I shopped at the better shops on East Tremont Avenue for the proper clothes to wear in September, when I started my job as a permanent substitute in P.S. 92. I wanted to be sure to blend in with the other teachers. Even though September was warm enough for summer clothes, I couldn't wear the summer clothes, frilly hats and the white gloves, I wore in June. I had to buy fall outfits, in fall colors, with hats, gloves and shoes to match.

Towards the end of the week, Joe called to make arrangements for our first date on the coming Saturday. The other two were not keeping the dates. We met in front of Patience and Fortitude, the two lions guarding the steps to the New York City Public Library. Little did we know then, how prophetic those two names were.

Before we parted, we made a date for the following Wednesday evening, still the date night. Even though the round trip by subway and by Third Avenue El took about three hours, Joe came to our house for our second date.

A few days before school started I joined the other teachers who went to decorate their rooms. We bought crepe paper to make curtains for the windows. We painted the flower pots to match or contrast the curtains and planted geraniums. We mounted pictures on two contrasting sheets of construction paper, as directed by the District Superintendent, and tacked them neatly on the cork bulletin boards that separated the clothing closets along the door wall.

I was grateful to be teaching at P.S. 92, a silk stocking school in a silk stocking district. The teachers were competent, the children were well behaved and the classrooms attractive.

Among the first things I had to do the first day of school was to fill out a schedule for my fourth grade class, for every day of the week, with the exact starting and ending times. Each day started with arithmetic and every subject was scheduled for exactly thirty minutes.

A few days after school started I received a very thin business-sized envelope from the New York City Board of Education. In it was an onion-thin certificate naming me a Probationary Teacher. At the completion of a satisfactory three year probationary period, I would become Permanent. I had passed the speech part. But I don't think it was because I had improved that much. The Board, faced with so many classrooms without teachers, relaxed their standards.

My elation soon turned to worry. The test had been given to fill the vacancies in schools that were losing the greatest number of permanent teachers. Teachers were retiring and many were using their seniority privileges to transfer from the problem schools to better schools. Schools in Harlem were left with mostly substitutes. As more and more classes were taught by *per diem* teachers, their discipline deteriorated. The newly certified probationary teachers were scheduled to be appointed to these schools. If we refused the appointment, we forfeited the license. I thought of the young teachers that Mussolini had sent to the hills of Lucania and I felt hopeless.

I showed the certificate to the newly appointed principal, Charles Thomas, a psychologist. He was delighted to ask the Board to appoint me to P.S. 92. He wanted to staff the school with new teachers. He could train them to use the new methodology that the older teachers were resisting.

164

Twenty-eight

As soon as Mr.Thomas received the official confirmation of my appointment he started his monthly visits that would last throughout my three year probationary period. He appeared unannounced, with a folder in one hand and a pen in the other, walked silently along the clothing closet to the back of the room and sat in an empty seat. By looking at the schedule I had filled out on the first day of school, he knew what subject I should be teaching. At the end of the lesson, he came up to my desk to look at my plan book. He wanted to see if I had prepared one, and if I was really doing what I had indicated I'd doing at that time.

Days later, he called me to go to his office to discuss the visit. He commented on the content of the lesson, its presentation, the behavior of the children and the appearance of the room. A few days after that, we had a follow-up meeting to go over his written report. By signing the report I agreed with its contents. He kept the original and I kept the carbon copy. We both held on to our copies in case there should be any questions about the issuance of my permanent license.

Joe and I kept seeing each other downtown on week-ends and in the Bronx on Wednesday evenings. My father made no objections to my dating but some Southern Italian fathers were still as tyrannical with their daughters as they had been before the war. I don't remember the reason I went with a friend to the house of a neighbor of the Lufranos. Aunt Filomena often praised the accomplishments of the four sons, who were all professionals, and the daughter who owned her own millenery shop in Manhattan.

The daughter, in her early thirties, let us in. She had a terrible twitch in one eye. Without smiling, she led us to the dining room where we sat at the table with her four brothers and the father. She disappeared into the kitchen and after a while came out with refreshments and served us with the air of an unhappy and unwilling servant. She may have owned a business of her own, but at home she was still subservient to the men in her family. The four year war had shaken the whole world but had not disturbed her father's world at all.

165

He continued to run the family as if they were still in Southern Italy.

After a few weeks of dating, Joe and I looked at our situation realistically. Joe lived with two sisters, a younger brother and his widowed father, in the apartment of his childless married sister and her husband. He supplemented the small stipend that he received from the government, along with the free tuition, with a part time job and contributed towards the running of the household. With three more years of college to go, he was in no position to get married. Besides all that, he was two years younger than I. (The man was supposed to be a few years older than the woman). We decided not to see each other any more.

Late one evening, a few weeks afterwards, Joe called. We resumed dating with the understanding that we would get married as soon as he got a job after graduation. Joe had little money to spend on our dates. (Women did not pay on dates). We went to the Metropolitan Museum of Art. We often walked across Central park and ended at the Museum of Natural history. We sat near the dinosaur that had been so carefully assembled from the fossil bones. We got to know every bone. (Years later we found out that its head really belonged to another type of dinosaur). We ate in the coin operated Horn and Hardart where the coffee was always fresh. In the Bronx we visited the Bronx Zoo and Bronx Botanical Gardens. On bad days we went to the movies on Tremont Ave. We spent a lot of time just walking and talking.

That winter I met Ondina, a young woman who worked in an office and kept house for her widowed father and her two brothers. She was following the Southern Italian custom of taking over her mother's responsibilities. She didn't question the reason why. She just resigned herself to spinsterhood. She was planning to go on a tour to Canada in the summer of 1947, led by the Cook Agency, the first international tour operator. I accepted her invitation to go with her without worrying about what my father would say. By then, he had come to the conclusion that it was best to trust me to do the right thing. I bought a Brownie camera to document my trip.

Soon after I started to teach, the Board decided that, in order to eliminate the teaching time lost during the transition between the A and B semesters and to minimize the emotional trauma of the children to adjust to a new teacher every six months, the classes stayed together with the same teacher for the whole year. But, even changing teachers once a year was too disruptive for first graders. The first grade teacher would stay with the class through the second grade.

I was assigned one of these first grade classes. Except for the few who might have gone to kindergarten, the first grade would be their first experience with school. As a group, they would not know the alphabet or numbers. The Board of Education followed the recommendation of two researchers who maintained that children should not be taught to read before the age of six. The parents left the teaching to the teachers.

A few days before school started I went to my assigned room. In rearranging the supply closet I found thin pamphlets of different colors stacked neatly on the very top shelf. I hadn't seen them since my teachers took them out of the bottom drawer of their desks. They were the syllabi for the different subjects to be covered, during the A and B semester of each grade. All the material to be taught in the semester was listed in detail. There were proverbs to be taught like, "A stitch in time saves nine". The teacher was warned never to mention alcohol or smoking within earshot of the children. Even though the syllabi were no longer used, the retiring teacher who had the room before me could not bear to throw them out. Neither could I, until much later. I kept them because we were not given any type of guidelines to replace them.

I wanted to make the first day of school as enjoyable and rewarding as possible for the children in my class. I walked several miles to the Woolworth store on East Fordham Road because they had better picture books than the one near-by, on East Tremont Avenue. I bought two illustrated books. Each page showed a large numeral, the corresponding number of birds and underneath, the corresponding word for the numeral. I spent hours cutting and mounting the pictures on colored construction paper with a contrasting border, consistent with the color scheme of the room. I tacked them on the cork panels separating the doors of the clothing closet.

When the children walked by the pictures on their first day they stopped to admire and count them. Their enthusiastic reaction to the display was ample reward for all my work.

A few days later, the Assistant Principal came in and looked around the room.

167

Glancing towards the pictures he asked me,

"Have you taught the concept of each of those numbers?"

I hadn't. The pictures were there to introduce the numbers.

He ordered me to take the pictures down. I could show the numeral and it's written name, only after I had taught every concept about that number.

A few days after that, he looked in and told me to erase the "Good morning, children", I had printed on the board. No words were to appear any where until I had taught them through experiences. The alphabet chart also had to come down. Phonics were out.

Instead of books, we were given blocks, beads and wires. We were to develop reading skills and arithmetic concepts through the children's manipulation of these materials. But we weren't told what these concepts were. The seats were bolted and the class size was over forty. Somehow, the three of us first grade teachers managed to organize the children in various activity groups.

Getting a large class of 40 six year olds to walk quietly and orderly through the halls was not easy. I worked hard to train them to respond to my various signals. On our way back to the room one day, I was particularly pleased with their behavior. The class stopped before rounding the corner and waited for me to signal them on. We were so quiet, that Mr. Thomas, coming the other way, almost bumped into us. He took me aside. Instead of the compliment I expected, he criticized me for keeping the children so quiet. It was not natural for young children to be so quiet. Explaining that we did not want to disturb the classes working in their rooms, did me no good. He did not want to see such quiet, straight lines in the hall.

In the Spring, the Assistant Principal called us in his office to ask for the experience charts we had made.

What experience charts?

Oh, hadn't he told us that we had to write experience charts as we worked with the children? After the meeting, thick pads of wall-chart size, lined paper and thick pens began arriving at regular intervals.

At the beginning of the second grade we still handed in the same rigid schedule as before, even though our day was unstructured. One young teacher on the grade really got into the spirit of the change. She came to school in jeans so she could sit on the floor with

168

her second graders, while they played half the day or sewed for half the day.

At the end of the second grade, I felt I had taught those children very little. I still feel guilty.

The next year we were told that we were no longer imparters of direct knowledge, but rather, facilitators of learning. To convey the change in our status, we had to move our desks from the center of the room to the corner near the windows. It was even better if we moved it to the back.

The class size was reduced to under forty. Some seats were removed from the back of the room to free space for an activity table for projects, and two easels, to carry out the newly mandated art program. Except for the one second grade teacher who wore jeans, we all wore good dresses and suits. To protect our clothes from the mess of water paints, we all bought painter's smocks and kept them in our closets. We put them on as soon as we came in and didn't take them off until we were ready to go home. The children brought their fathers' old shirts, which they put on backwards, buttoned in the back. The painting went on all day long and all week long, as the children followed a painting schedule. The walls were covered with dripping paintings and room smelled of paint.

The Board of Education was busy trying out new things and the rest of America was trying to get back to living a normal life. Europe could not. The countries were in shambles, physically and economically. The United States started the European Recovery Plan known as the Marshall Plan. Relief packages could be mailed at a very low rate as long as they were tagged with the appropriate forms.

The letters from *Noepoli* begged for any kind of clothing. My mother became a one woman relief organization. She asked her friends and acquaintances for used clothing. They in turn asked their friends. As soon as she had enough for a twenty pound package, she sewed them up in a flour sack. I became accustomed to the packages on the kitchen table, with the yellow tags next to them, for me to fill out. She carried those heavy packages in her arms for about ten blocks to the post office. On the way she made friends with a Jewish woman who was sending clothes and food to her nurse daughter who was stationed in Germany, with her doctor husband. The woman spoke English with a heavy accent and my mother spoke very little English.

169

but the two of them chatted all the way to and from the post office.

Along with the Marshall Plan, the United States mounted a relentless campaign against Communism, anywhere on earth. The Italian radio and press kept exhorting all of us to write letters to our relatives in Italy, warning them not to vote for the Communist Party. If they did, they would be forever barred from coming to the United States.

I put away thoughts about the world's situation to think about Joe's graduation in February, 1949. Because the private sector job market was not good, he took a civil service exam and was appointed as an Investigator for the New York City Department of Welfare. Even though our wages were low, we both had steady jobs. We set the date for July 10.

My friends were buying *Brides* magazine to get ideas for wedding gowns, china, stemware and silverware. My colleague Helen's father, a supervisor for the Prudential Insurance Company, was going to pay for everything. Her only worry was how to tell her future Southern Italian mother-in-law that she and her Joe were not going to show her their wedding night sheet. Victoria, my immigrant friend from *Abruzzi*, a sewing machine operator, ordered an eight hundred dollar satin gown from a bridal shop.

I could not afford anything in the magazine or in the bridal shops. Not only didn't I have the money, I didn't even have the year's notice the bridal shops required.

Twenty-nine

The worry about paying for our wedding was overshadowed by the worry of finding an apartment. The post-war housing shortage was so great that newly married couples were forced to live in a room in their parents' apartments or houses.

Catherine, from my Italian class, and Ralph moved into her mother's apartment, a few blocks away from us. They stacked all the mother's furniture in one bedroom, leaving just enough room for the mother's single bed. Catherine, unable to teach Italian in High School, was subbing in Jr. High schools. Ralph worked and went to college at night to get a Bachelor of Science degree. The mother's friends visited on Ralph's school nights and made sure to leave before he came home.

A newly married teacher from P.S. 92 invited us to visit her and her husband in the apartment they shared with her parents. Her parents dominated the conversation and did not leave us alone for one minute. The couple's captive look was the same I had seen on the faces of those who had to live with their parents during the Depression.

One bride in the neighborhood spoke enough dialect to communicate with my mother. She visited regularly and did chores for my mother just to keep busy and to get out of the apartment she and her husband shared with his parents. Since her husband did not allow her to get a job, she had a whole day with very little to do.

We held off accepting my parents' offer of their front room. Joe and I were determined to find an apartment of our own.

The severe housing shortage had created a black market. Tenants advertised their apartment for sale. Once the new tenant moved in and was willing to pay the same rent, the landlord could do nothing about it. The practice was not ethical but not illegal. We followed every lead. We took trains, buses and trolleys everywhere, only to be disappointed when we got there. One trip to the South Bronx almost put an end to our search. We walked up three flights in an old run-down building. A woman let us in a dimly lit hall. When she turned on the light, the walls seemed to move. The black moving

171

dots on the walls were scurrying roaches.

While looking for an apartment we planned the wedding. Since we didn't want the traditional *football* wedding, we did not expect my parents to pay for the reception. However, we didn't have much money to spend on it. One day I spotted an ad by a wedding coordinator, a job I had never heard of. We met her in an office in Manhattan. After a few minutes of figuring on a legal yellow pad, she assured us she could arrange a wedding to fit our budget.

Instead of sending me to a bridal shop, she sent me to a factory, where I was fitted for a princess style, cotton lace, gown and veil for $75. She arranged for the limo, the photographer and the music. She planned a simple sit-down dinner for 50, in an air-conditioned room in a Manhattan hotel and reserved a room for us for that night. The total cost of six hundred dollars was less than most of the bridal shops' gowns.

In June, we followed a newspaper ad for an apartment only a few blocks from P.S. 92. The building was built in the 1920's to alleviate the housing shortage created by WW1. The fifth floor, front, three room apartment was immaculate and tastefully furnished. Everything was well coordinated and looked new. The kitchen sink even had the starched skirt, to hide the ugly pipes under it, that matched the starched ruffled window curtains. The apartment had everything and its location was ideal. We paid two thousand dollars, almost all the money the two of us had saved, but we wouldn't have to go shopping for anything.

We moved in our personal things. Our china was the dish set my mother had collected on her trips to the movies. She amazed us by giving us a complete, twelve place setting of Sterling silver, which she had been buying for years, one place setting at a time, from the Jewish immigrant jeweler on Tremont Avenue. She bought a set of expensive, embroidered sheets and pillow cases, besides the regular sheets. But, the twelve dish towels, were made out of flour sacks she had bleached, cut and hemmed.

Even though I had no boyfriend when she started the trousseau, my mother could not imagine my not getting married, some day. She never urged me to get married and whenever the subject of marriage came up, she would always caution me, in her very quiet, terse way, not to marry a drinking man or a gambler or a jealous man.

172

But the worst fate would be to marry a jealous man.

On the other hand, my father often said that since I was a teacher and financially capable of taking care of myself, I didn't need to get married. When he said it, his face reflected a mental picture of some painful situation he had no control over. From his other remarks I gathered he was afraid my husband would physically abuse me. Many Southern Italian men routinely vented their frustrations on their wives, most of whom had been brought up to believe it was their fault if the husbands hit them. My father had a hot temper which he struggled to control. He had never even been near to exploding with me. He and I never reached the point where we could show our feelings but I knew he would cut off his hand rather than strike me. After Joe and I set the date, he was so worried that he asked me what I would do if my husband hit me. Well, he wouldn't do it a second time because I would divorce him. When he heard divorce, he shook his head and gave up. Then he told me to keep my own name instead of changing it to my husband's name. It was my turn to look at him in surprise. It was such an usual request. He was ahead of the times by about 50 years.

July 10, 1949 broke a forty day drought. It was stifling hot and it poured all day. But when I stepped out on the front porch to get into the limo, the sun miraculously appeared through the storm clouds.

There were so many weddings, that churches scheduled the fifteen minute ceremonies every half hour. We walked up the aisle on schedule for our five o'clock ceremony and knelt at the altar. The priest opened his book to begin the ceremony and then stopped. He looked upset and whispered something to George, the best man. George walked behind me. The priest motioned impatiently for him to return to his place and he continued with the ceremony. We had to get out before the next bride showed up. Walking out of the church we found out what had upset the priest. A cat had stretched itself out on the train of my dress. George couldn't dislodge the cat. The photographer had no choice but to take our picture with the cat on my train.

The hotel was easily reached by the Third Avenue El. Everyone was surprised and delighted to enter the air-conditioned room. The three piece band played all the standard music plus the

Tarantella to which Joe and I danced and everybody joined in. The chicken dinner was very good except that instead of the potatoes we thought we were getting, we got potato chips. The *paesani* must have talked about that for a long time afterwards. At the appropriate time, instead of the guests coming to us, we went around to the tables to bid them goodbye. I gave my mother the satin purse with the *buste* to keep until we came back from the one week honeymoon.

We took the elevator to our room on the top floor. The room was large and had cross-ventilation, a mark of luxury in those pre-air-conditioning days.

The next morning, we took a train to a lake-side resort in Connecticut, that I chose for its modest price and accessibility. Unions that had struggled to establish themselves in the 1930's and 1940's, were beginning to negotiate higher wages, shorter hours and one or two weeks paid vacations for their workers. Resorts started to spring up in the Catskill Mountains and other areas easily accessible from New York City. To entice the vacationers, most of whom didn't own a car, the resorts sent cars to pick them up at the train stations.

After a week of fresh air and greenery we came back to the hot concrete of the Bronx. We were happy to go to our own apartment, even though it was sweltering under the tar roof. We had eight dollars and forty-one cents to our name. We hoped the *buste* would help us out until our next paycheck.

On Monday morning I started my life as a housewife and Joe went to work.

We had a General Electric refrigerator, with the motor on top. The freezer compartment was just big enough for two ice cube trays. The newer ones had larger compartments to accommodate several packages of the frozen Birds Eye foods which could be bought at the newly opened A&P Supermarket a few blocks away. The A&P sold fresh vegetables and a few in cans. At first the housewives resisted buying the cans for fear of being considered lazy. Little by little the convenience and availability of the cans lured the women to buy them.

One of the great attractions of the store was that the shoppers could walk along the many aisles and pick and choose the products they wanted instead of having to ask the small grocer behind the counter for each item. The refrigerator cases offered a variety of

174

cheeses and meats. Near the butter were lower priced plastic bags of white margarine with a colored globule inside each one. The housewife had to knead the food coloring into the margarine to turn it into the same color of butter.[13]

The other attraction were the lower prices. The A&P eliminated the customer tab book still kept by the small grocers and offered lower prices instead. To promote their products they created Anne Page whose smiling face appeared on all their products. She also offered recipes in their single folded sheet, *Woman's Day*, that was sold at the checkout counter for 2 cents.

The neighborhood small grocery stores started to shut down.

Since the A&P and other stores were several blocks away, I couldn't carry too much on each shopping trip. When Joe came home he did what the other husbands did. He rang the bell downstairs. I opened the front window, waited for him to come out of the building and then I told him either to come up or what to buy.

The following Sunday morning a friend called us on our party-line telephone to tell us to buy a copy of the Sunday Daily News. The picture of us kneeling at the altar, with the cat comfortably resting on my train, was in the Animal Corner section.

---

[13]The color globule was the concession made, after a series of law suits, by the Dairy Industry to the manufacturers of margarine, who were prohibited to sell yellow margarine.

Thirty

When I returned to school in September 1949, as a permanent teacher, with a salary of $2600 a year, Mr. Thomas' monthly visits came to an end. From then on, he would only visit once a year.

I was forewarned by the Assistant Principal that the third grade class I was assigned included Arthur. The office knew Arthur very well. He spent a lot of time there as punishment for misbehaving in the classroom. Everyone knew his mother. She was a large, tall woman who had roamed the halls of the school since Arthur started kindergarten. She was so attached to her only child that she couldn't bear to leave him. She walked the halls until she picked up Arthur for lunch and then did the same in the afternoon. Arthur's teachers got used to her peeking through their doors to see how things were going. Everybody was annoyed with her but neither the teachers nor the Principal wanted to risk possible repercussions by telling her to leave.

When she appeared at my door the first day of school I told her not to worry. I promised I would take good care of Arthur. But she still lingered, unsure of what to do. I had a feeling that if someone gave her a reason to go home she would be very grateful. I smiled and asked her,

"Would you do me a big favor?"

She looked eager to please.

"I love coffee but I never have time to have a second cup. Would she please go home and drink a second cup for me."

She was happy to oblige and left. We repeated this ritual for a few mornings. After a while she allowed Arthur to come up with the class. She never roamed the halls that year. After a few months the Assisted Principal came in to ask me what I had done with Arthur's mother. When I told him he laughed and shook his head as if to say,

"Who would have thought of that ?"

One day Arthur did something to disrupt the class. I asked him to stand up by his seat, the last in the first row. He looked at me with a defiant-expectant look. Waiting. Testing me. The rest of the class, used to his bad behavior, turned to look at him and then at me. I

176

could feel the tension in the room. I had everyone's attention. They were all waiting for me to explode and send Arthur to the Principal's office. If I did that, I would be the loser. I realized it was his way of escaping work. He didn't get punished in the office. Instead, to keep him from bothering them, the secretaries gave him "fun" things to do. I very carefully and calmly, explained that no child in my class was ever going be sent to the principal's office for misbehaving. They just better get used to doing their work. I told Arthur to please sit down and continue with his assignment. The rest of the children exchanged furtive looks and then bent their heads over their books.

Later that year I had to prepare a program for the Assembly period. Arthur had the best voice of all the boys. I chose him for the lead in the program. The other teachers thought I was crazy. How could I trust him not to ruin the performance? He surprised them all. They had to admit that he did a wonderful job.

At a faculty meeting we learned that the teachers were eligible to enroll in a low cost Health Insurance Plan, HIP, the first HMO. Some teachers thought it was not good enough for them. Others didn't want to leave their family doctors. I was very happy to enroll in the family plan. We wouldn't have to worry about medical or hospital bills.

At another meeting we were informed that holding children back to repeat a grade did nothing but hurt the child's self image. Social promotion was started and the marking system was changed. When I went to school the marks on the report card were numerical. Less than 65 was failing and 100 was perfect. Later, the letters A B C D F took their place. F was the failing mark. With social promotion, the report cards were marked O for outstanding, G for good, F for fair, N needs improvement. Nobody failed.

In effort to improve the quality of education more and more new activities were added to the curriculum without discarding any of the old ones. Requesting and returning visual aids from a central source meant setting up schedules to be followed. We continued with the non-teaching chores we performed before the nine o'clock bell. We collected money from each child for their 10 o'clock snack of milk and cookies and money for the Red Cross. In the spring we sold seed packets for the Botanical Gardens. Since the time in the teaching day remained the same, we began to feel the pressure of never having

177

enough time to do all we wanted to accomplish.

Changes in educational philosophies followed one after another. The mimeograph machine made the fill-the-blank tests popular both with pupils and teachers. The students were no longer expected to write the answers in full sentences. Filling in the missing word was enough. Compositions no longer had to have margins, be written in good penmanship and have correct spelling. Concern for spelling and penmanship would only stifle the child's creativity. We marked the composition for content only. We marked spelling during the spelling period and we marked the penmanship during the penmanship period. We taught reading through the whole language method instead of through phonics.

Besides adjusting to the educational changes, I had to adjust to being married and taking care of the apartment. Although I had helped my mother, I had never been fully responsible for cleaning, cooking and running a household. I was beginning to find the real answer to my teacher's rhetorical question, "How long does it take to clean a three room apartment". It took longer than I thought. I wanted to streamline the housekeeping chores. More than anything, I wanted to get rid of the dust mop. I hated shaking it out of the window, as the other women in the building did.

All the wonderful household appliances that I had glimpsed at the World's Fair were for sale at the local stores. Besides the modern stoves and the refrigerators, they were selling vacuum cleaners and fully automatic washing machines. The store owners enticed customers who had jobs but not enough cash, by offering convenient credit terms. (Credit cards for ordinary people were still unknown). The thought of owning these wonderful appliances, for just a few dollars a month, proved irresistible for a great many housewives.

Joe and I both dreaded owing money for any reason. We knew that there was no where to turn for financial help. We saved for each item and bought everything for cash. The first item was a vacuum cleaner. While we saved for a washing machine, we carried the clothes to my mother's house and used her brand new front loading Bendix. By the time we bought ours, Bendix's competitors made machines that were loaded from the top. They responded to the concern of the possible danger of the front loaders. One day, my mother noticed our cat, Fiorentino, was spinning with the clothes. It had crawled in between the sheets, while she had momentarily left the room. Luckily, she opened the door in time to save him.

Once we had the necessities we started to save for the latest marvel, a television set. When we got married in 1949, there were less than a million households with TV sets. The small screens were built into luxurious wooden cabinets. The set was the focal point of the living room. We chose the set in the least expensive cabinet. Not only to save money, but also because we thought the luxurious cabinet would be obsolete as soon as the receivers got larger.

There were only a few Channels and few programs on each. There were no programs after midnight. The Channels broadcast their test pattern until programming resumed in the morning. One program, *The Texaco Star Theater*, starring Milton Berle, enthralled all America. Owners of TV sets were prepared to play hosts to relatives and friends who came to watch Uncle Miltie, every Tuesday evening, from eight to nine. My parents climbed the four flights to watch the program with us. Store owners complained that business fell off on Tuesday evenings. The popularity of the show spurred the sales of TV sets and Uncle Miltie became known as Mr. Television.

We tried to live just on Joe's salary and banked mine. Our frugal, three year courtship had prepared us well. We found leisure activities that either cost nothing or cost very little. We were delighted to go along with the Biondis (Catherine and Ralph) on their house hunting trips to Long Island, where Ralph worked. By then, their apartment had become even more crowded by the arrival of their little girl. They could move near Ralph's job without worrying about Catherine's substitute teaching job in New York City. Ralph told her to stop teaching as soon as the baby was born.

Arthur Levitt, who was the first to recognize the housing needs of the young veterans, started the housing boom on Long Island. By adapting the assembly-line method created by Ford to build cars, to the building of homes, he built about fifty affordable houses a day, on what had been potato fields. The houses had two bedrooms on the ground level and an expandable dormer to be finished later as the family and income grew. They were built on a slab, had radiant heat, had no porches, and instead of a garage had a car port. Arthur Levitt made the GI's dream of owning a home a reality by pricing the first houses at around five thousand dollars and accepting the government insured FHA mortgages.

By the time we went with the Biondis, Levittown had been there for several years. As the economy expanded, other builders started to build bigger and better houses. The later house hunters looked down on Levitttown and looked up to the newer and more expensive houses. We spent many wonderful week-ends tramping through the freshly excavated ground where new houses were being built on plots of 60x100 feet. Some places just had the model houses. In others, couples were living in newly finished houses, while bull dozers, and carpenters worked all around them, building others. No matter where we went all the new houses had one thing in common - no porches.

Stepping into the models was like stepping into a fantasy world. The kitchens were equipped with modern stoves, refrigerators and even dish washers. The walls were lined with cabinets above and under the formica counters. There were no frilly skirts to hide the ugly water pipes under the sink. The sink was completely enclosed in a cabinet.

Joe and I enjoyed going househunting with the Biondis but we never even gave a thought to buying one. We both worked for New York City and had no need to move. Besides, we couldn't afford even the cheapest of them. Joe did not earn enough to get a mortgagee and the banks did not count my salary.

The beautiful, modern houses were being built for the post-war ideal nuclear family. They were not suitable for the Biondis. They looked in more established areas of Long Island and couldn't find anything they liked. They later found out that some would not show them their houses because they were Italian. The owners were afraid Italians would spoil the neighborhood with their guitar playing and noisy, loud family get-togethers. We all had a good laugh at that. If ever there was a couple who didn't fit the stereotype, it was the Biondis. Eventually, they bought an older, large colonial house with four bedroom.

Thirty-one

I became pregnant just before our second anniversary. I had to notify the Board immediately. No pregnant women were allowed in the work place. I was placed on a mandatory, unpaid maternity leave for two years. In the fall I shopped for a maternity dress, a new concept in women's clothing, and started to think about what we would need for the baby's arrival in March.

When I felt pains on the morning of Feb.8, 1952, I thought they were false labor pains and I told Joe he could go to work. When the pains intensified I called my mother but she was outside and didn't hear the phone. I called Joe to tell him to meet me at the hospital. I carefully went down the four flights and hailed the first cab.

"Are you having a baby, lady?"

He took me to the hospital as fast as he could. They placed me in a wheel chair and whisked me to the delivery room. While the doctor and nurses told me what to do, I looked at the clock. I was shocked into motherhood at 11:25 A.M. Michael was born, six weeks premature. Dr. LaVine assured me that although Michael weighed only three pounds and twelve ounces, he was healthy. He'd have to stay in the hospital until he weighed five pounds. I started to worry that the baby might be blind, a common defect of *preemies*. The doctor said that Michael was not going to be put in an incubator, as had been the practice up to a short time before. They had since learned that the blindness had been caused by too much oxygen. Besides being concerned about Michael being premature, I was scared of the responsibility of motherhood. I didn't dare to voice my fears to anybody. Young mothers were supposed be ecstatic.

Michael was born in a private hospital on the Grand Concourse. My first meal was served on an attractively arranged tray. The cup cake had a tiny flag for Lincoln's Birthday. The first day, I was not allowed to move off the bed. The second day, I was allowed to sit up and dangle my legs, under the supervision of a nurse. The third day, I could step down after dangling, and finally, on the fourth day I could take a short walk. On my first walk I met another patient pacing the hall. She had come in bleeding and had been ordered to bed. Her doctor countermanded the order by telling her to walk. He hoped the walking would induce a miscarriage. It was the alternative to the abortion she had asked for and which he couldn't perform because abortions were illegal.

I went home without the baby at the end of the week's maternity stay. Once the baby was home, I moved objects in front of him whenever I picked him up or went near him. Even though I was sure he could follow the objects I didn't stop worrying until the pediatrician assured me that there was nothing wrong with his eyes.

Freud and the behaviorists had done their jobs well. We young mothers strove to be perfect. We were convinced that our child's success or failure depended entirely on us. Anything wrong with the child was the mother's fault. No questions about it. One of the "musts" was to take the child for a daily airing. I dreaded carrying the baby in one arm and dragging the carriage down the steps with other. Coming home, besides the baby and the carriage, I also had some groceries to carry. The shoemaker across the street offered to rent us a space for the carriage, for two dollars a month.

There was no solution for managing on one salary. After I set aside the thirty-five dollars for the rent and then the money for the utilities, there was not too much left. Baby shoes, baby food and other baby items were disproportionately high priced. I economized on the baby's clothes but never on his shoes, even though they cost over twenty dollars a pair. Diaper service was a must. I had to be sure I always had enough sterile diapers on hand. Most of that summer I wore the same black cotton dress, with tiny rose buds all over it. I hoped I wore it as graciously pushing the carriage, as Dorothy had worn her dress going back and forth to the blackboard in high school.

As my two year leave was coming to an end, I was torn between the baby and the job. Some men insisted that their wives stay home even if there were no children. Those modern enough to allow their brides to hold jobs, insisted they stay home once they became mothers. Joe, knowing how hard I had worked to get my license, left the decision up to me.

If I didn't return I would lose my job. No extensions were allowed. The thought of having no means of support, should Joe lose his job, scared me. Yet, I didn't want to do what Helen, my friend at

P.S. 92, was doing. She bundled up the baby and brought him to her mother on her way to school and picked him up on the way home. But she had a car. I would have to walk seven long blocks to my mother's house every morning, rain or shine.

Our problem seemed to have no solution until my father told us his tenants were moving out. If we moved into the apartment, my mother would take care of the baby while I went to school. After thinking about the pros and cons, we moved into the apartment as paying tenants.

That summer the temperature was over one hundred for several days. The apartment was like an oven. When I went to check on Michael, I found him having convulsions. I immediately applied an ice pack on his head and called the doctor. Even though there had been no damage, the doctor wanted us to take Michael to a HIP affiliated hospital in Harlem.

We entered a large, dingy, basement ward, with cribs lined up, wall to wall. The small windows on level with the side walk, were dirty and had iron bars. Joe, my mother and I sat by the crib, anxiously waiting for the pediatrician. He examined Michael and told me,

"You'll have to leave the baby here overnight."

"I can't leave him."

"All these babies have mothers and *they* had left them."

"I don't care what the other mothers did".

Reluctantly, he told us we could have a private room on the top floor but it was expensive and the insurance would not pay for it.

The room was so high up above the hot pavement that the breeze through the open balcony doors was cool. The nurses immediately packed ice around Michael. The doctor explained, "Desperate situations require desperate measures". His fever went down to normal. Michael was given continuous care and attention. When the doctors and nurses in the hospital heard about the case they came in just to see how he was doing. During our three day stay I pondered his fate had he stayed in the basement. I thought not only of the poor babies in the basement, but also of the helpless mothers in *Noepoli* and of *Noepoli*'s doctor. Perhaps it was not lack of concern but the knowledge that he had no way to help them, that made him go

183

hunting. I came to the conclusion that poverty was the worst disease of them all. I made up my mind then, that no matter what, I would keep my job.

As soon as we got home we bought the latest luxury appliance on the market, a window room air conditioner. The unit was large enough to cool our bedroom, Michael's bedroom and adjoining living room.

At the end of my maternity leave and before returning to school, I had to go for a medical exam at 110 Livingston Street in Brooklyn. After the physical, the woman doctor engaged me in a lengthy conversation about the medical advances in child care. I had a feeling she wanted to make sure I wasn't suffering from *post partum* depression.

The baby boomers were beginning to crowd the schools. P.S.92 was operating on a split session. The overcrowding upset the calm teaching conditions we were used to. One of the teachers invited us to her Manhattan apartment to attend a meeting of the Teachers Guild, an organization that was trying to encourage teachers to become politically involved, to better bargain for improvements in the teaching conditions.

We met in her spacious living room. The leader discussed the agenda in a very calm and dignified manner. We balanced the coffee cups and cookies on our laps, as if we were attending an afternoon tea. Nothing came of the meeting. As a group, teachers were just too timid. Even though the salaries in the private sector were going up and ours were not, we were still so grateful to have secure Civil Service jobs that we didn't want to jeopardize them. We were willing to forgo money for security. Besides, P.S. 92, was still considered a silk stocking school. The teachers still came to school well dressed, the classrooms were attractive and most of the children well behaved.

At the end of the school year, I applied for my second maternity leave.

By then, the front room in my parents apartment was occupied by two cousins, both named Antonietta, from *Terranova*. They were the daughters of the two teen-age American-born daughters of Giovanni and Brigida who had been so kind to me when my mother sent me ahead to *Terranova*. To thank the Italians for not voting for the Communists after the war, the United States relaxed the

184

immigration laws. The two mothers were able to transfer their American citizenship to their daughters. My father sent them the money for the boat tickets and offered to house them. The two Antoniettas got jobs in a dress factory and soon were able to repay my father. Eventually they saved enough for their trip back to *Terranova,* where they married the boyfriends they had left behind. They returned with their husbands and moved into their own apartments.

Whenever Mrs. Soda, a short, round, vivacious woman, came to visit my mother, she usually came up to visit me. While we chatted over a cup of coffee she warned me, in a roundabout way, of the pitfalls I should avoid to make sure my husband didn't stray. With gestures and rolling eyes she warned me never to allow a young woman relative to live as a boarder with us, as so many families were doing. She told me that men didn't get married to get a cook or a laundress. There were plenty of restaurants and laundries. She tilted her head to one side and asked me if I got her drift. She was the only woman, young or old who ever mentioned the intimate part of marriage.

Finally, even Carlo gave up the hope of returning to *Noepoli,* and sent for his family. By then, his *bossa* and her husband had divorced. When Carlo bought a house for his family, in a better part of the Bronx, he bought one that had an attic apartment for her. His wife Isabella, who had ignored the squabbles of us children, ignored the husband's motivation for the arrangement. She befriended Millie and treated her as part of the family. His daughters with whom I had played every day, had been traumatized by the fears and deprivations of the war. They had not been bombed but they had lived in constant fear. We no longer had anything in common.

On nice days I took Michael to Crotona Park, two blocks away. The iron fence around it was torn down. The fountain no longer had water and the flowers around it were gone. There were only patches of crab grass. But on hot days, the park was the only place where Michael could run around under the shade of trees. Except for an occasional walker using the park as short cut, Michael and I were the only ones there.

One day another pregnant woman came in from the street, speaking Italian to a little boy about Michael's age, who answered to the name of Sidney. She sat down next to me, on the only bench still

185

left. Curiosity about the boy's name prompted me to speak to her in Italian.

She met her husband, who had lost his wife and children in a concentration camp, in a Jewish refugee camp in Italy. They knew no one in the neighborhood. They were the only family left in the row of buildings facing the park. The buildings, that at one time had been the envy of the neighborhood, had been condemned by the City. Her husband was waiting for a better job in New Jersey before moving. Sidney was being raised as a Catholic and she was worried about finding godparents to baptize the new baby, due in a few weeks. I told her that Joe and I would be glad to be the baby's god-parents.

I was expecting in July but July came and went and there was no sign of the baby. The prolonged, record-breaking heat wave was making matters worse. An elderly woman on the block assured me that the baby would come as soon as there was a break in the weather.

Sure enough, in the early hours of August 8, 1955, as a storm was brewing, the pains started. Joe took me to the Veteran's Hospital on the Grand Concourse, where I was taken to the hallway near the delivery room. I was left there, on the gurney, to wait my turn in the crowded delivery room. While there, a hurricane hit the Bronx, ending the heat wave. The baby was born at 6:00 A.M. and we named her Mary Diane. I was in my room by lunch time. My meal was cold spaghetti and string beans, a far cry from the elegant first meal I had after Michael was born. The hurricane, coincidentally named Diana, had flooded the kitchen and this was the best they could do. But nothing could take away the happiness of knowing that Mary was healthy and weighed enough for me to take her home with me at the end of the week's stay.

By the early nineteen fifties, TV had become a major influence in American life. Day time viewers became familiar with Senator Estes Kefauver questioning important Mafia members in his fight to break up the different crime families. Perhaps the most familiar witness was Frank Costello, who made the Fifth Amendment a household expression by his pat answer to the Senator's questions,

"I refuse to answer on the grounds that it might incriminate me."

If invoking the Fifth wasn't appropriate he answered the

other questions with

"I don't remember."

Senator Joseph McCarthy's fanatical determination to rid the United States of Communists also engaged the viewers' attention. They watched him during the Senate hearings as he relentlessly questioned well known people to force them to admit that they belonged to the Communist Party.

There were early morning shows to entertain the preschoolers. No matter where I was in the apartment I could hear it and I could easily go into the room to watch the program Michael was watching. In the morning he watched Miss Frances on *Ding Dong School, Romper Room* and *Mr. Wizard.* In the late afternoon it was *Howdy Doody.*

Romper Room was a simulated pre-school classroom that used children chosen at random from the names submitted by their parents. I was surprised when I received a reply to my letter telling me when to appear for the show. For a week I took the train down to the studio and sat in a booth with the other mothers to watch the program. I submitted Mary's name but the show went off the air before she was called.

The daytime shows were hosted by women who tried to convince homemakers to buy the new convenience products. They reconstituted frozen orange juice or instant coffee crystals in elegant pitchers and then served it in elegant glasses to their guests. Working couples, eager to watch the evening news, ate their dinners by their TV sets on the newly marketed TV snack tables. In 1953 Swanson Co. started to market frozen turkey TV dinners, ($1.29) in a three sectioned aluminum pan with the picture of a TV on it. Pop the dinner in the oven, carry it to the TV table, remove the foil, eat it while watching the news, and then throw away the pan.

In 1957, during my second maternity leave, my mother returned to *Noepoli* to sell all our property. Uncle Raffaele had died and my parents decided that holding on to the property was more trouble than it was worth. Besides, none of us was ever going to return. She came back disillusioned with the town and the relatives. She stopped corresponding with Uncle Raffaele's daughters. Along with her disillusionment, she brought back the 1957 European flu, which, one by one, we all caught.

187

Many in my Italian class went to Italy to work as translators. Some became so fascinated with Italy, that everything Italian was the best. Other Italian girls took vacations in Italy in the hopes of finding a husband. Most came back disappointed but some were successful. One day, the names in a story in the newspaper caught my attention and brought back memories. A daughter had shot her father in an apartment in the Italian section of Arthur Ave. She no longer could tolerate his abusive behavior towards her for having married a man in Italy without his consent. The daughter was the milliner with the tick who had served refreshments to my friend and me, years before.

When the second maternity leave was over, I didn't have to go the Board for a medical exam. The teacher shortage was so acute that I don't think they cared what shape I was in. Just so I showed up. When I returned in September, I found more changes.

The new Principal and Assistant, were both Jewish. As the Irish teachers retired, Italians and Jews took their places. One new teacher wore no make up. The principal was upset about it but he was afraid to say anything to her. Since she was Italian, he asked me if I would talk to her about it. She agreed to wear lipstick. Another had a lisp and still another spoke with a Southern drawl. (The Board no longer could afford to worry about the applicants' dentilization or the proper pronunciation of the long i). The Kindergarten teachers were complaining about the effect of TV on the behavior of their classes. Used to watching TV shows, the children became restless and easily bored with the slow pace of the classroom. Throughout the school system there were so many Jewish teachers, that during the Jewish Holydays it was impossible to cover all the uncovered classes. The Jewish Holydays became school holidays.

One morning the Assistant Principal walked in during the arithmetic lesson. I was using flash-cards to drill arithmetic facts, even though they had been banished just before my maternity leave. When I saw him, I jokingly hid the flash cards behind my back. He laughed with me and said,

"Don't worry, Rose. Go ahead and use them. They're back. Only now, we write the answers on the back and call them "thinking cards".

The discipline problems were increasing. The Board of Education was offering free tuition to teachers to take guidance

188

courses. The principal offered to submit my name to study for a Masters' Degree in Guidance. I would have loved it. But for me to go to Manhattan for the evening courses, I would have to leave the children at supper time. Regretfully, I declined.

The next year, I was assigned a fourth grade class of middle ability. (Homogenous grouping was back). Besides teaching the New Math, we had to teach Social Studies in a new way, through units. We had to integrate any relevant curriculum area, such as spelling, composition and arithmetic with each Social Studies topic. At the beginning of the term we submitted an outline of each unit, along with the starting and ending dates.

For each unit, we discussed the subtopics we wanted to study. There was a flurry of activity while the children chose their topics and then formed committees. I decorated the back wall with appropriate pictures, put up large envelopes marked with the name of each committee and its members. During the Social Studies period the committees sat together and worked on their reports. I was there only for consultations. At the end of the period the children stored their work in the envelopes until the next period. At the end of the unit the children read their individual reports to the class.

The day before we were to finish the reports on the New York City government, the principal called the fourth grade teachers into his office to alert us that the District Superindent, well known for her inflexibility, was coming the next day to evaluate us on how well we had grasped the concept of teaching through units. She expected us be working on Hawaii, our new fiftieth state. We looked at each other in surprise. If we weren't, we'd better be. The other teachers said they would take everything down and prepare for Hawaii. I panicked.

The three boys who were scheduled to report the next day were academically at the bottom of the class. They had worked diligently and enthusiastically during every period. They couldn't wait to read their reports. I could not disappoint the boys. More importantly, I was afraid I could not pull off the deception. I begged the principal to please explain the situation to the Supervisor. We would start Hawaii the following day. With the pained expression of a man caught between two inflexible women, he sided with the one he had to live with every day.

The next day the principal escorted the Superintendent into my room. They stood against the closed door just as Charles was getting up to read his report. Thrilled to have such an audience, Charles read with evident pride. The Superintendent, looking at me with a vindictive smile but addressing Charles,

"Did your teacher tell you what to write"?

Charles, indignant at the thought, pulled himself up to his full height and looking straight at her, answered,

"No. I did it all by myself".

Defeated in her attempt to trick Charles into saying I had told him what to write and so have reason to discipline me, she turned the knob and walked out without even examining the work on the back wall.

Besides adjusting to the changes in the curriculum, we old timers were adjusting to the young teachers' attitude towards the rules we had so rigidly observed. It didn't bother them if they returned from lunch to find their classes waiting for them at the door creating a disturbance. The secretary had long ago stopped underlining the time book for lateness. She was happy if the teacher came in by nine.

Things at home were changing too. Joe attended evening classes at New York University and received a Master's degree in Business Administration. He left the job with the Welfare Department for a better paying job with Mergethaler Linotype Industries, in Brooklyn. When the firm moved to Long Island we had to buy a car. Until he got his driver's license, Joe took a bus to meet a co-worker who gave him a ride to work. In the spring we bought our first car, a 1958 Rambler. Once we had the car, we started to think how we might escape the hot Bronx during the coming summer.

For years we had observed the end-of-school ritual of the families who lived in the building across the street. It was a building with elevators, the only modern one in the neighborhood. Most of its tenants were the families of Jewish business men. Although by 1958 many of the original tenants had moved away, the rest still followed the same summer routine. As soon as school ended, the women packed up their children and left for the family oriented resorts in the Catskills. During the summer the husbands came home to empty apartments. On week-ends, when the husbands left to visit them, the building was almost deserted. Joe thought that I should follow their

190

example.

I too, wished we could escape the heat. I could no longer take the children to Crotona Park. The black iron gate that used to be locked at night had long disappeared. Most of iron fence was missing. What little grass still grew was strewn with litter and broken glass. The only ones in the park were the vagrants. Much as I wanted to escape the heat, I didn't want to separate the family. On our rides with the Biondis we had seen the open spaces on Long Island. It was not as good as going to the mountains but it certainly was better than the crowded Bronx. Since Joe was working on Long Island why not rent a house there for the summer? Our friends shook their heads and made faces at the idea. Joe was skeptical but agreed to pursue the idea. I looked through the newspaper ads and one day I spotted a summer rental of a house in Levittown.

Following the directions carefully, making sure we wouldn't get lost going in out of the curved streets of Levittown, we stopped in front of a Cape Cod, the first style Levitt built. The couple and their two teen-age children greeted us warmly. They showed us the house and the back yard. The picnic table, in the shade of the peach tree, one of the fruit trees that Arthur Levitt planted in the back yard of every house he built, was set with colorful dishes. During lunch, the owners confided to us that renting the house was a first for them. They wanted to go away for the summer but didn't want to pay for running the house while they were gone. Their friends were just as skeptical about the idea as ours. After lunch, we walked the few blocks to the community swimming pool, another of Levitt's innovative ideas. Each section of the development had its own pool.

The place was ideal. Joe's job was only fifteen minutes away. Michael and Mary had children to play with. We could walk to the pool and to the Bohack supermarket. We signed the papers right away and couldn't wait to move in.

We had an idyllic summer except for the fear we shared with all the other parents, that polio might strike at any time. The fear was so pervasive that we looked at every ailment as a symptom of the disease. One day Michael started to limp. We rode to the Bronx to see our doctor, who told us that whatever it was, it was not polio.

(The Salk vaccine had been approved in 1955 but its use was discontinued for a while because of problems with it. When inoculations restarted, Michael was not in the targeted age group.)

At the pool the next day, I noticed that Michael was imitating the Life Guard's walking with one foot on the top ledge of the pool and the other on the lower ledge.

Thirty-two

After having had a taste of life in suburbia, when we got back to the Bronx our neighborhood looked worse than we remembered. The windows and doors of many apartment buildings were boarded up. The nice shops on Tremont Ave. had disappeared, one by one. More families in the building across the street had left. Even the elderly Mr. Seigel and Mr. Klein were missing. We had become accustomed to them sitting on the sidewalk in front of the building, reading the Jewish paper the *Forward*. As the afternoon wore on, they moved their chairs little by little to follow the sunshine as it moved closer and closer to the building. Some of our neighbors had moved into new housing projects in the northern part of the Bronx. Some friends had moved to Westchester. The middle class steadily moved up to Yonkers, Westchester or out to Long Island. Poor whites from everywhere were moving in. They came from other cities and other states to take advantage of New York City's generous Welfare program. Italian immigrants and Puerto Rican families were moving in. Because of our Civil Service jobs and the arrangement we had with my parents we had not thought seriously about moving. Now we wondered how long we would be able to live there.

The children in my second grade class that year were not as well dressed or as care free as in the previous years. A waif-like, blonde Jenny never said anything and always looked as if she were waiting for the other shoe to drop. One day her mother came to object to the mention of God in the classroom.

"My husband and I are atheists and Jenny tells us that God will take care of everything."

I explained that most of the class was excused early one afternoon a week to go to religious instructions. I had no way of controlling their conversations about God.

Little Carmen walked in ten minutes late every morning. She stood in the front of the room, rigid, her Madonna like face inscrutable. When I asked why she was late, she just looked at me with her sad eyes and said not a word. I could sense that she was inwardly quivering. After a few mornings I stopped asking. I greeted

193

her with a smile and told her to sit down. She never failed to give me a grateful look as she scurried to her seat.

We were all aware of three siblings who came to school unwashed and in dirty clothes. One day they came to school squeaky clean. The Welfare Department worker had come to take care of them while the mother was sick. As soon as she left, they were dirty again.

We had to mark attendance very carefully because it determined the amount of state aid the school received. After three days of unexplained absences we had to send post cards. If there were no response, we notified the truant officer. The number of absentee cards I had to send kept increasing. Children came and left after a few months. Some moved without notifying the school. The class register began to look like a hotel register.

More and more children had both parents working. They came to school with keys dangling from thick strings around their necks. After school, these latch key children let themselves into empty apartments. To make sure the poor children and the latch key children had a healthy meal, the New York City schools started to serve lunch. The children on Welfare received it free. Others bought it at subsidized prices. Soon, even the mothers who were home took advantage of the supervised lunch time by giving their children bag lunches. Fewer and fewer children went home for lunch. The teachers had one more round of duty - lunch duty. The children eating lunch made so much noise, that even after the bell rang, it was difficult to get them to line up in an orderly fashion.

The formality of Friday assembly disappeared. So many boys came to school without white shirts and ties that it became impossible to enforce the regulation. But once a month one of the classes still staged a performance. I was responsible for the Christmas program. The principal gave me strict orders not to use religious symbols or references. I had to make do with Santa Claus, his elves, and Rudolph, the Red Nose Reindeer. As the time for the performance approached, he nervously kept asking me if I was sure that there would be nothing religious in the presentation. The many non-Christians in the system had forced the Board of Education to eliminate the religious carols and religious symbols from the celebration of Christmas.

The continuing deterioration of the neighborhood and Joe's

194

two hour daily drive convinced us to make a move to Long Island. By then, except for my job, there was nothing to keep us in the Bronx. Aunt Filomena's generation was gone and their children were scattered in the various suburbs. My parents also had no reason to stay. My father would soon be receiving his first Social Security check and my mother would receive half of his.

The problem was finding the right house to meet all our needs. It had to be close to the Queens' border so I could continue to teach in New York City and it had to have a separate apartment for my parents. The houses in the new developments were being built for the post-war nuclear families. No room for grandparents.

We made the rounds of Realtors and builders in search of a solution. Finally we found a Spot Builder, one who built custom homes on scattered lots he owned all over Long Island. He showed us an oversized, wooded plot on Alice Court, a cul-de-sac in Balmor in Nassau County. It was the last empty lot in a cluster of new, big, split levels. Even though the area was zoned for one family homes he could legally by-pass the law by building a new category of homes called Mother-daughter. To qualify, the house had to have just one entrance, the tenant had to be a member of the family and the neighbors must not register any objection.

The location was ideal. It was about a half hour's drive to Joe's job and according to the builder's blurb, twelve minutes to the toll booth on Southern Parkway, near the city line. It was also ideal for my parents. The church, doctor, dentist, notion store and two supermarkets were all within a good peasant walk along level, tree-lined streets. The back yard was full of trees. We cut down some to make room for a fig tree, a vegetable garden and for my mother's flowers.

Because it was a custom house, the builder would not accept the government insured mortage. We had to pay a higher mortage rate than the other veterans. We also had to put down a larger down payment than usual because the bank still did not consider my salary.

As soon as we signed the contract I wrote to the Board of Education for a transfer to one of the two schools right over the city line and another letter asking for a six month unpaid leave to help my children adjust to the move.

During the spring we visited the house as it was being built.

We met our neighbors and introduced my parents. When we mailed them the mandatory notification that my parents were moving in, no one objected.

Towards the end of school year, I received a notice from the Board that I was granted the six month unpaid leave but denied my transfer to either of the schools I had requested. The reason was that both schools were classified as above index schools. The term was coined to denote the schools that had more tenured teachers than substitutes. I could only be transferred to an under index school, one with the reverse proportion. The index had been started to slow down the rate of transfers of permanent teachers from the deteriorating schools to the more desirable ones. I had no choice but to accept a transfer to the nearest under index school, P.S.163, an all Black school in St.Albans. My friends at P.S.92 gave me commiserating looks and said,

"Lots of luck"!

It being an all Black school did not bother me. I had no preconceived notions about Blacks. There were no Blacks in my childhood and there were none in the neighborhood. Slavery was just a fact of history. The Black girls at Hunter College ate together at the same table in one corner of the lunchroom. I didn't think anything of it. We Italian girls also sat together. My only concern was its location. The only way to get to P.S. 163 was by car. I didn't know how to drive! But the excitement of moving to Suburbia's open spaces, trees and fresh air distracted me from my disappointment over the transfer. We couldn't wait to move into our new house.

The house looked like a large expanded Cape Cod. By cantilevering the second floor in the back, the builder made the second floor almost as big as the first. The front door opened into a small foyer leading to our living room and to the staircase to my parents' apartment. We could go down to the full, unfinished basement, both from our apartment and also from the back yard. The house was very basic. It had five rooms and one bath on each floor. It didn't have the luxury feature of other new homes - a recreation room, with a wet bar and space for the TV and HiFi. Our kitchens didn't have dish washers. But we made sure we had separate thermostats that were not preset to go off at ten o'clock.

The nine families of Alice Court reflected Balmor's religious mix of Jews, Protestant and Catholic. The nearby Methodist Church's minister and his family lived in the corner house. Inspired by the ecumenical spirit of the times, the minister's wife invited the "Ladies of the Court" to her house to promote understanding among the three religions. Unlike the women in the new housing developments, we were of different ages and our families were in various stages of development. But like most of the women on the Island, they were all housewives, except for Goldie who was also a teacher in New York City. She taught in one of the above index schools over the Nassau line and offered to take me to the bus stop where I could take the bus to P.S. 163. Joe, who was working the night shift, would come for me at three o'clock.

I was extremely relieved but I could not depend on Goldie to solve my transportation problems forever. I started to take driving lessons from a professional. After two of the five lessons I had signed up for, he came into the house and told Joe,

"About two percent of the people will never be able to drive. Your wife is one of them".

Joe told him that I would continue to take the rest of the lessons, anyway. After the instructor left, Joe offered to teach me. I accepted Joe's offer and disregarded everybody's advice,

"If you value your marriage, don't let your husband teach you how to drive".

Joe took me to empty parking lots and patiently tutored my driving. It was the most difficult thing I ever had to do. But if I didn't learn to drive I'd have to give up my job.

Thirty-three

At exactly 7:30, on the first day of the February 1960 term, Goldie pulled up in front of our house where I was waiting, ready to step into the car. About fifteen minutes later she dropped me off at the bus stop in Queens. As I got off the bus in St. Albans and started to walk the three blocks to the school, I noticed debris in the back yards and rotting window frames. St. Albans had been a beautiful neighborhood of middle class Blacks. When the Black middle class moved out, the poorer Blacks from other neighborhoods and from the South moved in.

P.S.163 was a large three story brick building, (similar to all the other schools in New York City), with classes from Kindergarten through the eighth grade. A wide stairway led from the sidewalk to the first floor. The double doors led into an open area large enough to accommodate classes for recess and for the children to line up in bad weather. There were classrooms at each end. I went up the Up staircase to the second floor. The walls along the staircase were scratched and peeling. The large general office was cluttered with steel cabinets, their open drawers bulging with files. The sign-in book was almost covered by other papers. Over the years I had noticed the gradual increase of papers on the desks of the secretaries at P.S. 92. But I was completely unprepared for the volume of files that I saw in P.S. 163.

The two secretaries, one black and the other white, sat at facing desks, under the two large windows. They were both busy looking through stacks of papers. They looked up when I introduced myself and motioned for me to go into the adjoining principal's office. It was dingy and just as cluttered as the outer office. The filing cabinets along the wall had stacks of papers and folders on them. The principal was sitting at her cluttered desk. After a few introductory remarks she warned,

"Be prepared to handle some very bad discipline problems."

Then she confided.

"I have a gun in my closet."

I left the office with some apprehension. I walked down to

my classroom on the first floor. The other two third grade teachers were standing in the hallway waiting for the classes to come in. Vanessa, a cheerful, friendly, young Black teacher and Marilyn, equally friendly but serious Jewish woman about my age, greeted me warmly. We chatted for a few minutes. Marilyn asked me if I was married to an Italian.

When I said, "Yes" she looked at me in wonder and with a look of bliss on her face, she exclaimed,

"How romantic!"

I did a double-take and thought of the effect of the movies in our lives. Italian movies were very popular after the war. Visions of leading men like Marcello Mastroianni and Rossano Brazzi must have been going through her head. I just smiled.

At least her remark was better than the one Goldie repeated to me on the way to school. The neighbors were worried when they heard that Italians were moving in. They were afraid we were going to be loud, uncouth and that our children would be hoodlums. They had been pleasantly surprised when we showed up. She chuckled when she added that our children turned out to be the best behaved on the block.

P.S.163 reflected the postwar changes in the New York City school system. There was only one Irish teacher and she was near retirement. The Principal and the Assistant Principal were Jewish. The faculty was about equally divided between Blacks and Whites. Until my transfer, the Whites were all Jewish except for two Italians.

The three of us teaching the third grade took advantage of our proximity and the few minutes we had in the morning, to discuss common problems and to plan common activities. The three classes met together for recess, either indoors on the first floor or in the outside yard. We took turns taking charge of the period while the other two assisted. Except for the one period a week when the librarian took over the class in the school library, we were always with our classes. I felt a special empathy with the librarian. Her son had been born prematurely a few years before Michael and he was blind.

Every morning, at about 11:30 A.M. we heard the custodians open the stacked tables and their attached benches. They transformed the play area into a lunchroom. One teacher supervised the children eating lunch until twelve thirty. Then another teacher took over to supervise them at play either in or outdoors. It wasn't long before I had my first lunch room duty. Most of the children in the school qualified for free lunch, consisting of soup, and either a sandwich, boiled eggs or franks, fruit and a half pint of milk. As they came in, many of them looked over the trays of other children before deciding whether to stay for lunch or not. If they didn't like the food, they made fun not only of the food but also of the children eating it, and left the building. Those who took the food ate only what suited them and threw the rest in the trash cans. Very few ate the whole lunch. I was so hungry I would have loved a bowl of soup or a boiled egg, but I wasn't allowed to have any.

I watched the workers dump gallons and gallons of unserved soup and milk down the drain. They threw the unused food in the garbage cans. They had notified the Board several times to cut down on the shipment. The answer was always the same. The amount they sent was correct according to the number of children enrolled in the school's lunch program.

Supervising the children eating lunch was bad enough but supervising them afterwards, while they played, was worse. When bad weather forced them to assemble in designated seats in the auditorium, their noise was deafening. The seventh and eighth graders, most of whom were taller than I, didn't sit for long. They milled around, fooled around and spoke loudly. I soon learned what the other teachers had learned. It was impossible to keep them quiet. I tried to spot the beginning of arguments and stopped them from flaring into fights. I often glanced at the clock on the wall and sent its minute hand silent pleas to move faster. One lunch hour was so bad that I took out my little note pad and did the arithmetic to see how much I was earning a minute.

Even the supposedly formal Assembly periods were noisy. It was never absolutely quiet even during the salute to the flag or the Bible reading. I don't think the children really noticed or cared when the reading of the Bible stopped in 1963 after the Supreme Court ruled the practice unconstitutional. (The mother of my second grader who had complained about the mention of God in the classroom had been joined by many others. Several groups filed suits against the practice of reciting prayers or reading the Bible in public schools. The most well known of these was the one brought by Madalyn Murray O'Hair.)

That summer we experienced the negative aspect of Suburbia. The streets were deserted. The children Mary and Michael had played with during the first summer and after school, were enrolled in Day Camps or were with their families at the private beach clubs. Michael and Mary found the days long and boring.

Everyone around us, except maybe, the Minister, had more money than we had. The men were lawyers, partners in accountant firms or owned auto dealerships. Joe and I had long before accepted the fact that no matter where we went there were always going to be people who had more than we. We did not waste time or energy envying them or trying to keep up with them.

We looked for nearby family things to do that didn't cost too much. We went to Jones Beach, Drive-in movies and to the picnics sponsored by Michael's Cub Scouts and by Mary's Blue Birds. We went to Salisbury park for the Fourth of July celebration, or just to walk on the tree-shaded paths and around the Golf Course. When the County announced the first of a series of free summer evening music programs in the park, we drove to the almost empty, designated parking area. Near it, a makeshift wooden platform was set up under the trees. We opened up our chairs and joined the handful of people there. Three musicians played popular music. We were delighted to be listening to music under the trees, even though we had to swat mosquitoes all evening. The mosquitoes did not stop us from attending the later concerts. The crowd remained very small all through the summer.

In the evenings the children, home from the Day Camps and days at the private beaches, played on the street. To get relief form the heat we sat out and watched them play. One particularly hot evening a man dressed in suit and tie came by selling the Encyclopedia Britannica. We bought a set. As a gift we received a set of the Jr. Britanica. It turned out to be a wonderful investment. It saved us many trips to the library.

More worrisome than the children's boredom was the news that for some unknown reason, the incidence of breast cancer among the women on Long Island was the highest in the nation. HIP was given a government grant to conduct a ten year study to establish a profile of the women most at risk. I received a letter notifying me that I had been picked at random to be one of the women in the study. I became one of the very first women to have a mammogram. It was a lengthy procedure. I had to lie down on a table, which the radiologist moved by inches, as he took one x-ray after another. He must have taken at least 50 pictures. Year after year, the letter came and I reported for the test.

When school started, Mary and Michael resumed their piano lessons. Michael started his visits to the orthodontist. Shortly after, Mary joined him. A few days into the school year, Mary told me, in a grieved tone of voice, that a girl in her class had a pair of shoes to match every outfit. Before that, even more aggrieved, she told me Judy next door had her own bathroom. Also, how come she and Michael only got a hug and a kiss when they got good grades and the other children got expensive presents. Since both she and Michael had an excellent grasp of arithmetic, I felt the best explanation would be a discussion of our family's finances. They were shocked to see the many deductions from my gross pay. They understood where the money went and what we were saving for. We could afford what we needed but we could not afford to be extravagant. After that, when we said we couldn't afford something, they knew what we meant.

We found our way of celebrating as soon as *Friendly's* opened a store near us. It was *the* place to go for ice-cream. Every time Michael or Mary brought a good report card or received some honor, we went to *Friendly's*. We went there so often, that we named every happy event a *Friendly's Occasion*. These celebrations continue to this day.

When I started my second term, I drove our new car to school. I kept looking back at it as I walked towards the school. I couldn't believe I was leaving two thousand dollars at the curb. As it turned out, about a year later I had a good reason to worry.

One afternoon the new Principal came to tell me he'd take over the class while I went to look at the damage done to my car. It had been pushed onto sidewalk by a hit and run driver and it was undriveable. Joe had to come to get me. After that, I took even more care to park the car on quiet side streets. One morning I was positively sure I had parked the car in a safe spot, on a quiet tree-lined street, three blocks from the school. At dismissal time I found the side of the car bashed in by another hit and run driver, but at least it was driveable.

A few weeks into the term there was talk of a strike by the United Federation of Teachers, UFT. The strike became a daily topic of conversation. Some teachers were definite about not going out on strike. It was unprofessional. Some were afraid of losing their jobs. The rest of us came to no decisions. When the strike was called for November 7, 1960, I still hadn't made up my mind and so I started out for school as usual. I found teachers milling around on the sidewalk, near the steps of the school. I and the others who came after me, joined them. A few teachers gave us disapproving looks as they climbed the steps. Others sympathized with us but didn't have the courage to join us. Teachers had never gone on strike. We were afraid of being fired. We aired our grievances to each other and gave reasons why we should get a raise. When one teacher mentioned the generous contract the Sanitation workers had negotiated with Mayor Wagner, we became indignant. We felt that if they got a raise, we should too. When the bell rang, signaling the start of classes, we were still talking. Without taking a vote, we walked away from the building.

We had no idea of how to spend the day. No one had the nerve to go home. We car-pooled to a nearby Diner. We drank coffee, ordered food and drank some more coffee until it was time to order lunch. We listened to the radio but there was little news about the strike. No one, including the leaders of the strike, had any idea of its outcome. We encouraged each other by saying that the teaching conditions were so bad that maybe it would be best if we were fired. Then we could look for a better job. Reports about the strike trickled in after lunch. The number of teachers who stayed out was so great, that by mid-afternoon, Mr. Cogan, the union leader, jubilantly announced that the strike had been a huge success. The Board had agreed to negotiate with the Union.

As a result of the negotiations, a guidance counselor and two remedial reading teachers were appointed to our school. A class of five, very disruptive boys was formed and two full time teachers were assigned to teach it. The classroom teachers were given two preparation periods a week. We were hopeful that the teaching conditions would improve.

Our general mood of optimism was boosted by the

announcement that in January 1961, the United States was to launch the astrochimp, Ham, in preparation to sending a man into space. On the morning of the launch we all hoped that it would be successful and so help to heal the wounds that Russia's *Sputnik* had inflicted on our national pride. Unfortunately, the flight self aborted in just ten minutes. However, Ham had performed so well, that the scientists were sure they could safely send a man in space. Little did I know then, how much Ham had done for our family.

But even with the improvements negotiated by the Union, the day did not get any easier. The changes generated meetings to discuss their implementations. Scheduling the meetings became a problem. After school we had staff meetings, travel to attend mandatory in-service courses and take care of our families

To avoid staying after school, we scheduled meetings during our preparation periods or during the few duty-free lunch hours. (The lunch hour was 50 minutes but it shrank to around 15 minutes when we had lunch duty.) We sat in the children's seats in the classroom of the teacher who called the meeting. We ate our bagged lunches and drank the coffee provided by the hostess. Soon, all our clothes' closets had electric coffee makers to make real coffee instead of new instant coffee, which was very convenient, but none of us liked.

Much as I had dreaded the drive back and forth to school, I soon began to appreciate it. The drive was the only time I had to be alone and catch my breath. When I got home my daughter was waiting for me at the door to show me her work. She couldn't wait to read the story the class had learned that day. When she was in the same grade I was teaching, I had all I could do to act enthusiastic while I listened to her read the same story I had just taught. After a few such afternoons we came to an agreement. I would first go into the kitchen for a drink of water, start supper and then I would listen to her.

No matter what, I aimed to serve supper when Joe came home at 5:30. The new refrigerators came with large freezer compartments to hold the great assortments of frozen foods available. I filled our freezer with meat, chicken and plain vegetables. I didn't like any of the frozen entrees or frozen French fried potatoes that were widely promoted. Having an early supper and at the same time every evening, gave us all a fixed schedule to do homework, take

204

baths and get to bed in time to be able to get up at six the next morning.

On Sundays, my parents joined us around the dining room table for the big afternoon meal. By the time we cleaned up it was around four o'clock. Reluctantly, we decided to eliminate the Sunday meals in order to have time together for recreational activities.

I made changes in our lifestyle to make life a little easier at home and the Board made changes to improve the curriculum. A second language was to be taught in some elementary schools. I took the test for an Ancillary License to teach Italian. (A test for a regular license to teach Italian in the high schools, still had to be given). I received my license but P.S.163 did not qualify for the program. The schools nearby did, but I could not be transferred from the under-index P.S. 163.

To avoid another boring summer, we enrolled Mary and Michael at Camp Bauman Day Camp in Freeport. The bus came for them in the morning and brought them back late in the afternoon, five days a week. On week-ends the four of us used the facilities. We continued to go to Jones Beach and attend the concerts in the park, which were only slightly better attended the second year.

The following September we had a new Principal and Assistant. I was assigned the brightest of the second grade classes and a room right next to the Principal's office. Had the class been in one of the better schools, it would have qualified for the foreign language program. I taught them a few words of Italian. Pretty soon the PTA president, the mother of one of my students, routinely poked her head in my room and cheerfully greeted me with *"Buon Giorno!"*

That spring, the parents of the brightest students took advantage of the new school choice policy and transferred them out of P.S. 163. At the end of the year, all of my bright second graders transferred to other schools.

As more and more of the bright students left, the discipline deteriorated. The Civil Rights marches created tension. One morning, one of my second graders refused to come into the room. The Assistant Principal stood with her near my door and asked me if something happened the day before. I couldn't think of anything. The girl looked so sad that I started to put my arm around her shoulders but he stopped my arm in mid air. Quietly he told me not to touch.

Later that day I found out that one of the teachers was being threatened with a law suit for touching a sixth grader on the shoulder, when she told her to get into a straight line. The next day, I was relieved to learn that the reason the little girl didn't want to come in was that she didn't want to leave her mother home alone with the new baby.

One day the parents boycotted the school. Not one child came to school. A reporter from the *Daily News,* on the way to the Principal's offices saw me busy at my desk. Seeing a quick end to his assignment, he came into the room and asked if he could take my picture. To my amazement the picture appeared in the next day's issue.

The Administration fearing accusations of racial prejudice, condoned behavior that previously had been considered unacceptable. In the Teacher's Lunchroom we talked of possible ways to stop the discipline from deteriorating further. Our morale was getting lower. We were unsure of what to do. If we marked too strictly, we might be accused of prejudice. If we were too easy, we might be accused of not expecting any better. Things got so tense that even Vanessa, a Black teacher, received a phone call from an irate mother, accusing her of prejudice.

One very dedicated young teacher left after one year. She could not keep up the effort it took to achieve the results she wanted. She left to teach in a Catholic school, at a fraction of the salary. Another young one left in tears, after two years. One lunch hour I was in the office when a very tall woman strode in. On top of her voice she said to the two secretaries,

"I'm leaving and I'm not coming back this afternoon. Don't ever call me to sub in this school, again".

She dropped the room keys on the desk and strode out.

She had been teaching a kindergarten class. The Principal was left with an uncovered class and no teacher in sight. He broke up my class among the other classes and told me to take the class for the afternoon.

Near the end of every school year the teachers of each grade met with the Principal to discuss class assignments for the next year. It was customary for the Principal to ask for a volunteer to teach the slowest class on the grade. I had no qualms about volunteering. I had taught slow learners before. I had often seen the class at dismissal time. Their first grade teacher hugged each one as she said good-by to them. She told me that they were lovely children but very slow.

"Just keep them happy!"

Thirty-four

I put off worrying about how slow my class could be to prepare for Michael's first summer at Camp Balfour, in the Adirondacks. Unlike the one or two week camps sponsored by the Boy Scouts and Catholic Youth Organization, this was a resident camp that lasted the whole summer. We bought the clothes and items on the list given to us by the camp at a shop in town that specialized in outfitting campers. My mother, happy to help, sewed name labels on every item. On departure day, we drove Michael to the appointed pick-up point. We wouldn't be allowed to see him until parents' visiting week-end, in four weeks.

The camp was about an hour's drive north of Lake George. Mary was the first to glimpse the glistening patches of Lake Balfour through the trees on our left. The small eating place at the edge of the lake was our landmark to make a right into the gravel parking area of the three story hotel, half hidden from the road by the tall trees. At one time, it must have been a luxury hotel. The rooms were clean and had private baths. But the furnishings that once had been expensive and fashionable were being replaced, piece meal. The setting reminded me of Dr.Riis and Dr.Rae. The hotel and the lake fit the description of their vacations in the Adirondacks. After visiting Michael we visited Camp CHENAWAH, the girl's camp across the lake from Camp Balfour, to see if Mary would like it.

During that summer we finished the basement to give Michael and Mary a place to entertain their friends while we had our friends in the living room. The room was large and cheerful and had two small windows but still no wet bar or TV or HiFi. It was to be for the children to play in and have sleep overs. Joe refused to use the basement as part of our living quarters. He had seen too many Italian families living in their basements so they wouldn't mess up the upstairs.

Michael had such a good time at camp that we enrolled him for the next summer and enrolled Mary at Camp CHENAWAH. They were among the few Christians in the two camps of Jewish children. But every Sunday, someone took them to church in North Creek. (A

208

few years later Michael became a counselor at the camp and he did the driving.)

Driving to school on the first day of the September term I thought about my new class. Their IQs ranged from 57 to 91. One lived with her parents and one with her grandparents. The rest lived in foster homes. Several were in their third home. Eddie was blind in one eye, an injury he suffered as a baby, when his mother scalded him in the tub.

Within a few minutes of meeting the class I knew just how slow they really were. The thirty three children had spent the whole year in first grade but they did not recognize one letter or number. They could not read their names. They didn't speak clearly. They substituted the sound of one consonant for another. I had trouble understanding them. Oh! If only the examiners who had failed me for dentalizing and for mispronouncing prescient, could be there.

Driving home that first afternoon, I felt defeated. I couldn't possibly follow their first grade teacher's suggestion to "Just keep them happy", without teaching them how to read and write. There was nothing in the classroom that could hold their interest. The situation was too desperate for normal teaching methods. I needed to think of unusual things to do, day by day, just to survive.

Besides that, I was in a fish bowl. Every time the principal left the office to make his frequent rounds of the school, he looked in my room and again when he returned. I alerted him that he might see some strange things happening in my room. He smiled and told me that whatever I did would be all right. What he really meant was that as long as I kept the class under control, he wasn't going to ask too many questions. The desperate situation and his confidence gave me the courage to try things that I would not have even dared to think about, let alone try, in P.S. 92.

Not only didn't they know the alphabet or numbers, they didn't listen when I spoke. They went on with what they were doing as if I weren't there. I was at a loss to explain it. They were too young to make such a concerted effort to ignore me. In a flash I saw myself in the corner in the classroom in America, hearing the teacher but not understanding one word she was saying. Something was stopping them from processing what I was saying.

I deliberately slowed down my speech to an unnatural slow

rate and enunciated every word carefully. It was like magic. They turned towards me, paid attention and followed the directions. I spoke that way from then on. I kept my directions brief. My speech was so exaggeratedly slow and precise that the other teachers teased me. But they marveled at the results. The class was the best behaved of any in the hallways. They beamed at the compliments they received and were very proud of themselves.

When the monitors delivered the reading texts to my classroom I told them to return them to the office. The Assistant Principal, who couldn't send the books fast enough to suit most teachers, quickly came to ask me why. I explained that since the children didn't recognize any of the letters, the books would only add to their frustration. They would end up scribbling in them. He reluctantly agreed.

Even though reading was once again taught through phonics, I'd have to use the discarded whole word method. I made a list of the words in the primer and planned activities involving those words. We made up sentences with the words. We wrote experience charts that I tacked on the walls around the room. Each child chose a sentence, read it aloud and then drew a picture about it. We read and re-read the charts and pointed to the words until they could recognize them in isolation.

One morning the children were especially talkative. They were discussing *Batman*, the TV program they had watched the evening before. I postponed the arithmetic lesson that traditionally started the day and used their enthusiasm to allow each one to say something about the program. We wrote stories, drew pictures and learned words. I mentally thanked the sponsors of the program. I watched it regularly. The day after the show we had a highly motivated language arts lesson.

Every subject became a reading lesson. In writing the experience charts, no matter the subject, I made sure I used the reading words in the sequence in which they appeared in their reader. When they knew all the words in the primer, I asked for the books. The children eagerly opened them and cried with delight when they recognized the words. They showed the pages to each other as if to confirm the fact that it was really so.

I didn't give up on the alphabet. For each letter I found a

colorful picture of a food. Soon they could associate the sound of "B" with "banana" and "M" with "milk", etc. After a few months they could associate the sounds with the letters but blending the sounds was still difficult and I still could not depend on phonics as a teaching tool.

In the classroom I hardly ever sat down at my desk. To maintain their short attention span I had to be up, directing and supervising their activities. Driving home each afternoon and while I did household chores, I thought of something new to do the next day. Teaching this class to read and write and do some arithmetic, became almost an obsession.

We started a terrarium and placed a frog in it. We made a schedule so that each child was responsible to give food and water to the frog. When they got too noisy I reminded them that "Harry" was trying to sleep. During our discussion on bread making we planted wheat kernels in a window box and they took turns watering them. Each morning we looked for the green shoots to come up. Willie, with the 55 IQ, was fascinated by the plants. He never raised his hand for any answers except when I asked what wheat was used for. His hand waved wildly and his whole body vibrated. He said "bread" with such enthusiasm that I tried to fit that question in as often as I could.

The second grade social studies book dealt with "*Our Helpers*", like the policemen, firemen, sanitation workers, and other workmen. I refused them, too. They were too difficult.

Instead, I gave the children a form to be signed by their guardians, giving me permission to take them on neighborhood walks, whenever I wanted. When we heard some interesting noise outside, we put on our coats and went out to see what was happening. The principal never stopped to ask where we were going. He just smiled and said, "There she goes again". We saw policemen, firemen, sanitation men and postmen. We took several walks to the house that was being built nearby, and observed the different types of workers. When we got back from our walks, the children wrote individual stories and we made a class experience chart.

I went to school even when I didn't feel well. But one day I was too sick to go. I stayed out for two days. A few weeks later a man and a woman came in and introduced themselves as the two psychologists who had tested the class while I was out. They were curious to see what I looked like. Every one of the thirty-three children had severe emotional problems. Eddie was so sick that if he were institutionalized he would have no chance to adjust to the real world. They wondered how I could teach these children day in and day out.

Among the many non-teaching chores was the collection of bank books the children brought in once a week. The books were sealed in small brown envelopes, along with their small deposits. I collected them and sent them to the office. A few days later, the bank books were brought back and I returned them to the children.

One morning Mary's grandparents came to see me. He had on a white shirt, with a starched collar, and tie. She wore a hat and gloves. They looked very distinguished and dignified but nervous. The grandfather twisted his hat in his hands and the grandmother clutched her bag. (I thought of my father getting all dressed up to go to see my third grade teacher). They wanted to know what had happened to the money they had been giving Mary. The bank book did not show any deposits for several weeks. In effect, they were accusing me of pocketing the money. I didn't feel insulted. Instead I felt sorry for them. They were raising Mary for their daughter who seldom visited them. Mary was tall for her age, had an IQ of 60 and resented her mother for not visiting her. Every Friday afternoon she loudly announced to me and to the class that her mother was going to visit her over the week-end. I dreaded Monday mornings. Invariably, the mother did not visit and Mary was more disruptive than usual.

I calmly explained to them that Mary had not handed in her bank book for several weeks. I suggested they talk to her when she got home. I was sure she would be able to explain what had happened to the money. I thanked them for coming instead of ignoring the situation. A few days later they both came back to apologize. Mary had spent the money at the candy store.

To boost the school's morale, one of the eighth grade teachers, who had a Ph.D. in folk dancing, planned a May Day celebration in the outside yard. The second graders had to learn two circle dances with words to the music. Through activities and charts the class learned the words and sang the songs in the room but when we tried the dance in the play area on the first floor, they got confused. The area was seldom quiet. Classes moved through,

212

children used the bathroom and custodians made noise. It was difficult for them to follow my directions. The thought of disgracing ourselves in front of the whole school gave me the courage to do something I thought I would never have the nerve to do.

A few years back, I had taken piano lessons which I had to stop for lack of time. The only thing I could do was pick out a simple melody with my right hand. I went to the old piano in the corner of the room, dusted off the fine flakes of paint that continually fell from the ceiling, and picked out the melodies to the dances. The next time we went down to recess I swallowed my pride and played the tunes on the old piano there. Luckily I didn't need its broken keys. After a few tries, the class did the dances perfectly. The other two teachers asked if they could join us when I "played the piano".

I had become so used to having people poking their heads in my room on their way to and from the Principal's office, that I almost ignored a very tall, pleasant lady who came to my door one spring morning. She introduced herself as the District Supervisor in charge of the study the Board was conducting on the teaching of reading in the second grade. I had heard about the study but I was too busy trying to teach the class to pay too much attention to it. She started to look through a rather complicated schedule to find a convenient time for her to observe my class during our reading lesson. I suggested it might be easier for her to come whenever she could fit me in. I would teach the lesson then. She gratefully accepted the offer.

When she came in later that morning, she informed me, in a confidential tone of voice, that the Principal had briefed her on the makeup of my class. The inference was for me not to worry if the children didn't do well. She found a seat in the back of the room and took copious notes. At the end of the lesson, she told me she was impressed not only by the fact that despite their limitations most of the children were reading on the second grade level, but also by how well the two groups worked independently, while I worked with the third.

"If only I could put you in all the second grade classrooms, there wouldn't be a reading problem". Her remark took me entirely by surprise. I didn't think I was doing any thing fantastic. I was just trying to live through each day as best as I could.

The compliment was followed by a request. Would I speak at

the district wide meeting to be held in a few weeks, to explain my method of "Teaching Reading Through the Curriculum", to the supervisors and other second grade teachers of the district.

After the presentation, several people waited in line to speak to me. The woman at the end of the line waited patiently. I was flattered that she waited so long. When she finally reached me, she looked at me as if she were about to consult an oracle. She wanted to know how I came up with all the ideas. I told her that I thought about the class while I cleaned, cooked and whenever I wasn't thinking about my family.

Her face dropped with disappointment.

"Oh! That's too much work!"

She abruptly turned around and left.

I have never forgotten that gesture. As a result, I don't ever offer advice and if I'm asked, I try to evade the question or say very little.

After the presentation even more people poked their heads to say,

"I just want to see what Mrs. Tangredi looks like."

The May Day celebration was a huge success but it didn't improve the discipline in the school.

The teachers usually returned to their classrooms after escorting their classes to the outside doors at three o'clock. At the next faculty meeting, we were told that for safety precautions, effective immediately, we had to leave the building with our classes. Noone would be re-admitted after the three o'clock dismissal. Dismissals became very precise. We lined up in the classroom, ready to leave as soon as the first bell rang. Then, we lined up in the hallway near the exits, ready to follow the last class down from the floor above. We heard the clanging of the fire doors, as the custodians shut and chained them as soon as the classes walked through them. It reminded me of the prison lock-ups I had seen in the movies).

Professionally, I was having the best year of my teaching career. But the intensity of my commitment was beginning to take its toll. I developed ailments I hadn't had before. Some afternoons I was so tired I could barely get myself out of the car to walk up the few steps into our house. I weakly waved back at my next door neighbor, Sheila and her neighbor, sitting on their lawn chairs. I fleetingly wished I could afford to stay home.

One afternoon my father was sitting on the front steps when I got out of the car. The expression on his face reflected what he must he have seen on mine. He, who had always encouraged me to keep my job so I would collect a pension, told me to stop working and enjoy life like the other women on the block. But I couldn't stop. I would lose my retirement benefits. All my hard work would have been for nothing.

A few years later, when I asked my daughter why she never wanted to be a teacher, she looked surprised that I should even ask such a question.

"Because I saw what you looked like when you came home in the afternoon".

One day I saw the mother of one of my daughter's friends in Macy's perfume department spritzing on the different perfumes. She wasn't buying anything. She explained that she did it just to pass the time. Her eyes were so dead that I did not envy her leisure one bit.

She was one of the many brides or young mothers who had moved to Long Island in the fifties, expecting to live an idyllic life. They were happy to escape the crowded neighborhoods where they had to carry the babies, carriages and groceries up the many stairs of their apartment houses. They looked forward to putting the babies in the carriages in their back yards, where they could keep an eye on them while they did their household chores. They enjoyed the open spaces, the trees and the fresh air.

Most of their husbands had long ommutes into Manhattan. In the morning, wearing slippers and only a robe or coat over their night gowns, they dropped their husbands off at the nearest Long Island Railroad station, just as the train was coming in. In the evening, they sat in their idling cars, ready to pick up their husbands as they stepped off the train. Away from their families, childhood friends and the old neighborhoods, the young couples in the housing developments socialized with the couples near them. They met in each other's houses to have a drink, eat finger foods and discuss common problems and successes. In the summer, they had barbecues and dined informally on their patios. Some bought boats and joined boat clubs. Some couples drove the short distance to Jones Beach, spread their blankets by the water, drank their customary pre-dinner cocktails and ate their picnic supper while enjoying the cool sea breeze. The Long Island couples were the envy of those in the crowded city.

The television program, *Leave It To Beaver*, idealized the nuclear family of the 1950's. The episodes started with the Cleaver father and two sons, fully dressed, sitting at the kitchen table, discussing a potential family crisis. June Cleaver, fully made-up, without one hair out of place and wearing a frilly apron to cover her fashionable dress, cheerfully served advice and a full breakfast. She was never without a string of pearls around her neck, even while she pushed the vacuum cleaner. At supper, the scene was repeated in the dining room. After placing the food on the table, June joined them in eating supper and in resolving the problems discussed at breakfast.

Unlike June Cleaver, the young mothers wore their husbands old shirts, rough jeans and colorful bandannas to hide curlers in their hair while they gardened, painted furniture and did housework. I wore a housedress while I cleaned the house on Saturdays. Every time I went by a mirror, I felt worse than I looked, when I compared myself to June.

After a while, the 60 by 100 plot that had given their children a safe play area, became a play pen for the young mothers, too. It isolated them from casual interaction. One of my friends felt so lonely for adult conversation that she wished she were back in the Bronx, pushing the baby carriage through the crowded neighborhood. Carrying the carriage and the baby up and down the stairs of the apartment house didn't seem so bad after all.

In the 1960's, when their children started school, many housewives relieved their boredom by becoming active in the schools, Cub Scouts, Girl Scouts and Blue Bird groups. Some got jobs. Others roamed the newly built shopping malls. Those with maids had even less to do and had more time to be bored.

One afternoon I met Mrs. Fried with an armful of books in the town's library. She was looking for a special fish recipe that required some very exotic herbs. I knew she was just killing time. The first time Emily, her oldest daughter and Mary's classmate, came to visit, Mary offered her some chocolate pudding. Emily had no idea what it was. In the morning it was Emily who fixed cold cereal for herself and her two younger siblings while her mother stayed in bed.

Some women turned to drink. When we arrived at a

neighbor's New Years' party, the husband greeted us. We joined the other guests in the living room where all sorts of finger foods had been put out. The husband served the drinks and nervously explained that the wife was taking a nap and would soon join us. Midnight struck and she still didn't appear. While we ate the food the wife had put out before "taking her nap" we all made polite conversation, pretending that none of us thought it strange that the hostess never showed up.

There were news items that some housewives were recruited to act as companions for business men in Manhattan. They met the men for lunch, where they could pass for their wives, and then went to the hotel rooms. The police broke up a prostitution ring, run by a Madam in Levittown. There were stories of key swapping parties. At the end of a social evening in a neighbor's house, the men went home with the owner of the keys they picked up at random from the bunch thrown on the table.

Even the women who did all the right things, seemed to be disillusioned. The promises of suburbia in the 1950's had not come to pass in 1960's. Did I really want to be a full time, Long Island housewife in the 1960's? Not really. I wished I could find a middle ground between being extremely exhausted and being extremely bored. I didn't want to quit teaching but I was beginning to have doubts about how long I'd have the strength to stay in the classroom at P.S.163.

Perhaps, this was the time to get a Master's degree, even though I'd have to pay for it myself. Since the District Supervisor thought I had done such a good job, I considered becoming a Remedial Reading Teacher. I discussed the idea with my husband and children. I would not be able to do it without their help and cooperation.

Michael, in Jr. High and Mary, in the fifth grade, encouraged me to do it. They would not feel neglected if some afternoons I didn't come straight home from school. They had enough afterschool activities to keep them busy. My husband, as usual, gave me the support I needed. I enrolled in the Master's degree program at Hofstra University on Long Island, and signed up for courses in both summer sessions.

Near the end of the term, the principal offered me the chance to stay with my class through the third grade. No other class had affected me so much. I worried about them and dreamed about them. I would have liked to be their third grade teacher but I was physically and emotionally exhausted. I knew that I could not go at the same pace for another year. Reluctantly I refused. To this day I wonder what has happened to them. I don't remember all their names but I can still see their beaming faces when they received a compliment from the principal or another teacher.

In September I enrolled in an evening class. The whole family became involved to make it possible for me to continue teaching and also go to Hofstra in the evening. My husband continued to do the bulk of the marketing for us and drove my parents to places too far to walk. He drove Michael and Mary to and from Cub Scouts, Blue Bird meetings and their other activities. Michael and Mary did their homework without any reminders. They got up promptly with their alarms and started their day without any prompting from me. While I had my breakfast, I made lunches for the four of us. I was the last to leave, promptly at 7:30. None of us was ever late.

On the course day I drove home, talked with Mary and Michael about their day and discussed supper. The burners on the electric range had numbers to regulate the temperature. I left directions as to when to put what on, at what setting and for how long.

When my parents moved in upstairs I made it very clear to my mother that I didn't want her to do any housework or cooking for me. I didn't want her to be my maid. She did enough by just being home to greet Michael and Mary when they came home from school. But when she offered to broil a chicken for us, in her brand new rotisserie, on the course night, I gratefully accepted. They still ate supper at 5:30 and then cleaned up. As a treat we started to go out to eat on Friday nights. We often combined a shopping trip to Roosevelt Field Mall with supper at Horn and Hardart. It was no longer a coin operated, self service cafeteria but a Restaurant with waitresses and bartenders.

I was granted a six month sabbatical in which I carried a full load of courses. P.S. 163 had no openings for a *Remedial Reading Teacher* and neither did any of the nearby schools. On the other hand, the school systems in Nassau County were all hiring reading teachers for their summer remedial reading programs. With no real expectation of an answer, I wrote an informal note to Mr. Foster, the Supervising Principal of the Balmor School system, asking for a position in the summer reading program.

A few mornings later, the phone rang at 7 AM. It was Mr. Foster asking me to attend a meeting in his office, late that afternoon. I was hired after a short interview with Mr. Foster and Mrs. Gray, the Curriculum Coordinator. On the way out, Mrs.Gray confided that she had looked up the records of my two children, who by then were out of the school. Their excellent marks and conduct helped her make the decision.

About a week into the program, Mary woke up in the middle of the night, complaining of a pain in the right side of the abdomen. At 2 AM we were on the highway, hoping we wouldn't get lost on the way to the HIP hospital in Queens. It was almost dawn before we found out that it was not appendicitis. Waiting for Mary's discharge, we drank coffee in the cafeteria and watched the sun rise. There was no way I could be in Bayer school by eight o'clock. The custodian answered the phone and assured me he would notify Mr. Foster.

When we got home my mother told us that Mr. Foster had come to the house looking for my plan book. All my mother understood was "book". She showed him around the house and asked him to look for himself. He found it on my night table. I had diagnosed each child's reading problems and indicated the proposed remedy. He was very impressed. Were it not for the emergency, he never would have seen it.

The other reading teacher in the summer program was the regular reading teacher in the school. A few days before the session ended she told me that she was leaving for California and suggested that if I wanted the job I'd better ask Mr. Foster the same day she gave him her notice.

Mr. Foster asked why I wanted to leave the New York school system. I started to describe the conditions in the system but after a few sentences I noticed the look in his eyes. He just could not conceptualize the situation. It was beyond his understanding. I cut the explanation short.

He was pleased with my work and I was hired. He added, with an impish smile, the other reason he was hiring me was that there was no one else asking for the job. There weren't enough reading teachers to fill the demand on Long Island. I accepted the job and promised to take the remaining courses towards my Masters degree.

I wrote to the principal of P.S.163 to tell him of my intention to leave. He called and spoke to Joe. He begged him to dissuade me. I was leaving a tenured job with a good pay and excellent pension benefits, for an untenured one with less pay and fewer pension benefits.

As I listened to my husband's recital of what I was giving up I thought of how hard I had worked to get and keep that job. But I had nothing left to give to the children in P.S. 163. I was so drained that I had finally found the courage to leave.

Meanwhile, Joe had made another career move. Mergenthaler Linotype had not kept up with the times. It was losing business to companies using more modern methods. When the layoffs started, Joe started to look for another position while he still had a job. He answered a newspaper ad by the Grumman Aerospace Corporation. The company had a government contract to build a vehicle that would meet President Kennedy's challenge to the nation, to land a man on the moon before the decade was over. Joe joined the company as an Industrial Engineer, in Bethpage where the Lunar Module was to be built. Thanks to Ham's success, Joe had a new job.

Thirty-five

On the first morning of the 1967 school year, instead of getting on the Parkway to go to P.S. 163, I continued straight on Derrick Ave. and in ten minutes I was in Bayer School's parking lot, a two level, red brick building, for the kindergarten through the sixth grade. As I got out of the car I was both optimistic about the new start and nervous about the possible outcome. If things didn't go well I might be without a job at the end of the year. I hadn't had that worry since I had received my tenure.

The grass-scented breeze, blowing from the field next to it, followed me to the side entrance and fanned my optimism. Without a thought to the car, I walked in by the parking lot entrance and headed for the Principal's office. I went by the classrooms where teachers were already at their desks preparing for their classes. The gleaming hallway was deserted. The Principal's outer office had no window and was just big enough for the secretary's desk and a few metal cabinets behind her. The private office was spacious and bright. Thelarge windows overlooking the lawn and Derrick Avenue, took up the entire wall. Mrs. Hutton was sitting at her gleaming, glass covered desk which had nothing but a calendar and holders for pens and pencils.

She was near retirement but still wore a bow on the back of her hair, for which she was known by all educators in the area. She graciously walked with me to my room, across the hall from her office. We met the stream of orderly children coming in as they were discharged from the buses. Mrs. Hutton smiled at them and they all smiled back.

The Remedial Reading Room was the size of a large closet and as dark despite the one tiny window. My desk was under it. One long wall was covered with a chalkboard and the other was lined with bookcases. The room was just big enough for a round table and six chairs.

After a few minutes I smelled coffee. It came form the lunchroom diagonally across from my room. One of the lunchroom women made a large pot of coffee for the teachers to buy for a dime a

221

cup. I thought I had died and gone to heaven. I finally could have a second cup of morning coffee.

In a few days the teachers sent me the list of children who needed help. I tested them individually and placed them in appropriate groups of four to six. I gave the teachers a schedule and it became their responsibility to follow the schedule. The children came unescorted, in an orderly fashion, discreetly whispering to each other. They left the same way.

The majority of the teachers lived locally, had been in the school for years, dressed well and were very proper in every way. They took pride in a job well done and felt secure in their position. They acquiesced to Mrs. Hutton's treatment of them as students at a finishing school. Occasionally they made remarks about her bows and wondered what had caused her divorce, many years before.

Unlike the teachers at PS 92 and PS 163, the teachers at Bayer had no yard duty because the children were bussed in and no lunch hour duties because the girls' gym teacher and the boys' gym teacher, both referred to as Coach, supervised the children at lunch and during the play time afterwards. We all ate together in the teacher's lunchroom which reeked of stale smoke even more than the ones in the other two schools. Most of us brought our lunch but we could buy the school lunch. Except for the two male six grade teachers and Marie, the music teacher, we were all married women.

The lunchroom conversations gave glimpses of our lives away from the classroom. We expressed our frustrations at our husbands' idea that our job was a hobby they allowed us to have as long as it didn't interfere with our real job of caring for the family and the house. We could have our full time job as long as we cleaned, cooked, wrote the greeting cards, arranged for family celebrations and baked the cup cakes for our children's classes. We older wives complained to each other but none of us confronted our husbands with our grievances.

The younger teachers were having varying degrees of success in convincing their husbands to help them around the house. Linda's husband of a few months took excellent care of her when she was home with a cold, including serving her meals in bed. Her delight turned into disappointment when she finally walked into the kitchen. All the dishes and pots he had used were piled high, for her to clean.

The women's attempt at equality since the 1960's had some strange consequences. Except for Arlene who used Chanel No.5 cologne, none of us used perfume. It was quite a change from my first days of teaching. Then, everybody wore perfume. When one of the teachers became an Avon representative, the different fragrances vied with each other in the halls.

The birth control pill had given women unprecedented freedom to have casual sex just like the men. The part-time, married librarian, told one of the teachers (who told all of us in the lunchroom) that she was having an affair

After a few weeks at Bayer, my euphoria over the morning coffee started to diminish. I was informed that along with the Supervising Principal, the three school principals and the other special teachers, I had to attend all the monthly School Board meetings. I also was expected to attend all the PTA meetings and any other function sponsored by the school. I was at the disposal of the community.

Unlike the Board of Education in NYC, a mysterious group of people none of us ever saw, the Board in Balmor was a group of well known and respected members of the community. The Board members took their job very seriously and their expectations were reasonable. They were happy with the instruction in the school. The basal reading program was working well for the great majority of the students. The Reading Teacher in each school was there to help those who were falling behind. The meetings were friendly and we showed each other mutual respect. We settled differences amicably. The woman member invited the faculty of the three schools to her house for a Christmas party.

During one of the meetings, the Board approved the controversial sex education course for the sixth graders. In preparation for the course the staffs of the three schools had to attend several after school meetings in the Bayer's gym, to listen to Dr. Calderone, a leading Long Island authority on sex education. The doctor enjoyed shocking us by using the correct vocabulary. She wanted to desensitize us to the curriculum. We cringed every time she mentioned the sex organs, but not as much as poor Mrs. Hutton, who looked as if she were going to explode. But she just twisted her pencil over and over again on the little note book she clutched over her primly crossed knee.

The mother of one of the girls in my fourth grade reading groups stopped me in the hall to voice her strong objection to the sex education program. She didn't want her daughter, who knew nothing about sex, to be exposed to such knowledge. I had to bite my tongue. Just the day before, I had overheard her daughter discuss sexual matters with her friend.

My daughter had started to ask questions about where babies came from when she was in kindergarten. I always answered truthfully, within her ability to understand, cautioning her to keep our talks to herself. One afternoon she was playing doctor with three of her kindergarten friends. Judy, obsessed with child birth, was the doctor and told Mary to lie down, so that she could cut up her stomach to take out the baby. I held my breath, waiting for Mary to tell her that the baby was in the uterus. But she didn't say a word and did what Judy told her to do. After that I had no hesitations about discussing anything with her.

When the sex program started, Mary was in Jr. High. I asked her if she thought the sixth grade was too early to start sex education. She gave me one of those teen-ager "are you joking"? looks.

I was not prepared for her answer.

"It's too late. By then, some are already having sex ".

(Many years later the US Surgeon General publicly voiced the same opinion.)

The program started despite some parents' objections. The male gym teacher taught it to the boys and the female gym teacher taught it to the girls.

I usually spent my preparation period in the large closet, accessible only through the gym, to use the mimeograph machine to duplicate material for my groups. During one of those periods, a class of boys come into the gym. After a few minutes I realized they were there for the sex education class. I was stuck in the closet. I was surprised at the boys' frank questions and I could sense their relief when the Coach answered them.

To fulfill my commitment to Mr. Foster, I took the last two courses at Hofstra during that summer. I had to administer individualized IQ tests to ten children and ten adults, interpret them and write them up. Mary and Michael recruited their friends and their parents.

224

The Hofstra Reading Clinic assigned me a boy to tutor at the college. I had to tape the twenty one hour lessons and transcribe them. Hoping to kill the proverbial two birds with one stone I offered the transcribing job to one of my housewife friends who wanted to earn some money. She returned the tapes the next day. I could not give her money enough to make her transcribe the *verbatim* tapes! I spent many evenings in the basement listening and typing. I scared the whole family when I sent up a loud "whoopee" after I struck the last period.

To make sure we passed the qualifying test, my class decided to meet for several study sessions. Rather than leave the family, I invited them to our house to meet in the privacy of our basement family room. They came from all over Nassau County and took turns bringing the cake and cookies. I supplied the coffee and the tea.

At the end of summer, after three years, I received my MA degree.

In September the conversations in the Teachers' Room reflected our concerns with the unanticipated changes in our society. Our generation had worked hard to buy bigger houses, better cars and to give our children all the advantages we never had. Instead of being grateful, the over-indulged youth were openly criticizing our materialism and challenging our lifestyles. Those who saw their parents under the influence of alcohol or drugs or not practicing what they preached about extramarital sex were especially disillusioned. The most innocuous form of rebellion was their way of dressing. Some boys had pony tails. Others had hair as long as the girls. Both girls and boys wore frayed jeans with a hole in each knee and scuffed-up shoes. Many acted out by smoking, drinking, being promiscuous and challenging authority. They questioned school practices that made no sense to them. Why were the study periods scheduled for the middle of the day? They should be scheduled at the end of the day. Amazingly, enough parents sided with them that the local High Schools gave in. The result was that very few students stayed in to study. Many either loitered on the school grounds or left the grounds all together.

The parents of girls worried about out-of-wedlock pregnancies. One fifth grade teacher took her young teen-ager to the doctor for a prescription of the pill. Another didn't know what to do about her twelve year old girl who used drugs and periodically ran away from home.

Drugs were no longer just the problem of the ghetto teens. Joe and I attended a meeting on the subject of the spreading drug use among the teenagers in Suburbia. The speaker was an Episcopalian priest who ran a shelter in New York City. The young people in the shelter were not underprivileged. Instead, they had been indulged in every way. Everything had been done for them. The first thing the counselors did was to show them the kitchen and teach them how to boil an egg. Many had no idea of what to do.

Subjects that had never before been mentioned in public were topics of TV programs. More and more promiscuous life styles were being accepted as normal. Anne was scandalized by the TV program *Maude* with Bea Arthur, which dealt with pre-marital sex and abortion. Yet, she never failed to watch it and to tell us all about it the next day. Younger married women (the Korea War generation) did not hesitate to talk about their marriages and husbands. Arlene, a forty year old mother of two school age children still talked about her teen-age conquests. She called her husband a "big nothing" and was thinking of "dumping" him. The only time she said something good about him was the day after he had a vasectomy. He was so proud of it that he wore a tiny, red lapel pin to promote the procedure.

The Broadway's success of *Hair*, with its nudity and obscene language, led the way to the very successful run of the raunchy *O Calcutta*. Books dealing with explicit sexual matters were on the best seller list. One dealing with the pill was popular with the adults and sparked the curiosity of the teens. I asked my daughter if she had heard of the book. She told me that several girls were reading it, without their mothers' knowledge. (I thought of how far we had come since Marilyn hid *The Grapes of Wrath* under her desk). When she repeated the mis-information her friends were passing along, I got the book. We both read it and talked about it. One afternoon we spent a long time discussing pre-marital sex and it's ramifications. I was happy to note that her questions and comments proved her ignorance of first hand knowledge of the subject. She showed more fear and concern than anything else. We were both exhausted but glad we had the conversation.

As if the sexual revolution weren't enough, the Vietnam

226

conflict added to our anxieties. Besides worrying about our teenage daughters getting pregnant, we worried about sending our teenage sons to war.

Finally something happened to lift our generation's spirits. The projected launch to the moon was announced. We were especially excited. Joe had been part of the team that built the Lunar Module, the LEM. On July 20, 1969, we sat glued to our chairs, watching TV and we heard Neil Armstrong triumphantly announce,

"The Eagle has landed".

At about two AM we watched Neil Armstrong step down from the LEM, in slow motion, put one foot on Tranquillity Base and say,

"That's one small step for man, one giant leap for mankind".

We, as a nation were very proud. We had beat Russia in the space war.

(In April of the next year, the next moon landing almost came to a tragic end. The command ship of the Apollo 13 flight lost power and there seemed no way for the three astronauts to survive. By moving into the LEM, which was not meant to hold three, they were able to survive. Just before going back to the command ship, for the splash down, they used the netting of the LEM to hold the scientific instruments. The LEM had saved them. That netting was later cut up into small pieces, mounted, signed by the three astronauts and framed. One of those framed pieces was given to everyone who had been associated with building the LEM. Joe's is hanging in the family room. Years later, this episode of space travel was made into the movie *Apollo 13.*)

The successful moon landing didn't stop us from worrying about Vietnam. Thousands of young men went to Canada to avoid the draft. The war that had divided the country for years, was about to touch Michael's class. One of Michael's friends went to Cuba to cut sugar cane for Castro. College students all over the country held rallies protesting the escalation of the war. Others, like Michael, held candle-light vigils along Derrick Avenue. By the time Michael registered, the draft lottery was in effect. We prayed his number would be exempt.

While we hoped that Michael would be going to college in September instead of Vietnam, we started to worry about paying for his college tuition. Our combined income was slightly above the qualifying minimum for government aid. The banks didn't consider my salary when we applied for a mortagebut the government did, in calculating the formula for school aid.

Michael scored 1553 out of a possible 1600 on the SAT (Scholastic Aptitude Test). He scored a perfect 800 on the math part. Sure to be accepted, he submitted an application to Stonybrook, the new tuition-free, state university on Long Island. Instead, he received a letter of rejection. Because of its policy of *affirmative action*, the college had no room for him.

The Grumman Corporation solved the tuition problem. It offered a merit scholarship to their employees' children who scored a minimum of 1550 out of 1600 on the SAT test. As soon as Michael received the scholarship, he applied to the college of his choice, The Massachusetts Institute of Technology, MIT. He was ecstatic when he received notification of early admission.

Thirty-six

Along with the four year scholarship came a summer job with the Grumman Corporation. Michael used my car and I walked wherever I could. On Friday afternoons I walked to the supermarket and he picked me up after work. One Friday afternoon I nervously pushed the shopping cart waiting for the lottery numbers to be announced over the radio. Michael walked in just as they announced his number. He was excluded from serving!

Relieved that Michael was not going to Vietnam we went shopping for the things we thought he would need for college life. We made sure we bought him a nice sport jacket along with shirts and ties etc. (We found out later that both students and professors wore cut-off shorts and polo shirts to class).

When we drove him to MIT for the beginning of the semester we were given a tour of the school. One of the highlights was a visit to a large, sterile-looking, air-conditioned room, filled with about 20 white units, the size of washing machines. Each had a horizontal slot from which came out large sheets of papers with squiggles on them. They were the precious computers that needed to be housed in a temperature controlled place. We were duly impressed but we did not really understand their importance.

Relieved that Michael was in college instead of in Vietnam, I started the school year expecting to have a year without problems. But when two women took over the positions of the retiring Board members, things started to change. They both had sons with discipline and academic problems. They hinted that the school system was to blame. During the next few meetings they stopped hinting and blamed the district's old fashioned curriculum. With each meeting they became more and more adversarial. The school system was too old fashioned. The Basal Reader program should be replaced by the new Individualized Reading program. For several meetings, Mr. Foster and the rest of us tried to persuade them that the change was not necessary. No one reading system could be completely successful with every child in the school. The small number of children who were not learning to read could be helped in other ways. It was not

229

necessary to spend almost one hundred thousand dollars for the new materials. But we could not convince them. Eventually all the members of the Board voted to replace the basal Reading program with the new Individualized Reading Program.

I asked Mr. Foster if he could stall them. The whole thing would go away in about three years.

"If only I could"!

Soon after, in a defeated voice, he informed the three Reading teachers and the Curriculum Coordinator to prepare for the change. Mrs. Hutton and Mrs. Gray retired rather than implement the new system. Mrs. Hutton was replaced by Dr. Taylor, who had just received his Ph.D. in Individualized Reading from Hoifstra University. Mrs.Gray was replaced by an expert in Individualized Reading.

Years before, the teachers at Bayer had made the successful transition from teaching reading to the whole class to teaching it to three ability groups, with names like Bluebirds and Robins. They became very anxious when they heard of the imminent change and insisted on guidance. We had meeting after meeting to introduce them to the lengthy diagnostic test they had to administer to each child. The test came in a work book format with detachable pages that I duplicated to supply all the classes. I arranged the pages in the filing cabinets that had been brought into my already overcrowded room. Fearful of the change but eager to do a good job, the teachers came before, after and in between classes, to get the sheets.

As soon as the teachers received the new multi-level reading materials, they sent the Basal readers to me. The custodian, a Navy veteran, would Deep Six them after school. Within a short time we destroyed hundreds of perfectly good readers.

Individualized Reading was capturing the attention of Long Island's school systems. Dr.Taylor wanted to establish his name in the field as soon as possible. He told the Curriculum Coordinator to order materials and me to transform one of the large, airy, former kindergarten rooms into the Resource Room.

Soon the room was so full of materials that I had to store some in the closet. One day I received a catalogue and a note from Mr.Foster asking me to order five hundred dollars worth of materials. I looked at the catalogue and at the crowded closet. I answered that we didn't need anything. An immediate message came back.

"Order something or we'll lose the five hundred dollars in next year's budget".

The Resource Room was among the first in the area. Dr. Taylor sought every opportunity to publicize it. Pictures of me in the room appeared often in *Balmar Life*, the local newspaper. As more and more school systems changed over to Individualized Reading, reading teachers and Curriculum Coordinators, came to visit. A school supervisor from Australia, who happened to be in the area, came to interview me carrying a small tape recorder that was replacing the reel to reel recorder. Dr. Taylor invited an entire class of future Reading Teachers from Hofstra to visit after school. I was to explain how I had set up the Resource Room and how it was used.

A few weeks before the scheduled visit of the Hofstra students I was undergoing the stress brought about by the Sandwich Generation phenomenon. Joe and I were caught between obligations to my mother and obligations to our children. My father's fatal heart attack while working in his vegetable garden two years before left the care of my mother, who showed signs of dementia, to us.

Michael was at the University of Wisconsin on a fellowship, studying for his Ph.D. in mathematics and Mary was spending her Junior year at the University of Madrid in Spain, sponsored by Georgetown University. We got passports and made arrangements to visit her during the Spring vacation with the intention of leaving my mother in a nursing home for the duration of our visit. We spent days going from nursing home to nursing home, trying to decide on the best one. But every time I had to sign the papers, the thought of leaving her in unfamiliar surroundings stopped me. The date to decide was approaching and I kept agonizing over it.

One morning I woke up with Bell's Palsy and we canceled the trip.

My face looked like the before of a before and after ad for plastic surgery. Although in most cases the face reverts to normal after a few days, mine never would. The best I could hope for was for an 80% restoration and that, would take years. I felt awful and looked even worse. There was nothing for me to do but settle for inner beauty and return to work.

The first group of children who walked into my room silently questioned me with their eyes. I explained that I was all right and that it didn't hurt. They were relieved. One second grade girl touched my hand and said, "Don't worry. It'll get better". The groups that came later also accepted the explanation and never mentioned it again.

I was apprehensive about speaking to the class from Hofstra. I had poor control of my lips and had difficulty making the labial sounds. Considering the widespread use of drugs and alcohol, I was afraid they might come to the wrong conclusions. I started my presentation by explaining the reason for my slow speech and distorted face. Their questioning looks disappeared and we proceeded with the presentation.

During the individualized reading periods students worked independently at their own pace and used the teacher as a resource person. After they finished a unit of work, they took a self administered test to advance to the next level. The reading periods were no longer quiet. It was impossible to stop the chairs from scraping the floor as the students moved back and forth to get materials. The children whispered to each other to share materials or asked each other for help. The teachers lost some of their lady-like composure in trying to keep up with the daily reading progress of the 35 or so children. More and more of them started to look harried. In the mornings I'd find them waiting to ask me about class management. The skills that had been incorporated sequentially in the basal readers were a little harder to schedule as the days became increasingly more chaotic.

Soon we discovered that while the educational philosophy of the IndividualizedReading specialists was impeccable, their knowledge of flesh and blood children was not. It was impossible for one teacher to keep track of 35 children, all doing different assignments. After a while the least able had the best scores. They didn't learn to read better but learned instead, that if they looked up the answers first, they didn't have to do the reading. Even after we challenged them, they continued to cheat.

The old classroom order was further disrupted by the addition of more special teachers. Besides the Reading Teacher, each school had a nurse and a special education teacher. The three schools shared a speech teacher, a music teacher and a child psychologist. As a result, the classroom teachers had children coming and going to different specialists all day long. They hardly ever had the whole class to teach at one time.

The students who saw the psychologist usually belonged to multiple special groups. When the psychologist scheduled conferences with the parents, all the special teachers involved with the child had to attend. I had to attend several. After a few months a secretary was hired just to take care of the paper work generated by these meetings

The school district had to hire extra staff to serve the children with disabilities who had been mainstreamed from the special schools they had been attending. As new programs were started and extra teachers were hired to implement them, the school budget increased.

The public blamed the extra costs on the teachers' salaries and benefits. Since the teachers' salary is one of the few items in the budget that is not mandated by the state, it became a sore subject of negotiations each year. One of the Board members wanted to deny health insurance to the married women teachers. One year the school budget was turned down three times, tripling the cost of the voting process. The result was an austerity budget which cut out very little because the state-mandated programs couldn't be cut.

The amicable contract negotiations of the past turned bitter. During one stalemate we picketed before and after school. Neither the Board nor the public sympathized with us. Finally, the teachers took the unprecedented step of joining a union. The endless negotiation sessions started. As the Secretary of the District's chapter, I hosted several evening meetings in our basement. Prior to the first meeting, I received a call from one of the art teachers. He was afraid of being sued by the District or maybe jailed if he came. It took me a while to convince him that nothing would happen to him just for attending a meeting. After several meetings with the Board we signed a contract and didn't have to go on strike.

But all this unrest proved too much for Mr. Foster, who had been used to genteel negotiations with the Board and the teachers. One day, while making his rounds in the school, collapsed and died.

Settling our differences with the Board was about the only thing settled around us. There was unrest in all aspects of our society. The economy was so good that there was a shortage of workers. One Saturday afternoon, while walking along the aisles of Grant's

Department Store in Levittown I saw something that took me back to my days at Grant's. I watched in disbelief. How things had changed! A sullen, teen-age sales clerk, with folded arms, was standing by a counter of unfolded face towels. The manager walked over and asked her to please fold them. She refused. Why bother. They would only get messed up again. She didn't unfold her arms until the manager pleaded with her,

"Please, fold the towels".

Books like the *Joy of Sex* and *The Women's Room* added to the unrest started by the *Feminine Mystique*. A couple wrote a best seller praising the wonders of an "Open Marriage" in which both were free to have affairs. (The couple eventually divorced.) Young women felt they could do anything they were capable of doing. They didn't need a husband. One young woman chose a man to father a child and then had nothing more to do with him. Divorce was no longer a stigma. Instead, it was glamorized in books and films. Some women were sending out invitations to Divorce Parties. Arlene divorced her "Big Nothing", with the expectations of marrying someone better. (About a year later I saw her ex-husband at a conference. The little red pin was on his lapel and a good looking blonde on his arm).

The feminist movement influenced Congress to pass an Equal Rights Amendment (ERA). The school secretary, a divorced mother of two teen-age boys, greeted us almost every morning with the latest progress of the amendment and urged us to vote for it. But the amendment was not ratified. Many women didn't really care about the ERA. Some argued that their husbands allowed them enough freedom and they didn't need the amendment. I refrained to remind one of them that her husband had *forbidden* her to go back to teaching after she had the children. They neglected to notice that wives' salaries were still not counted by the banks, that single women couldn't buy houses and women still had trouble getting credit unless they mentioned their husband's name. The militancy of the proponents of the ERA, however, raised the lawmakers' consciousness enough for them to enact the Title IX legislation that provides that funds for the girls' school sports be equal to the funds for the boys. It influenced the banks. They started to give credit cards to women who insisted on having one issued to them alone and not jointly with their husbands. It even reached the churches. The women had grown up hearing only these words from the pulpits,

"Wives, submit to your husbands...wives should submit to their husbands in everything." Now they finally heard the sentence after it, "Husbands love your wives..."[14]

The Hippie movement of the Sixties was in full swing in the Seventies. Not only teens but older men wore their hair in pony tails. They wore earrings in their pierced ears, chains around their necks and carried shoulder bags. Young women used no make-up, burned their bras, and wore short-short shorts. The ones who believed in the curative power of crystals and massage therapy had long hair, wore long skirts and long chains of beads. Some took up Eastern religions and philosophies, yoga and Transcendental Meditation, (TM). Some moved out of their middle class homes into Hippie communes. Jewish Mrs. Ronald's daughter joined the Jesus moment and was living with other members of the sect. Some visited psychics. Our School Nurse visited one once a month. The college graduate spoke of the psychic with the fervor of my illiterate Grandma Rosa.

The political activist "Yippies" that disrupted the 1968 Democratic convention didn't upset us for long. But the shooting of the protesting Kent State University students by the National Guard, on May 5, 1970, shocked the nation. It made young people even more nervous and disillusioned with the Establishment.

Somehow our family escaped much of the turmoil of the Sixties. We were all so busy and routinized that we didn't have time to get into trouble. Even though we were all doing different things in different places, we each knew what the other was doing. We lived with Michael's long hair and old shoes with the flapping soles, and Mary's frayed bell-bottoms with gaping holes in the knees. Considering the messes they both could have gotten into, we thought it best not to make a fuss about their dress code.

In 1972 our daily lives were disrupted by a severe oil shortage. It meant waiting a long time at the gas pump and sometimes by the time it was your turn there was no more gas. Members in a family took turns waiting in line. To alleviate the problem they instituted the system that licenses ending in even numbers gassed up one day and uneven numbers gassed up on another. Our Jewish

---

[14]Ephesians 5:22-25

friends were worried that the oil shortage would start a back-lash against the Jews. Some Jews from Canada immigrated to US, feeling they would be safer here.

The sexual revolution that was abetted by the pill, gathered momentum when the 1973 *Roes vs. Wade* decision made abortions legal.

We at Bayer tried to hold our own. We continued to wear make-up and our bras. But even those of us who had frowned on wearing pants were forced to wear them. The hem line was steadily going up. When the hems got so high that skirts barely covered the buttocks, we chose to wear pants. Before long we were all wearing pant suits. We soon began to appreciate the easy movement afforded by the pant suit and their easy care. Most were made of a new synthetic material, polyester, which was washable and needed no ironing. The material was also widely used to make men's suit. The pant suits gave us another advantage. We wouldn't have to buy panty hose as often since the pants covered any runs we may have in them. By then we had discarded stockings and the garters or garter belts we needed to hold them up.[15]

Michael was still in Wisconsin working on his Ph.D. Mary graduated from Georgetown University and found a job in the office of an insurance company in the Washington area. We realized that like many of their generation, Michael and Mary were not coming back home after college.

Even though both Michael and Mary were away, Joe and I were still house bound. My mother could not be left alone for more than a few hours at the time. She died in her sleep in January, 1977.

Shortly after her death, three of the older teachers decided to enroll for an evening course at the local High School, to learn how to play Bridge. They asked me to be the fourth. At first I refused, explaining that I didn't even know the suits. When they persisted I reconsidered. All I had ever done was study and work. Playing Bridge would be a good leisure activity during my retirement. The hardest part of the course was holding the thirteen cards without dropping them. I eventually became a good bridge player. Through the game I've met many wonderful people and become part of several groups.

---

[15]Panty hoses came on the market in 1963.

But I still get teased for not shuffling the cards well.

In June, exactly ten years after I was hired, the School district eliminated one reading teacher. Since I was the last hired, I was the first one to go. I was offered a class for the next year but I refused it. I chose early retirement at age fifty five.

The mother-daughter house that had served us so well was no longer useful. The Court had changed. The minister had died. The Banks next door had moved several years before, to a newer, more affluent neighborhood. When last we visited them, Sheila was obese and Judy was anorexic. The family that had moved into their house was moving into a ranch type house. The wife had muscular sclerosis and could no longer use the stairs in the split level. Goldie and her husband had moved to Florida. Sheila's neighbor had died of breast cancer and her husband had remarried. The house across the way had been sold three times. We decided to move.

Thinking we were going to grow old and feeble in the house we bought, we fought the temptation to buy one of the beautiful spit levels and looked only at one level houses. We found one in Massapequa. We had no trouble selling our house. By then, the mother-daughter type house had become very popular.

For various reasons, people all over Long Island were moving. There were garage sales everywhere. We didn't have one. We donated items to charities and put out our junk on the curb. Amazingly the junk was gone the next morning. Scavengers picked up the items to sell them either at their garage sales or at the increasingly popular flea markets. The largest of these was in Roosevelt Field, departure spot for Charles Lindbergh's famous solo flight to Paris in 1927 and later used as a Race Track.

Thirty-seven

In the summer of 1978 we moved to Massapequa, two blocks west of the Suffulk County line, in a house just north of Merrick Road.

For the first time since I started kindergarten, except for the two maternity leaves, I wasn't going to school in September. I had become a full time housewife. Once Joe left for work I had the whole day to myself. I didn't need a whole day to do a housewife's work. I had done all that while I raised two children, held a full time job, took courses, wrote papers, went to meetings, and attended conferences.

I was not alone. I was one of a large group that had never existed before - retirees on pensions, in good health and with a long life expectancy. We had vacuums, washing machines, dryers and dish washers to help us with our housework. Our refrigerators with large freezers saved us shopping time by allowing us to stock up the food we bought at the one-stop Supermarkets. Cooking for two was easy. It was made even easier by the latest wonder - the microwave oven. Besides, we could afford to go to restaurants when we didn't feel like cooking.

The retirees who couldn't find enough things to do, found jobs. But most of us looked forward to having less responsibilities and more leisure time. We had lived through the Depression, World War II, Korea, Vietnam, raised our children, sent them to the best colleges, and taken care of our parents. We searched for rewarding activities to take up the time we had spent on the job.

Institutions and community organizations were aware of us and found ways to persuade us to donate our time, talents and money. I helped with the Red Cross' blood drives, did clerical work in the church office and visited some shut-ins in the parish.

Hofstra University sponsored the Learning Institute For Elders, LIFE. The program offered a variety of non credit courses aimed at both college graduates and those who had never been to college. For a yearly fee, we could attend as many or as few classes as we wished. Through this program I met people with a variety of backgrounds. We socialized in between classes, had lunch in the

238

cafeteria and planned activities outside the college.

One of the LIFE members, Cynthia, divorced, vivacious and very friendly, was very popular with the men. The women admired her for her masterful handling of Bob, the second boyfriend since her divorce. She invited a group of us for lunch and we found out that she would not serve anything in the nightshade family. It was the latest fad aimed at curing arthritis. She was one of many of a growing number of people who sought medical cures through special diets. Nutritionists vied with each other in promising us the fountain of youth, if we followed their advice and bought their books. Adele Davis endowed her morning cocktail of essential nutrients with almost magical powers. She touted the Mediterranean (peasant) diet I had grown up with as the healthiest. (One woman in the LIFE class cooked a big pot of dry beans at a time and ate some every day). Some restaurants started to feature *ratatouille*, the French version of our *ciambotta*. Pritikin promised to reverse heart damage by following his no fat diet. On the radio, Carlton Fredericks promoted *Prevention Magazine* and mega doses of vitamins. All three died rather young.

Meanwhile, Julia Child, the French chef that had captivated the TV audiences for years refused to change her ways. She continued to cook with lots of butter and top every dessert with lots of whipped cream. Ironically, she is still going strong at age 88.

For those who were forever looking for a magic diet to lose weight, there was yet another diet to try. It was Dr. Atkins' high protein diet that some authorities thought dangerous.

Plans and suggestions for healthy living bombarded us daily but there was little outcry against smoking. Joe and I still suffered from inhaling other people's smoke. We didn't have the nerve to tell our friends not to smoke in our house. Instead, I dutifully put out the ashtrays I received at my bridal shower. The house stank of smoke for days after their visits.

I joined the Great Books discussion group that met one evening a month in the cramped upstairs room in The Massapequa Library. For a small fee I also joined the Literature and Life book discussion group, sponsored by the Adult Education Program, that met in its basement, one morning a month. The group was led by a Jewish woman who was studying for a Ph.D. in English Literature.

We read whatever books she was assigned to read for her courses.

One of the books was *Ulysses* by James Joyce. Since only a few of us were Catholic, we were sure the others would look to us to explain some terms in the book. We were all surprised to hear Norma, a Jew, who spoke English with a heavy German accent, explain all the references. She had spent the four war years in a convent, hidden by the nuns. She praised the nuns for never trying to convert her.

I continued to play bridge with my friends from Bayer and found out that soon after I retired the Board abandoned the Individualized Reading program, *three years* after it was started. They ordered a brand new set of basal readers.

Within a short driving distance from home there were several commercial Bridge Clubs. Elaine, from the Literature and Life group, suggested we play in The 110 Bridge Club, in Farmingdale, sanctioned by the A.C.B.L, American Contract Bridge League. It was the nearest and the nicest around. The players met in a large, cheerful room with lots of windows. For a three dollar entrance fee, we could have coffee and bagels while we listened to Irma, the director, give a lesson. Play started at ten. In between directing the game Irma cooked a hot lunch for us. After lunch we played until three o'clock. It was a very pleasant and economical way to spend a day.

It was there that one day I saw my classmate Shirley and her husband for the first time since we left Hunter High. I recognized her characteristic beaming wide smile. All through High School I had admired her smile. Anybody with that smile had to be happy and at ease with the world. After catching up with the events of our lives, I told her that I all through High School I had admired, and sometimes envied her, for being so happy.

" Happy? I was miserable."

As we played I saw that the wide smile I had envied was just a facial feature that had nothing to do with being happy. Her eyes were not happy. I didn't envy her one bit for the wary way she catered to her husband at the bridge table. I was very sad to lose my happy memory of Shirley.

Elaine and I shared the driving. She lived in a big split-level in the affluent Bar Harbor section of Massapequa, South of Merrick Road. It was a post-war development of very expensive houses that got progressively more expensive the closer they were to the Bay.

Those on the Bay were priced at around a million dollars. One of those belonged to Carlo Gambino, the well known member of the Mafia. Elaine's house was close to Merrick Road, needed painting and the lawn, though mowed, was full of weeds. It represented the rise and fall of her husband's business in the garment industry on Seventh Avenue in New York City.

Her diabetic husband was housebound and the children had health and marital problems. She blamed all the family's misfortunes on having too much money. They had spent excessively on restaurants, vacations and on their three children. At the time Elaine was the one who managed the purse strings. She was proud of her frugality and to be driving the economical Ford Escort. According to her if the parents had taken away their children's credit cards, the Kent State students would not have demonstrated and would not have been killed. After listening to her repeat this opinion a few times, I almost came to agree with her. Perhaps one of the reasons our family escaped the turmoil of the Sixties was that we didn't have the money for the excesses.

Elaine's theory and the worst characteristics of the 1970's were tragically demonstrated when six members of the DeFeo family were brutally murdered by the oldest son. The father had made enough money in Brooklyn to buy a dream home in the sleepy village of Amityville, south of Merrick Road, just over the border of Suffolk and a few blocks away from our house. It seems that instead of spending time with the son when he misbehaved the father showered him with expensive gifts, including an expensive car. The gruesome murder received national attention when it became the subject of the national best selling novel, *The Amityville Horror*.

Massapequa was often referred to as *Matzapizza* because most of its residents were Jews and Italians. On the many rides to the Bridge Club, Elaine and I often discussed the common prejudices people had about Jews and Italians. Mario Puzo's best seller *The Godfather* had helped to reinforce the misconception that all Italians are somehow connected to the Mafia. I jokingly mentioned Michael's experience at the University of Wisconsin. When his fellow students found out he was Italian, and that he came from Long Island, they asked him if he belonged to the Mafia. When I made some disparaging remarks about members of the Mafia, Elaine strongly disagreed with me. She and her husband had been invited to their houses for social events. When the bank was about to foreclose on their house, Tommy Gambino and Bobby Lucchese paid off the mortage. They also gave their younger son a job delivering legitimate merchandise to and from their garment factory. Had she been Catholic, she'd probably pray the Rosary for them every day.

While Joe was at work I kept busy with my various activities but on weekends we did a lot of sightseeing of scenic and historic spots on Long Island and continued to attend the concerts in the park, which had been renamed Eisenhower Park. The performances had become so elaborate and popular that the County built a large shell at the edge of a man-made lake at the bottom of a wide based, low hill. The sloping lawn could accommodate thousands. They had to set up portable toilets for the performances which became occasions for friends to meet and have picnic suppers. We too, went with some friends early enough to place our folding chairs and snack tables in a good spot from which to view the performance. We never missed a performance. But when it took us over an hour to get out of the parking lot, we stopped going. We felt good that we had been there at the beginning, when they had needed the encouragement.

Our generation had lived through the rebellion of our Baby Boomers, the Hippies, Flower Children and the demonstrations against the Vietnam War. Despite it all, most of our sons were doctors, lawyers, engineers and other professions. Our daughters were no longer restricted to be secretaries, nurses or teachers. The Boomers were getting married and giving birth to the Y generation. But things were not as great as we would have wished. Wherever I went, I saw discontent and the breakdown of relationships.

Many young people wanted to escape the responsibilities of adulthood. When they found married life too confining, they left their partners. Sons and daughters of friends, whose wedding receptions we had attended, were getting divorced after one or two years. The twenty-two year old hairdresser in the Balmor salon used her free time to talk to the lawyer who was arranging the divorce from her husband, and to talk to her new boyfriend. The twenty year old hairdresser in the Massapequa salon was divorcing her immature husband. Another, a mother of three, tearfully told us that her husband left for work one morning and never came back.

The emphasis on self discovery and self fulfillment was also affecting our generation. Anna in the Literature and Life group bitterly told us that her husband of thirty years left her to find himself. The favorite destination for those in search of themselves was Denver, Colorado.

Some older couples were divorcing for financial reasons. The cost of Nursing Homes was so high that the well spouse divorced the spouse in the Nursing Home to avoid losing all the assets.

In the summer of 1981, Michael finished his thesis for his Ph.D. On the day he was scheduled to defend it orally, Joe and I stayed by the phone. I jumped to pick it up on the first ring. The operator said the words we had been waiting to hear,

"A collect call from Dr.Tangredi. Will you accept ?"

Michael liked living in the Middle West so much that he got a teaching position at a College of St. Benedict at St. John's University in Minnesota. By then he had met Julie, his future wife.

Mary's boss and his wife introduced her to the son of their good friends from Wellesley, a suburb of Boston. Once they set the date, Mary asked if she could wear my wedding gown. I was completely surprised by the request. I hadn't looked at or thought about the gown since my wedding day. I dreaded opening the box. I feared it would be in shreds and Mary would be heart broken. Instead, it was in perfect condition! The expensive satin gowns of my friends had not lasted. But my inexpensive cotton one, had. Mary and Ron were married in 1981 and moved into the house they bought in Northern Va.

Thirty-eight

Joe and I found ourselves part of the growing number of empty nesters, parents living alone in the big houses they had been so proud to buy for their growing families. Empty nesters continued to spend week-ends doing repairs and mowing the lawn. In the winter, they shoveled the snow. The houses were too big. The constant maintenance was getting burdensome.

Neighborhoods were changing. As more and more young families moved on their streets, the seniors moved to escape the basketball hoops on the neighbors' driveways, the balls bouncing on their lawns and the big wheels rattling on the sidewalk.

After the war, builders catered to the housing needs of the financially strapped young veterans. In the Sixties, the builders thought of ways to meet the housing needs of the same veterans who now were ready to retire, financially secure, and in good health. Ads on the radio and in newspapers lured many seniors to these gated Retirement Communities for Active Adults. The comfortable, smaller houses, with maintenance free grounds, built in peaceful locations, proved to be irresistible. Seniors looked forward to living their retirement years as if on a permanent vacation.

At first we ignored the ads. But when the family to the right of us installed the loud compressor for their swimming pool right under our bedroom window, and the neighbors on the left started to shoot baskets at seven in the morning, we began to pay attention to the radio and newspaper ads. We started to pay closer attention when the five and half hour ride to our daughter's house kept getting longer and longer due to the increased traffic. The day the 40 minute drive from the Verrazzano Bridge to Massapequa stretched to two hours, we started our search.

There were no such communities in Virginia. We sent for brochures from several communities in New Jersey, looking for one that would shorten our trip to Mary's house. After reading the information and examining the floor plans of the model homes, we decided to visit Homestead at Mansfield in Columbus, New Jersey.

When we turned onto Rte 206 from the New Jersey

Turnpike, we started to have some qualms. The only sign of civilization on the road that was flanked by corn fields, were a few scattered houses and a gas station. The sight of the first house on Columbus Road, leading to Homestead, added to our misgivings. It had rotting, bilious green shutters. The column that was meant to support the extension over the porch was leaning and barely touching it. Several roof shingles were missing. We became even more doubtful as we rode by more old houses and more corn fields. We were relieved to spot the entrance to Homestead.

The uniformed guard directed us to the Models. From the models we went to the Club House, where the welcoming lunch was being served. There was an air of excitement in the room. We met the other couples who like us had decided to leave their old neighborhoods behind. They were from Long Island, Queens, Brooklyn, Staten Island and from the congested towns of Northern New Jersey. We were all eager to get to know one other. We compared notes about other places we had visited in trying to find the best community. We exchanged addresses and promised to keep in touch.

After the sales presentation and lunch, the Activities Director herded us into a bus to tour the nearby area. The tour was designed to dispel any hesitations we might have about moving into such an undeveloped area. The Director pointed out all the conveniences available within a few minutes drive from Homestead. We ended the tour with a walk through the bright, new Burlington Mall. The tour accomplished what it was designed to do. On the way back to the Clubhouse, we all felt better about moving to the area.

We visited Homestead several times. We walked through the models, visited the Clubhouse, looked at the outdoor swimming pool, rode around the community and spoke to the residents. Finally we signed the contract. We continued to visit Homestead to monitor the building of our new house. Each time we trudged through mounds of earth to look at it, we thought of the days when we had trudged over mounds of earth with the Biondis. Then, we could not even afford the *thought* of buying a house. Now, we were about to move into what was advertised as a luxury adult community.

Each time we went through the security gate we saw one of the residents, Mike, a short, gray haired man, sitting on a utility post.

245

In one hand he held a cigar and with the other he waved cheerfully to all who drove in. Mike spent a lot of time on that small post. His wife prohibited smoking in the house. Everyone who moved to Homestead got to know Mike.

Finally the moving day was set. We put out our discards on the curb. Among the first things to go were all our ash trays.

On June 24,1988 we left Massapequa for Homestead. We were looking forward to helping establish a community built especially for seniors who were eager to begin a new phase in their lives.

When we turned onto the Columbus Road, banners announcing Columbus' three hundred anniversary celebration greeted us. The sight of the banners brought back the thoughts I often had when we visited Homestead. By American standards, Columbus is a very old town. Many of its 2000 residents can trace their origins to the American Revolution. We were moving to an old farming town about the same size as *Noepoli*. The natives of Columbus like those in *Noepoli* were wary of strangers. Except for the manager of the Bank, they thought of us Homesteaders as intruders.

This time, when we reached Homestead's entrance, instead of driving up to the gate marked Guests we headed for the one marked Residents. An electronically operated wooden bar stopped us from entering. It was a reminder that, although man had conquered the oceans and the continents, broken the sound barrier and landed on the moon, he still had not conquered his primeval fear of fellow man. We, in the twentieth century, were moving into a modern version of a feudal village. As a child I had walked through the Door of *Noepoli*'s ancient, once protective, crumbling stone wall. As a senior citizen, I was entering its modern version by riding through a protective, modern electronic Gate.

Joe stopped at the post that supported the bar and slid the electronic card in the slot. Waiting for the bar to lift, we glanced at Mike sitting on the utility post, resting the cigar on his knee. He smiled and raised his free hand in greeting. The sun light playing on his glasses momentarily blurred Mike's gray hair, round face and smile. I gulped. For a split second I thought I was seeing my father. He was smiling that special smile of his that over the years I had learned meant,

"Well done".

As we drove through, the slight rattle of the coffee pot in the well of the car brought me back to the present. I waved to Mike and turned my thoughts to greeting the movers with coffee and cake and to our future as Golden Agers.

Homestead at Mansfield, NJ

June 2000

www.ingramcontent.com/pod-product-compliance
Lightning Source LLC
Chambersburg PA
CBHW020456030426
42337CB00011B/132